Air Fryer Cookbook for Beginners

Top 600 Tasty, Crispy and Delicious Recipes to Fry, Bake, Grill, and Roast with Your Air Fryer

By
Scarlett Wilson

TABLE OF CONTENTS

Introduction 1

    Air Fryer Technology 1

    Benefits of Using an Air Fryer 2

    How to Use an Air Fryer 3

    Getting the Most Out of your Air Fryer 4

    Air Fryer - Cleaning & Maintenance 5

    Air Fryer - FAQs 6

Air Fryer Cooking Charts 7

    Frozen Foods Chart 7

    Poultry Chart 8

    Vegetables Chart 9

    Fish & Seafood Chart 10

    Beef Chart 11

Breakfasts 12

    Nuts and Zucchini Bread 12

    Vanilla Banana Bread 12

    Bananas Bread 13

    Special French Toasts 13

    Pineapple Corn bread 13

    Tasty Tuna Sandwiches 14

    Pumpkin and Yogurt Bread 14

    Tasty French Toasts 14

    Tasty Cream Bread 15

    Mushroom and Tomato Frittata 15

    Cheese Omelet 15

    Tasty Apple Muffins 16

    Sausage Frittata 16

    Egg Yolks with Squid 16

    Chocolatey Peanut Butter Bread 17

    Mini Tomato Quiche 17

    Carrot Muffins 17

    Blueberry Muffins 18

    Delicious Ham Rolls 18

Pumpkin Bread 19

Bacon and Hot Dogs Omelet 19

Nuts and Banana Bread 19

Zucchini Omelet 20

Italian Eggplant Sandwich 20

Chicken Omelet 20

Green Beans Omelet 21

Banana Muffins 21

Zucchini and Chicken Tortillas 21

Raisin and Oat Muffins 22

Fruity Casserole 22

Bread and Bacon Cups 22

Apple and Zucchini Bread 23

Potato Rosti 23

Trout Frittata 23

Butter Banana Bread 24

Dates Bread 24

Jalapeño Cornbread 25

Easy Cornbread 25

Chocolatey Banana Bread 26

Spinach and Egg Cups 26

Eggs and Mushroom Scramble 26

Eggs and Tomatoes Scramble 27

Zucchini Fritters 27

Mustard Toasts 27

Vanilla Cinnamon Toasts 27

Breakfast Potatoes 28

Scrambled Eggs 28

Breakfast Biscuits 28

Tomato and Eggs 28

Roasted Peppers Frittata 29

Bacon and Egg Cups 29

Chicken and Spinach Casserole 29

Leek and Potato Frittata 30

Chicken and Broccoli Quiche 30

Creamy Peas Omelet................................... 30

Easy Onion Frittata 30

Hash Browns Breakfast............................... 31

Squash Breakfast 31

Chili and Parsley Soufflé 31

Sausage Bake 31

Breakfast Sausage Rolls 32

Vanilla Toast 32

Herbed Tomatoes Breakfast 32

Sausage Omelet 32

Parmesan Muffins....................................... 33

Polenta Cakes 33

Breakfast Potatoes 33

Pumpkin Oatmeal....................................... 33

Apple Oatmeal... 34

Corn Pudding... 34

Delicious Doughnuts 34

Blackberries and Cornflakes 35

Fried Mushroom 35

Smoked Bacon and Bread 35

Pancakes.. 35

Creamy Mushroom Pie............................... 36

Cheesy Hash Brown................................... 36

Pear Oatmeal 36

Ham and Cheese Patties.............................. 36

Peppers and Lettuce Salad.......................... 37

Cod Tortilla... 37

Artichoke Omelet....................................... 37

Carrot Oatmeal 37

Chicken Burrito 38

Potato Frittata.. 38

Herbed Omelet... 38

Cheese Toast.. 38

Carrots and Cauliflower Mix 39

Vanilla Oatmeal 39

Fish Tacos Breakfast 39

Tuna Sandwiches.. 39

Tofu and Bell Peppers................................ 40

Chicken & Poultry....................................41

Chicken with Potatoes 41

Cinnamon Chicken 41

Chicken Wings and Endives 41

Cheese Stuffed Chicken Breasts.................. 42

Sweet and Spicy Chicken Drumsticks 42

Herbed Chicken 42

Parmesan Chicken 43

Lemon and Garlic Chicken 43

Buffalo Chicken Tenders............................. 43

Fried Chicken Wings 44

Ginger Chicken Drumsticks........................ 44

Duck Breast with Figs 44

Lemon Chicken and Asparagus.................... 45

Crispy Chicken Tenders 45

Crispy Chicken Burgers.............................. 46

Chicken with Carrots.................................. 46

Salsa Verde Chicken Breast. 47

Chinese Chicken Drumsticks....................... 47

Sausage Stuffed Chicken Breasts................. 47

Spinach Stuffed Chicken Breasts................. 47

Awesome Oregano Chicken Thighs.............. 48

Turkey Meatloaf 48

Crispy Chicken Thighs 48

Turkey Legs... 49

Chicken Cutlets.. 49

Crispy Chicken Wings................................ 49

Chicken Breasts and Veggies. 50

Chicken with Broccoli and Rice 50

Chicken and Dates 50

Sweet Chicken Kabobs 51

Turkey and Parsley Pesto 51

Chicken and Veggie Kabobs 51

Spicy Chicken Legs 52

Chicken Tenderloins 52

Bacon Wrapped Chicken Breasts 52

Glazed Chicken and Apples 53

Chicken and Scallion Kabobs 53

Chicken Wings 53

Herbed Roasted Chicken 54

Spicy Roasted Chicken 54

Oats Crusted Chicken Breasts 54

Crispy Chicken Drumsticks 55

Chicken Thighs and Rice 55

Glazed Turkey Breast 55

Fried Whole Chicken 56

Chicken Breasts 56

Chicken and Leeks 56

Chicken and Pancetta 57

Turmeric Chicken Legs 57

Spiced Chicken 57

Herbed Turkey Breast 58

Turkey Chili 58

Turkey Rolls 58

Sour and Sweet Chicken Thighs 59

Beer Coated Duck Breast 59

Jerk Chicken, Pineapple and Veggie Kabobs 59

Tomato Chicken 60

Chinese Style Chicken Thighs 60

Buttered Duck Breasts 60

Honey Duck Breasts 61

Turkey Wings 61

Turkey Breast 61

Japanese Style Chicken Thighs 61

Blue Cheese Chicken 62

Herbed Duck Legs 62

Curried Chicken 62

Chicken and Pear Sauce 63

Mexican Style Turkey 63

Easy Chicken Thighs 63

Chicken and Green Coconut Sauce. 63

Chicken Breasts Delight 64

Honey Glazed Chicken Drumsticks 64

Tarragon Chicken Breasts 64

Chicken Thighs 65

Chicken with Apple 65

Marinara Chicken 65

Tomato Duck Breast 66

Chicken with Veggies and Rice 66

Turkey Wings Orange Sauce 66

Chicken and Yogurt 66

Chicken and Peppercorns 67

Duck and Sauce 67

Barbeque Chicken Wings 67

Turkey and Spring Onions 67

Chicken and Squash 68

Soy Sauce Chicken 68

Chicken and Veggies 68

Rosemary Chicken Breasts 69

Sesame Chicken 69

Turkey with Fig Sauce 69

Duck Breast and Potatoes 70

Cajun Chicken and Okra 70

Chicken and Beer 70

Turkey Meatballs 71

Chicken and Baby Carrots 71

Balsamic Chicken 71

Chicken Curry 72

Asian Atyle Chicken 72

Lemongrass Chicken 73

Chicken and Chickpeas 73

Beef, Pork & Lamb 74

Buttered Filet Mignon 74

Beef and Mushroom Meatloaf 74

Pork Meatloaf 74

Herbed Beef Roast 75

Buttered Rib Eye Steak 75

Pork and Cauliflower 75

Pork Rolls 75

Beef and Veggie Kebabs 76

Beef Cheeseburgers 76

Pork Chops and Mushrooms Mix 76

Spiced and Herbed Skirt Steak 77

Pork Chops with Peanut Sauce 77

Pork Spare Ribs 78

Beef Stuffed Bell Peppers 78

Bacon Wrapped Filet Mignon 79

Beef Tips with Onion 79

Beef Taco Wraps 79

Herbs Crumbed Rack of Lamb 80

Buttered Striploin Steak 80

Skirt Steak with Veggies 80

Simple New York Strip Steak 81

Pork Chops 81

Herbed Pork Chops 81

Crispy Sirloin Steak 82

Beef Jerky 82

Beef Short Ribs 82

Steak with Bell Peppers 83

Glazed Ham 83

Beef Roast 83

Pork and Bell Pepper 84

Cheesy Beef Meatballs 84

Pork Neck Salad 84

Lamb Loin Chops with Lemon 85

Sweet and Sour Pork Chops 85

Bacon Wrapped Pork tenderloin 85

Pork Loin with Potatoes 86

Beef and Chives Marinade 86

Herbed Lamb Chops 86

French Beef 87

Pork and Peanuts 87

Breaded Pork Chops 87

Pesto Coated Rack of Lamb 87

Glazed Pork Shoulder 88

Pork Tenderloin with Bacon and Veggies 88

Lamb Roast 88

Pork Tenderloin with Bell Peppers 89

Lamb Chops 89

Herbed Leg of Lamb 89

Beef and Sauce 90

Pork Sausage Casserole 90

Beef and Mushroom 90

Tarragon Pork Loin 90

Lamb Chops with Veggies 91

Smoked Pork Roast 91

Beef Roast and Grapes 91

Delicious Rack of Lamb 92

Nut Crusted Rack of Lamb 92

Pork and Bell Peppers 92

Spiced Lamb Steaks 93

Leg of Lamb with Brussels Sprout 93

Ground Beef 93

Rubbed Steaks 94

Fennel Pork 94

Mustard Pork Chops 94

Pork Steaks 94

Pork and Broccoli 95

Coconut Pork 95

Beef Roast 95

Jalapeno Beef 95

Oregano Pork Chops 96

Lamb Chops and Dill 96

Sage Pork 96

Pork and Chives 97

Pork Chops and Spinach 97

Pork and Sprouts 97

Cinnamon Beef 97

Beef and Celery 98

Crispy Lamb Recipe 98

Beef Kabobs Recipe 98

Marinated Lamb and Veggies 99

Garlicky Loin Roast 99

Lamb Meatballs 99

Hot Pork Delight 99

Paprika Beef 100

Lamb Ribs 100

Beef and Plums 100

Chinese Style Beef 101

Beef and Peas 101

Marinated Beef 101

Cumin Beef 101

Creamy Beef 102

Lamb and Beans 102

Delicious Sausage 102

Beef, Arugula and Leeks 103

Basil Beef Roast 103

Snacks & Appetizers 104

Simple Roasted Peanuts 104

Broccoli Poppers 104

Onion Rings 104

Easy Spicy Chickpeas 105

Salmon Croquettes 105

Broccoli Bites 105

Pepper Rolls 106

Mozzarella Sticks 106

Chocolate Cookie Dough Balls 106

Bacon Wrapped Shrimp 107

Cauliflower Poppers 107

Simple Roasted Mixed Nuts 107

Fried Corn 107

Simple Roasted Cashews 108

Potato Chips 108

Squash Fries 108

Zucchini Fries 108

Carrot Sticks 109

Beet Chips 109

Spinach Rolls 109

Banana Chips 109

Crispy Prawns 110

Tomatoes and Dates Salsa 110

Eggplant Slices 110

Spring Rolls 110

Potato Croquettes 111

Pork Bites 111

Basil and Cilantro Crackers 112

French Fries 112

Avocado Fries 112

Cauliflower Poppers 113

Cheesey Sandwich 113

Squash Dip 113

Buttered Corn 113

Apple Chips 114

Polenta Sticks 114

Dill Pickle Fries 114

Kale Chips 114

Coconut Shrimp Snack 115

Lemon Biscuits 115

Turmeric Carrot Chips.............................115

Rice Bites 115

Coconut Cookies 116

Balsamic Zucchini Slices 116

Cheesey Pastries 116

Bacon Croquettes 117

Buttermilk Biscuits 117

Tortilla Chips 117

Cod Nuggets 118

Cream Cheese Balls 118

Beef Dip 118

Veggie Bread Rolls 118

Lemony Apple Bites..................................119

Veggie Pastries..119

Lentils Snack 119

Carrot Dip 120

Minty Cauliflower Spread 120

Broccoli Bites...120

Banana Chips 120

Kale Crackers 120

Chili Dip 121

Coriander Bites..121

Tomato Dip...121

Crab Bites 121

Corn Dip...122

Sausage Bites 122

Zucchini and Mint Spread 122

Italian Mozzarella Sticks..........................122

Chives Radish Snack.................................123

Zucchini Balls 123

Potato Chips 123

Buttery Onion Dip 123

Cheesy Tomatoes and Sausage Dip 123

Lentils Spread 124

Cheesy Beef Meatballs 124

Minty Shrimp Mix 124

Lemony Endives Appetizer......................124

Chicken Sticks 125

Mushroom Salad 125

Leek Spread..125

Fish & Seafood... 126

Coconut Cod Fillets 126

Cod Cakes 126

Cajun Spiced Salmon................................126

Asian Style Cod 127

Sweet and Sour Glazed Salmon..............127

Salmon with Broccoli 127

Coconut Crusted Shrimp..........................128

Salmon with Shrimp and Pasta...............128

Eastern Style Catfish.................................129

Spicy Salmon 129

Prawn Burgers 129

Maple Glazed Salmon...............................130

Breaded Flounder......................................130

Easy Salmon...130

Salmon with Asparagus 130

Salmon with Green Beans 131

Zesty Salmon 131

Parmesan Clams 132

Crispy Cod Sticks 132

Buttered Scallops.......................................132

Salmon and Orange Marmalade Recipe 132

Creamy Tuna Cakes 133

Nacho Chips Crusted Prawns 133

Baby Shrimp 133

Cod and Veggie Parcel 134

Salmon Patties 134

Sesame Seeds Coated Tuna 135

Cheesy Shrimp 135

Creamy Breaded Shrimp 135

Glazed Calamari 136

Spicy Shrimp 136

Breaded Hake 136

Tuna and Potato Cakes 137

Pesto Haddock 137

Lemon Garlic Shrimp 137

Glazed Halibut 138

Bacon Wrapped Scallops 138

Rice Flour Coated Shrimp 138

Shrimp Scampi 139

Shrimp Kebabs 139

Chili Salmon Fillets 139

Breaded Shrimp with Lemon 140

Scallops with Capers Sauce 140

Bacon Wrapped Shrimp 140

Roasted Cod and Parsley 141

Salmon Fillets 141

Shrimp and Veggies 141

Crispy Scallops 141

Scallops with Spinach 142

Salmon Fillets and Bell Peppers 142

Maple Salmon 142

Crab Cakes 143

Balsamic Cod Fillets 143

Saffron Shrimp Mix 143

Salmon and Orange Vinaigrette 144

Tiger Shrimp 144

Coconut Shrimp 144

White Fish and Peas 144

Salmon and Balsamic Orange Sauce 145

Cod Fillets 145

Salmon and Fennel 145

Salmon and Capers 146

Shrimp and Mushrooms 146

Chili Tomato Shrimp 146

Butter Shrimp 146

Salmon and Carrots 147

Trout and Almond Butter Sauce 147

Rosemary Shrimp Kabobs 147

Tarragon Shrimp 148

Cod and Lime Sauce 148

Salmon and Blackberry Sauce 148

Pistachio Crusted Cod 148

Salmon Steaks 149

Cod Fillets with Leeks 149

Salmon Fillets and Pineapple Mix 149

Herbed Tuna 149

Shrimp and Tomatoes 150

Peas and Cod Fillets 150

Awesome Shrimp Mix 150

Pea Pods and Shrimp Mix 150

Halibut and Sun Dried Tomatoes 151

Baked Cod 151

Simple Lime Salmon 151

Sea Bass Paella 151

Spicy Cod 152

Cilantro Trout Fillets 152

Snapper Fillets 152

Salmon and Jasmine Rice 152

Mussels and Shrimp 153

Fried Salmon...153

Trout Bites...153

Shrimp and Spaghetti..................................153

Hawaiian Salmon Recipe.............................154

Easy Trout...154

Clams and Potatoes.....................................154

Mussels Bowls..154

Shrimp and Corn...155

Salmon Thyme and Parsley.........................155

Vegan & Vegetarian 156

Parmesan Broccoli......................................156

Radish Salad...156

Caramelized Carrots....................................156

Cauliflower Salad..157

Eggplant Salad..157

Lemony Green Beans...................................158

Potato Salad..158

Stuffed Pumpkin...158

Hassel-back Potatoes...................................159

Cheesy Mushroom Pizza.............................159

Curried Eggplant...159

Buttered Dinner Rolls.................................160

Garlic Broccoli..160

Veggies Stuffed Eggplants...........................160

Cheese Stuffed Tomatoes............................161

Cheesy Brussel Sprouts...............................161

Broccoli with Olives....................................162

Oatmeal Stuffed Bell Peppers.....................162

Parmesan Asparagus...................................162

Basil Tomatoes...163

Buttered Broccoli..163

Brussel Sprout Salad...................................163

Mixed Veggie Salad....................................164

Cheese Stuffed Mushrooms.........................164

Veggie Stuffed Bell Peppers........................165

Cheesy Dinner Rolls...................................165

Spiced Soy Curls...165

Honey Glazed Carrots.................................166

Zucchini Salad..166

Sweet and Sour Brussel Sprouts..................166

Sweet and Spicy Parsnips............................166

Cheesy Spinach...167

Pesto Tomatoes...167

Herbed Carrots...168

Spicy Potatoes...168

Tofu with Peanut Butter Sauce....................168

Beans and Veggie Burgers............................169

Herbed Eggplant...169

Stuffed Potatoes..170

Veggie Rice...170

Croissant Rolls..170

Rice and Beans Stuffed Bell Peppers............171

Ratatouille..171

Breadcrumbs Stuffed Mushrooms................171

Glazed Veggies..172

Jacket Potatoes...172

Salsa Stuffed Eggplants...............................172

Herbed Potatoes...173

Sautéed Green Beans...................................173

Sesame Seeds Bok Choy..............................173

Stuffed Okra...174

Almond Asparagus......................................174

Stuffed Tomatoes..174

Spicy Tofu..175

Sweet and Spicy Cauliflower.......................175

Tofu with Capers Sauce...............................175

Spiced Butternut Squash.............................176

Herbed Veggies Combo...............................176

Broccoli with Cauliflower 177

Sautéed Spinach 177

Crispy Marinated Tofu 177

Spices Stuffed Eggplants 177

Tofu in Sweet and Spicy Sauce 178

Rice Flour Crusted Tofu 178

Mushrooms with Peas 179

Desserts **180**

Fruity Oreo Muffins 180

Sweet Potato Pie 180

Brownies Muffins 181

Yogurt Cake 181

Fruity Crumble 181

Apple Cake 182

Butter Cake 182

Apple Crumble 182

Crispy Banana Split 183

Layered Cake 183

Walnut Brownies 184

Lava Cake 184

Orange Cake 184

Passion Fruit Pudding Recipe 185

Pear Pastry Pouch 185

Chocolate Yogurt Muffins 185

Cinnamon Apples 186

Shortbread Fingers 186

Pecan Pie 186

Milky Doughnuts 186

Vanilla Soufflé 187

Red Velvet Cupcakes 187

White Chocolate Cheesecake 188

Raspberry Cupcakes 188

Maple Apples 189

Apple Tart 189

Double Chocolate Muffins 189

Chocolate Cake 190

Fried Apples 190

Strawberry Cheesecake 190

Strawberry Cupcakes 191

Strawberry Cream 191

Mini Apple Pies 192

Stuffed Apples 192

Simple Cheesecake 193

Cream Doughnuts 193

Chocolate Cream Cake 194

Cinnamon Pears 194

Chocolate Mug Cake 194

Fruity Tacos 194

Fudge Brownies 195

Chocolate Soufflé 195

Apple Pie 195

Apple Pastry Pouch 196

Banana Cake 196

Strawberry Cobbler Recipe 197

Lemon Cake 197

Pear Delight 197

Butter Donuts 197

Apple Bread Pudding 198

Creamy Blackberry 198

Cranberry Jam 198

Yummy Rice Pudding 199

Chocolate Pudding 199

Apple Doughnuts 199

Coffee Cheesecakes Recipe 200

Grape Stew 200

Chocolate Banana Pastries 200

Raisin Bread Pudding 201

Apple and Cinnamon Sauce 201

Raspberry Wontons...201

Doughnuts Pudding...202

Cinnamon Rolls..202

Brioche Pudding...202

Pineapple and Carrot Cake 202

Rum Cheesecake 203

Amaretto Cream...203

Oreo Cheesecake..203

Cream of Tartar Bread..204

Pumpkin Cake 204

Introduction

This modern and innovative cooking tool will make cooking fun again for you. It doesn't matter how busy you are. You only need a few minutes and the right ingredients, and you'll enjoy some of the best meals ever. You can forget about using all those pots and pans, and you certainly don't have to be an expert cook to use the air fryer. Just follow its directions, and you'll be making some incredible and rich dishes in no time.

The air fryer uses the circulation of hot air to cook the food. This is called Rapid Air Technology, and it means that your food will be done faster and in a healthy way. The air reaches up to 400 degrees F, and it allows you to cook perfectly crispy but also tender and succulent foods in a few minutes.

This cookbook will also act as a guide on how to prepare some of your favorite meals that will not only be healthy but also packed with texture and flavor. Now most of us might be thinking that air fryers are limited to cooking only, but in reality, it is a multipurpose device as it can fry, roast, grill, and bake delicious, mouthwatery meals. And as such this book offers a various set of recipes ranging from breakfast, lunch, dinner, appetizers, side dishes, and desserts, which above all are easy to prepare just by using this kitchen appliance

Before embarking on this air frying recipes, you will get to know more about the air fryer itself as an appliance and the secrets behind it. It is a complete guide for your Air Fryer Cooking!

Air Fryer Technology

Air Fryer heats and cooks foods by circulating extremely high-temperature heat, up to 400 degrees F, at high-speed. At such a high-speed circulation, it only consumes a negligible amount of oil, usually about one tablespoon to prepare aromatic crispy foods

The hot-air technology cooks foods from different angles. More importantly, the technology maintains their great taste and essential nutrients. Meals prepared with such a meager amount of oil also free you from greasy stains on your fingers

This technology has brought a new era of cooking by using 80% less fat as compared to traditional deep fat frying. Air Fryer comes with an exhaust fan placed right above the cooking chamber; this fan provides the food required airflow. This modern heating technology ensures that food is cooked with constant heated air

As a result, the same heating temperature is maintained covering different parts of the added food ingredients. Air fryer is completely odorless and harmless making it a user-friendly kitchen invention.

Benefits of Using an Air Fryer

Time Saving:

With only 24 hours to complete everyday routine tasks, the time has become a genuinely luxury in our fast paced lifestyle. Air Fryers are designed to save your precious cooking time by serving you crunchy snacks and fried cuisines in a matter of minutes. If you are always on a tight schedule, Air Fryer is no less than a time savior

Superfast Heating:

Unlike traditional frying method, Air Fryers takes only a few minutes to heat and prepare foods. They are always ready to make meals whenever you crave for fried foods. Most Air Fryer models get ready in only 3 minutes to heat up properly and they can also go as high as 400 degrees F to make you crispy meals

Natural Food Taste:

It's quite common for anyone to worry about their food's ability to delight them with their mouthwatering flavors. When it comes to Air Fryers, things are no different. Air Fryers prepare meals without compromising on their taste profile. As far as the taste is concerned, they can easily be compared with deep-fried foods

Protect the Food's Nutrients:

Unlike deep frying, Air Fryers do not deconstruct the food's good nutrients and add on bad fats. If you think your yasai tempura (deep fried battered vegetables) are healthy, here is news for you; while they may look like they are full of nutritious elements, the deep-frying process would have destroyed the beneficial vitamins and minerals contained in the vegetables

Versatile Options:

Air Fryer allows you cook a diverse range of foods, be it chicken tenders, mushrooms, crispy fries, fried shrimp, mozzarella sticks, or grilled vegetables. You want to grill, fry, roast, or bake your foods? Air Fryers are there to prepare them in real quick time. Specific ultra modern range of Air Fryers also allow you make many recipes in a single cooking session

Space Saver and Ease of Cleaning:

Cleaning after cooking foods is also very easy as they are designed for effortless cleaning. On top of that, they don't take up much of your counter space and require quite less space to store

How to Use an Air Fryer

There are 4 steps in using an air fryer, follow this set of instructions when cooking anything in your air fryer:

Preparation:

To prevent ingredients from sticking to the air fryer basket, spray it with a nonstick cooking spray or add a tablespoon of oil. Don't over pack foods in your air fryer basket otherwise some parts won't be fully cooked thoroughly. If you are working with a marinated or wet ingredient, make sure you rub them dry, because this will help avert splattering or excess smoke

Pre-Heating:

Plug in your air fryer and preheat it. This usually takes around five minutes, although preheating is not that necessary, nevertheless it can reduce your time in cooking.

Cooking:

If you are cooking frozen foods or items with small ingredients, try shaking the air fryer many times to prepare it evenly and efficiently. Also, when cooking high fatty foods, you should have it at the back of your mind that, the fats will drop to the base of the air fryer, which will thereafter need cleaning

Cleaning:

To ensure your air fryer stays in shape, make sure you clean it properly by purifying the air fryer basket and the pan after using them. Most air fryers come with dishwasher safe parts which makes this process easy

Getting the Most Out of your Air Fryer

To maximize the benefits of using an air fryer, here are some tips that you should not overlook:

Getting Started

- Place your air fryer on a level and heatproof kitchen top, if you have granite surfaces this is perfect
- Avoid putting it close to the wall as this will dissipate the heat causing slower cooking times. Leave a space of at least five inches between the wall and the air fryer
- Oven-safe baking sheets and cake pans may be used in the air fryer on the condition that they can fit inside easily and the door can close

Before Cooking

- If you can, always preheat your air fryer for 3 minutes before cooking. Once the timer goes off it will be ready to rock and roll
- Use a hand pumped spray bottle for applying the oil. Adopting this method will cause you to use less oil and is an easier option when compared to brushing or drizzling. Avoid canned aerosol brands as they tend to have a lot of nasty chemicals
- Always Bread if necessary. This breading step should not be missed. Be sure to press the breading firmly onto the meat or vegetable so the crumbs do not fall off easily

Whilst Cooking

- Adding water to the air fryer drawer while cooking high-fat foods to will prevent excessive smoke and heat. Use this technique when cooking burgers, bacon, sausage and similar foods
- Secure light foods such as bread slices with toothpicks so they don't get blown around
- Avoid putting too many food items into the air fryer basket. Overcrowding will result in uneven cooking and will also prevent the food from getting that glorious crispy texture that we all love.
- Shaking the fryer and flipping the food halfway through the cooking process is advised to make sure that everything inside cooks evenly
- Opening the air fryer a few times to check how the food is doing won't affect the cooking time, so don't worry.

Once done:

- Remove the basket from the drawer before taking out the food to prevent the oil remaining on the food that you just fried.
- The juices in the air fryer drawer can be used to make delicious marinades and sauces. If you find it too greasy you can always reduce it in a saucepan to get rid of the excess liquid.
- Cleaning both the basket and drawer after every use is imperative

Air Fryer - Cleaning & Maintenance

The first thing you should have at your fingertips is that, if you do not clean and maintain your air fryer from time to time, it won't last long. Following these guidelines will secure the fact that your air fryer will remain effective and durable for years to come

How to clean your air fryer:?

1. Unplug your air fryer from the wall socket and allow it to cool until you can touch.

2. Using a wet rag, wipe the exterior part of your air fryer

3. Remove the air fryer pan, tray, basket and wash it with hot water and a dishwasher soap in your sink. These parts are removable and are safe for an easy cleanup.

4. Use a cloth or sponge to wipe and clean the inner part of your air fryer

5. If you find any ingredients sticking in your air fryer, scrub it off with a brush.

6. Before adding the pan, tray, and basket back into your air fryer ensure they are entirely dry

7. Once your air fryer is cleaned, store it safely.

How to maintain your air fryer:

Your air fryer requires a standard form of maintenance to ensure it does not get damaged or work erroneously. To do this, one needs to follow this instruction

1. Before using your air fryer, make sure you check the cord. That is, do not plug a damaged cord into an outlet; this can result in a ghastly injury or even death.

2. Make sure your air fryer is clean and free of any debris before you begin cooking. Check the inner part and make sure you remove anything redundant in there.

3. Ensure the air fryer is placed upright, on a flat surface.

4. Make sure that your air fryer is not too close to the wall or another appliance. Air fryers require 4-inches of space all around them.

5. One after the other, check each component of your air fryer, including the basket, pan, and handle.

6. If you find anything damaged or wrong with your air fryer, reach the manufacturer and get it replaced.

Air Fryer - FAQs

1. How many items can be cooked at a go in an air fryer?

Answer- You can easily cook two different items at a go in an air fryer but make sure to use the divider. This will help in proper cooking and less time will be consumed.

2. Do we need to preheat the air fryer?

Answer- No, there is no need to preheat the air fryer. However, pre-heating the air fryer for about 4 minutes can help in significant reduction of the cooking time.

3. Can we cook different varieties of food in an air fryer?

Answer- Yes, you can easily cook different varieties of food in an air fryer. One of the best things about cooking food in an air fryer is that it is healthy and free from oil. Items such as meat, potatoes, poultry and French fries can be easily cooked. Apart from these items you can also bake brownies and grill different vegetables.

4. Can we add more ingredients while the food is getting cooked in an air fryer?

*Answer-*Yes, you can add more ingredients while the food is getting cooked in an air fryer but make sure to add the ingredients immediately otherwise the heat loss may lead to more time consumption for cooking the food.

5. What is the input power range of an air fryer?

Answer- For the European market the input power range is 220 v and for USA market it is 110 v.

6. Does air fryer help in making food crispy and tasty?

Answer- Yes, the food that you cook in an air fryer is as tasty and crispy as it is with frying. One of the main reasons why air fryer cooks tasty and crispy food is because it helps in keeping the outer layer of the food crisp and the inside gets soft.

7. Is it possible to use baking paper or aluminium foil in an air fryer?

Answer- Yes, you can use a baking paper or aluminium foil but you need to make sure that appropriate space is given so that the steam can pass easily.

8. How much time an air fryer takes to cook frozen foods?

Answer- One of the best things to do while cooking frozen food in an air fryer is to use the knob as per the food that you are cooking. It normally takes some more time to cook frozen foods as compared to other food items.

9. Is there any specific type of oil required for air fryer?

Answer- No, there is no special oil which is required for cooking in an air fryer. You can use any type of oil such as olive oil, peanut oil, and even butter spray.

10. How much food can be cooked at a time in an air fryer?

Answer- It all depends on the capacity of the air fryer. Most of the air fryers come with 500g of capacity and you can also see a "max" mark on the basket of the air fryer which means that the air fryer can be filled up to this mark.

Air Fryer Cooking Charts

The below chart can be used for reference assuming that the food is flipped or basket shaken halftime during cooking.

Frozen Foods Chart

Frozen Foods		
Type	*Temperature (Fahrenheit)*	*Cook Time (Minutes)*
Thin French Fries (20 oz)	400	14
Thick French Fries (17 oz)	400	18
Onion Rings (12 oz)	400	8
Mozarella Sticks (11 oz)	400	8
Pot Stickers (10 oz)	400	8
Fish Sticks (10 oz)	400	10
Fish Filets (10 oz)	400	14
Chicken Nuggets (12 oz)	400	10
Breaded Shrimps	400	9

Poultry Chart

POULTRY		
Type	*Temperature (Fahrenheit)*	*Cook Time (Minutes)*
Bone-In breasts (1.25 lbs)	370	25
Boneless breasts (4 lbs)	380	12
Drumsticks (2.5 lbs)	370	20
Bone-In thighs (2 lbs)	380	22
Boneless thighs (1.25 lbs)	380	18 - 20
Bone-In Legs (1.75 lbs)	380	30
Wings (2 lbs)	400	12
Halved Game Hen (2 lbs)	390	20
Whole Chicken (6.5 lbs)	360	75
Tenders	360	8 - 10

Vegetables Chart

VEGETABLES		
Type	Temperature (Fahrenheit)	Cook Time (Minutes)
Asparagus (sliced)	400	5
Beets (whole)	400	40
Broccoli Florets	400	6
Brussels Sprouts(halved)	380	15
Carrots (sliced)	380	15
Cauliflower florets	400	12
Corn on cob	390	6
Eggplant (cubed)	400	15
Fennel (quartered)	370	15
Green Beans	400	5
Kale leaves	250	12
Mushrooms (sliced)	400	5
Pearl Onions	400	10
Parsnips (cubed)	380	15
Pepper (chunks)	400	15
Small baby potatoes	400	15
Potato (chunks)	400	12
Whole potatoes (baked)	400	40
Squash (chunks)	400	12
Sweet potatoes (baked)	380	30 - 35
Cherry Tomatoes	400	4
Tomatoes (halved)	350	10
Zucchini sticks	400	12

Fish & Seafood Chart

FISH & SEAFOOD		
Type	Temperature (Fahrenheit)	Cook Time (Minutes)
Fish Filets (8 oz)	400	10
Calamari (8 oz)	400	4
Salmon filets (6 oz)	380	12
Swordfish Steak	400	10
Tuna Steak	400	7 - 10
Scallops	400	5 - 7
Shrimps	400	5

BEEF		
Type	*Temperature (Fahrenheit)*	*Cook Time (Minutes)*
Burger (4 oz)	370	16 - 20
Filet Mignon (8 oz)	400	18
Flank Steak (1.5 lbs)	400	12
London Broil (2 lbs)	400	20 - 28
Meatballs	380	7
Bone-In Ribeye (8 oz)	400	10 - 15
Sirloin Steaks (12 oz)	400	9 - 14
Beef-Eye Round Roast(4lbs)	390	45 - 55

Breakfasts

Nuts and Zucchini Bread

(Prep + Cook Time: 35 minutes | Servings: 16)

Ingredients:
- 3 cups all-purpose flour
- 2 cups zucchini; grated
- 1 cup walnuts; chopped
- 2¼ cups white sugar
- 1 cup vegetable oil
- 3 eggs
- 1 tbsp. ground cinnamon
- 1 tsp. baking powder
- 1 tsp. baking soda
- 1 tsp. salt
- 3 tsp. vanilla extract

Directions:
1. Take a bowl and mix together the flour, baking powder, baking soda, cinnamon and salt.
2. In another large bowl, add the sugar, oil, eggs and vanilla extract. Beat until well combined.
3. After that, add in the flour mixture and stir until just combined.
4. Gently, fold in the zucchini and walnuts. Set the temperature of Air Fryer to 320°F. Grease and flour two (8x4-inch) loaf pans.
5. Place the mixture evenly into the prepared pans. Arrange the loaf pans into an Air Fryer basket. Air Fry for about 20 minutes or until a toothpick inserted in the center comes out clean.
6. Remove the pans from Air Fryer and place onto a wire rack for about 10 to 15 minutes.
7. Carefully, take out the bread from pans and put onto a wire rack until it is completely cool before slicing. Cut the breads into desired size slices and serve.

Vanilla Banana Bread

(Prep + Cook Time: 50 minutes | Servings: 5)

Ingredients:
- 2 ripe bananas, peeled and mashed
- 1 large egg
- 1/2 cup all-purpose flour
- 1/2 cup granulated sugar
- 1/4 cup plain yogurt
- 1/4 cup vegetable oil
- 1/4 cup whole wheat flour
- 2 tbsp. turbinado sugar
- 1/2 tsp. pure vanilla extract
- 1/4 tsp. baking soda
- 1/2 tsp. salt

Directions:
1. In a bowl, sift together the flours, baking soda and salt.
2. In another large bowl, mix well the egg, granulated sugar, yogurt, oil and vanilla extract.
3. Add in the bananas and beat until well combined. Now, add the flour mixture and mix until just combined.
4. Set the temperature of Air Fryer to 310°F. Place the mixture evenly into a cake pan and sprinkle with the turbinado sugar.
5. Arrange the cake pan into an Air Fryer basket. Air Fry for about 30 to 35 minutes or until a toothpick inserted in the center comes out clean, turning the pan once halfway through.
6. Carefully, take out the bread from pan and put onto a wire rack until it is completely cool before slicing. Cut the bread into desired size slices and serve.

Bananas Bread

(Prep + Cook Time: 30 minutes | Servings: 8)

Ingredients:

- 3 bananas, peeled and sliced
- 1 1/3 cups flour
- 1/2 cup milk
- 1/2 cup olive oil
- 2/3 cup sugar
- 1 tsp. baking soda
- 1 tsp. baking powder
- 1 tsp. ground cinnamon
- 1 tsp. salt

Directions:

1. Take the bowl of a stand mixer and mix well all the listed ingredients.
2. Set the temperature of air fryer to 330°F. Grease a loaf pan.
3. Place the mixture into the prepared pan. Arrange the loaf pan into an air fryer basket. Air fry for about 20 minutes or until a toothpick inserted in the center comes out clean.
4. Remove from air fryer and place the pan onto a wire rack for about 10 to 15 minutes.
5. Carefully, take out the bread from pan and put onto a wire rack until it is completely cool before slicing. Cut the bread into desired size slices and serve.

Special French Toasts

(Prep + Cook Time: 14 minutes | Servings: 2)

Ingredients:

- 4 bread slices
- 1/4 cup chickpea flour
- 3 tbsp. onion; finely chopped
- 1/4 tsp. ground turmeric
- 1/4 tsp. ground cumin
- 2 tsp. green chili, seeded and finely chopped
- 1/2 tsp. red chili powder
- Salt, to taste
- Water, as needed

Directions:

1. Add all the Ingredients except bread slices in a large bowl and mix until a thick mixture forms.
2. Apply the mixture over both sides of the bread slices using a spoon. Set the temperature of Air Fryer to 390°F. Line the Air Fryer pan with a piece of foil.
3. Place the bread slices in the prepared pan. set the Air Fryer to 355°F. Air Fry for about 3 to 4 minutes. Serve warm.

Pineapple Corn bread

(Prep + Cook Time: 25 minutes | Servings: 5)

Ingredients:

- 7 oz. canned crushed pineapple
- 1 (8½-oz.) package Jiffy corn muffin
- 1 egg
- 1/3 cup canned pineapple juice

Directions:

1. In a bowl, mix together all the ingredients.
2. Set the temperature of Air Fryer to 330°F. Grease a round cake pan. (6"x 3")
3. Place the mixture evenly into the prepared pan. Arrange the cake pan into an Air Fryer basket. Air Fry for about 15 minutes or until a toothpick inserted in the center comes out clean.
4. Remove from Air Fryer and place the pan onto a wire rack for about 10 to 15 minutes.
5. Carefully, take out the bread from pan and put onto a wire rack until it is completely cool before slicing. Cut the bread into desired size slices and serve.

Tasty Tuna Sandwiches

(Prep + Cook Time: 15 Minutes | **Servings:** 4)

Ingredients:

- 16-ounce canned tuna; drained
- 1/4 cup mayonnaise
- 2 tbsp. mustard
- 1 tbsp. lemon juice
- 2 green onions; chopped
- 3 English muffins; halved
- 3 tbsp. butter
- 6 provolone cheese

Directions:

1. In a bowl; mix tuna with mayo, lemon juice, mustard and green onions and stir
2. Grease muffin halves with the butter, place them in preheated air fryer and bake them at 350°F, for 4 minutes. Spread tuna mix on muffin halves; top each with provolone cheese, return sandwiches to air fryer and cook them for 4 minutes; divide among plates and serve for breakfast right away

Pumpkin and Yogurt Bread

(Prep + Cook Time: 25 minutes | Servings: 4)

Ingredients:

- 2 large eggs
- 4 tbsp. honey
- 6 tbsp. oats
- 4 tbsp. plain Greek yogurt
- 2 tbsp. vanilla essence
- 8 tbsp. pumpkin puree
- 6 tbsp. banana flour
- Pinch of ground nutmeg

Directions:

1. Take a bowl, add in all the Ingredients except oats and with a hand mixer, mix until smooth.
2. Add the oats and mix them well using a fork.
3. Set the temperature of Air Fryer to 360°F. Grease and flour a loaf pan. Place the mixture evenly into the prepared pan. Arrange the loaf pan into an Air Fryer basket.
4. Air Fry for about 15 minutes or until a toothpick inserted in the center comes out clean. Remove the pans from Air Fryer and place onto a wire rack for about 5 minutes.
5. Carefully, take out the bread from pan and put onto a wire rack to cool for about 5 to 10 minutes before slicing. Cut the bread into desired size slices and serve.

Tasty French Toasts

(Prep + Cook Time: 13 minutes | Servings: 2)

Ingredients:

- 4 bread slices
- 1/4 cup evaporated milk
- 2 eggs
- 3 tbsp. sugar
- 1/8 tsp. vanilla extract
- 2 tsp. olive oil

Directions:

1. Set the temperature of Air Fryer to 390°F. Grease an Air Fryer pan and insert in the Air Fryer while heating.
2. In a large bowl, mix together all the above Ingredients except bread slices.
3. Coat the bread slices evenly with egg mixture. Arrange the bread slices in the prepared pan. Air Fry for about 2 to 3 minutes per side. Serve warm.

Tasty Cream Bread

(Prep + Cook Time: 75 minutes | Servings: 12)

Ingredients:

- 1 large egg
- 4½ cups bread flour
- 3/4 cup whipping cream
- 1/2 cup all-purpose flour
- 1/4 cup fine sugar
- 1 cup milk
- 2 tbsp. milk powder
- 1 tsp. salt
- 3 tsp. dry yeast

Directions:

1. In the baking pan of a bread machine, place all the Ingredients in the order recommended by the manufacturer.
2. Place the baking pan in bread machine and close with the lid. Select the Dough cycle and press Start button.
3. Once the cycle is completed, remove the paddles from bread machine but keep the dough inside for about 45 to 50 minutes to proof. Set the temperature of air fryer to 375°F. Grease 2 loaf pans.
4. Remove the dough from pan and place onto a lightly floured surface.
5. Divide the dough into four equal-sized balls and then, roll each into a rectangle.
6. Tightly roll each rectangle like a Swiss roll. Place two rolls into each prepared loaf pan. Set aside for about 1 hour. Arrange the loaf pans into an air fryer basket.
7. Air fry for about 50 to 55 minutes or until a toothpick inserted in the center comes out clean.
8. Remove the pans from air fryer and place onto a wire rack for about 10 to 15 minutes.
9. After that, remove the bread rolls from pans and place onto a wire rack until they are completely cool before slicing. Cut each roll into desired size slices and serve.

Mushroom and Tomato Frittata

(Prep + Cook Time: 29 minutes | Servings: 2)

Ingredients:

- 1 bacon slice; chopped
- 6 cherry tomatoes, halved
- 6 fresh mushrooms, sliced
- 3 eggs
- 1/2 cup Parmesan cheese; grated
- 1 tbsp. fresh parsley; chopped
- 1 tbsp. olive oil
- Salt and freshly ground black pepper, as needed

Directions:

1. Set the temperature of Air Fryer to 390°F. In a baking dish, mix together the bacon, tomatoes, mushrooms, salt and black pepper.
2. Arrange the baking dish into an Air Fryer basket. Air Fry for about 6 minutes. Add the eggs in a small bowl and beat them well. Add in the parsley and cheese and mix them well.
3. Remove the baking dish from Air Fryer and top the bacon mixture evenly with egg mixture.
4. Return the baking dish in Air Fryer basket. Air Fry for about 8 minutes. Serve hot.

Cheese Omelet

(Prep + Cook Time: 13 minutes | Servings: 2)

Ingredients:

- 1/4 cup cheddar cheese; grated
- 1/4 cup cream
- 4 eggs
- Salt and freshly ground black pepper, to taste

Directions:

1. Set the temperature of Air Fryer to 350°F. Lightly, grease a 6"x3" pan. In a bowl, mix together the eggs, cream, salt and black pepper.
2. After that, pour the egg mixture into the prepared pan and Air Fry for about 4 minutes.

3. Once done, sprinkle the cheese over the top and cook for another 4 minutes at 350° F.
4. When the time is up, take out the pan from air fryer and use a spatula to flip the omelet onto the pan. Serve hot.

Tasty Apple Muffins

(Prep + Cook Time: 40 minutes | Servings: 12)

Ingredients:
- 1¾ cups plain flour
- 3/4 cup milk
- 1/3 cup applesauce
- 1 cup apple, cored and chopped
- 1/3 cup white sugar
- 1/4 tsp. ground ginger
- 1½ tsp. baking powder
- 1/2 tsp. ground cinnamon
- 1/4 tsp. salt

Directions:
1. In a large bowl, mix together the flour, sugar, baking powder, spices and salt.
2. Add in the milk and applesauce. Beat until just combined. Fold in the chopped apple.
3. Set the temperature of Air Fryer to 390°F. Grease 12 muffin molds. Put the mixture evenly into the prepared muffin molds. Arrange the molds into an Air Fryer basket.
4. Air Fry for about 20 to 25 minutes or until a toothpick inserted in the center comes out clean.
5. Remove the muffin molds from Air Fryer and place onto a wire rack to cool for about 10 minutes.
6. Carefully, invert the muffins onto the wire rack to completely cool before serving. Serve.

Sausage Frittata

(Prep + Cook Time: 26 minutes | Servings: 2)

Ingredients:
- 1 large potato, boiled, peeled and cubed
- 3 jumbo eggs
- 1/2 of chorizo sausage, sliced
- 1/2 cup frozen corn
- 1 tbsp. fresh parsley; chopped
- 2 tbsp. feta cheese, crumbled
- 1 tbsp. olive oil
- Salt and freshly ground black pepper, as needed

Directions:
1. Set the temperature of Air Fryer to 355°F. In the pan of an Air Fryer, heat the oil and cook the sausage, corn and potato for 5 to 6 minutes or until golden brown.
2. In a bowl, mix together the eggs, salt and black pepper. pour the eggs over the sausage mixture and top with cheese and parsley.
3. Air Fry for about 5 minutes or until desired doneness. Serve hot.

Egg Yolks with Squid

(Prep + Cook Time: 35 minutes | Servings: 4)

Ingredients:
- 1/2 cup Self rising flour
- 14 oz. squid flower, cleaned and pat dried
- 2 green chilies, seeded and chopped
- 2 curry leaves stalks
- 4 raw salted egg yolks
- 1/2 cup chicken broth
- 2 tbsp. evaporated milk
- 1 tbsp. sugar
- 1 tbsp. olive oil
- 2 tbsp. butter
- Salt and freshly ground black pepper

Directions:
1. Set the temperature of Air Fryer to 355°F. Grease an Air Fryer pan.
2. In a shallow dish, add the flour. Sprinkle the squid flower evenly with salt and black pepper.
3. Coat the squid evenly with flour and then shake off any excess flour. Place the squid into the prepared pan in a single layer.
4. Air Fry for about 9 minutes. Remove from the Air Fryer and set aside

5. heat the oil and butter in a skillet over medium heat and sauté the chilies and curry leaves for about 3 minutes. Add the egg yolks and cook for about 1 minute, stirring continuously.
6. Gradually, add the chicken broth and cook for about 3 to 5 minutes, stirring continuously.
7. Add in the milk and sugar and mix until well combined. Add the fried squid and toss to coat well. Serve hot.

Chocolatey Peanut Butter Bread

(Prep + Cook Time: 45 minutes | Servings: 8)

Ingredients:
- 3/4 cup all-purpose flour
- 1/3 cup creamy peanut butter
- 1/3 cup mini chocolate chips
- 1/3 cup unsweetened applesauce
- 1/4 cup plain Greek yogurt
- 1/4 cup cocoa powder
- 1/4 cup sugar
- 1 egg
- 1/2 tsp. baking soda
- 1/2 tsp. baking powder
- 1/8 tsp. salt
- 1/2 tsp. vanilla extract

Directions:
1. In a bowl, mix together the flour, cocoa powder, sugar, baking soda, baking powder and salt.
2. In another bowl, add the egg, applesauce, yogurt and vanilla extract. Beat until well combined.
3. After that, add in the flour mixture and mix until just combined. Add the peanut butter and mix until smooth. Gently, fold in the chocolate chips.
4. Set the temperature of Air Fryer to 350°F. Grease a loaf pan. Place the mixture evenly into the prepared pan.
5. Arrange the loaf pan into an Air Fryer basket. Air Fry for about 30 minutes or until a toothpick inserted in the center comes out clean.
6. Remove from Air Fryer and place the pan onto a wire rack for about 10 to 15 minutes.
7. Carefully, take out the bread from pan and put onto a wire rack until it is completely cool before slicing.
8. Cut the bread into desired size slices and serve.

Mini Tomato Quiche

(Prep + Cook Time: 45 minutes | Servings: 2)

Ingredients:
- 4 eggs
- 1 cup Gouda cheese; shredded
- 1/2 cup milk
- 1/4 cup onion; chopped
- 1/2 cup tomatoes; chopped
- Salt, to taste

Directions:
1. Set the temperature of air fryer to 340°F. In a large ramekin, mix together all the listed ingredients.
2. Arrange the ramekin into an air fryer basket.
3. Air fry for about 30 minutes. Serve hot.

Carrot Muffins

(Prep + Cook Time: 29 minutes | Servings: 6)

Ingredients:
For Muffins:
- 1 carrot, peeled and grated
- 1/4 cup whole wheat flour
- 1/2 cup yogurt
- 1/4 cup all-purpose flour
- 2 to 4 tbsp. water (if needed)
- 1 tbsp. vegetable oil
- 3 tbsp. cottage cheese; grated
- 1/8 tsp. baking soda
- 1 tsp. vinegar
- 1/2 tsp. baking powder
- 1/2 tsp. dried parsley; crushed
- 1/2 tsp. salt

For Topping:
- 7 oz. Parmesan cheese; grated
- 1/4 cup walnuts; chopped

Directions:
1. Set the temperature of Air Fryer to 355°F. Grease 6 medium muffin molds.
2. **For the muffin:** in a large bowl, mix together the flours, baking powder, baking soda, parsley and salt.
3. In another large bowl, mix well the yogurt and vinegar.
4. Add the remaining Ingredients except water and beat them well. (add some water if needed)
5. Make a well in the center of the yogurt mixture. Slowly, add the flour mixture in the well and mix until well combined.
6. Place the mixture evenly into the prepared muffin molds and top with the Parmesan cheese and walnuts.
7. Place the muffin molds into an Air Fryer basket in 2 batches. Air Fry for about 7 minutes or until a toothpick inserted in the center comes out clean.
8. Remove the muffin molds from Air Fryer and place onto a wire rack to cool for about 10 minutes.
9. Carefully, invert the muffins onto the wire rack to completely cool before serving. Enjoy!

Blueberry Muffins

(Prep + Cook Time: 27 minutes | Servings: 12)

Ingredients:
- 1/2 cup fresh blueberries
- 1/2 cup milk
- 2 cups plus 2 tbsp. Self rising flour
- 2 oz. butter, melted
- 2 eggs
- 5 tbsp. white sugar
- 2 tbsp. fresh orange juice
- 1/2 tsp. vanilla extract
- 2 tsp. fresh orange zest; finely grated

Directions:
1. In a bowl, mix together the flour and white sugar.
2. In another large bowl, mix well the remaining Ingredients except blueberries. Add in the flour mixture and mix until just combined. Fold in the blueberries.
3. Set the temperature of Air Fryer to 355°F. Grease 12 muffin molds. Put the mixture evenly into the prepared muffin molds. Arrange the molds into an Air Fryer basket.
4. Air Fry for about 12 minutes or until a toothpick inserted in the center comes out clean.
5. Remove the muffin molds from Air Fryer and place onto a wire rack to cool for about 10 minutes.
6. Carefully, invert the muffins onto the wire rack to completely cool before serving. Serve.

Delicious Ham Rolls

(**Prep + Cook Time:** 20 Minutes | **Servings:** 4)

Ingredients:
- 1 sheet puff pastry
- 8 ham slices; chopped
- 4 handful gruyere cheese; grated
- 4 tsp. mustard

Directions:
1. Roll out puff pastry on a working surface, divide cheese, ham and mustard, roll tight and cut into medium rounds.
2. Place all rolls in air fryer and cook for 10 minutes at 370 degrees F. Divide rolls on plates and serve for breakfast

Pumpkin Bread

(Prep + Cook Time: 40 minutes | Servings: 4)

Ingredients:
- 1/4 cup canned pumpkin
- 2 large eggs
- 1/4 cup coconut flour
- 2 tbsp. unsweetened almond milk
- 2 tbsp. stevia blend
- 3/4 tsp. pumpkin pie spice
- 1/4 tsp. ground cinnamon
- 1 tsp. baking powder
- 1/8 tsp. salt
- 1 tsp. vanilla extract

Directions:
1. In a bowl, mix together the flour, stevia, baking powder, spices and salt.
2. In another large bowl, add the pumpkin, eggs, almond milk and vanilla extract. Beat until well combined.
3. After that, add in the flour mixture and mix until just combined Set the temperature of air fryer to 350°F. Line a cake pan with a greased parchment paper.
4. Place the mixture evenly into the prepared pan. Arrange the pan into an air fryer basket. Air fry for about 25 minutes or until a toothpick inserted in the center comes out clean.
5. Remove the pans from air fryer and place onto a wire rack for about 5 minutes.
6. Carefully, take out the bread from pan and put onto a wire rack to cool for about 5 to 10 minutes before slicing.
7. Cut the bread into desired size slices and serve.

Bacon and Hot Dogs Omelet

(Prep + Cook Time: 20 minutes | Servings: 2)

Ingredients:
- 1 bacon slice; chopped
- 2 hot dogs; chopped
- 2 small onions; chopped
- 4 eggs

Directions:
1. Set the temperature of Air Fryer to 320°F.
2. In an Air Fryer baking pan, crack the eggs and beat them well. Add in the remaining Ingredients and gently, stir to combine. Air Fry for about 10 minutes. Serve hot.

Nuts and Banana Bread

(Prep + Cook Time: 40 minutes | Servings: 10)

Ingredients:
- 3½ oz. walnuts; chopped
- 2/3 cup plus 1/2 tbsp. caster sugar
- 2 medium eggs
- 2 cups bananas, peeled and mashed
- 1½ cups Self rising flour
- 5 tbsp. plus 1 tsp. butter
- 1/4 tsp. bicarbonate of soda

Directions:
1. In a bowl, mix together the flour and bicarbonate of soda.
2. In another bowl, add the butter and sugar. Beat until pale and fluffy. Put the eggs, one at a time along with a little flour and mix them well.
3. Stir in the remaining flour and walnuts. Now, add the bananas and mix until well combined.
4. Set the temperature of air fryer to 355°F. Grease a loaf pan. Place the mixture evenly into the prepared pan. Arrange the loaf pan into an air fryer basket. Air fry for 10 minutes on 355°F, then 15 minutes for 338°F.
5. Once done, remove from air fryer and place the pan onto a wire rack for about 10 to 15 minutes.
6. Carefully, take out the bread from pan and put onto a wire rack until it is completely cool before slicing. Cut the bread into desired size slices and serve.

Zucchini Omelet

(Prep + Cook Time: 29 minutes | Servings: 2)

Ingredients:

- 4 eggs
- 1 zucchini, julienned
- 1 tsp. butter
- 1/4 tsp. red pepper flakes; crushed
- 1/4 tsp. fresh basil; chopped
- Salt and ground black pepper; as your liking

Directions:

1. Set the temperature of Air Fryer to 355°F. Grease an Air Fryer pan.
2. Take a skillet, melt the butter over medium heat and cook the zucchini for about 3 to 4 minutes.
3. Meanwhile, in a bowl, mix together the eggs, basil, red pepper flakes, salt and black pepper. Add the cooked zucchini and gently, stir to combine. Transfer the mixture into the prepared pan.
4. Air Fry for 10 minutes or until done completely. Serve hot.

Italian Eggplant Sandwich

(**Prep + Cook Time:** 55 minutes | **Servings:** 2)

Ingredients:

- 1 eggplant; sliced
- 1/2 cup panko breadcrumbs
- 4 bread slices
- 1/2 cup mayonnaise
- 3/4 cup tomato paste
- 1/2 tsp. garlic powder
- 2 tsp. parsley; chopped
- 1/2 tsp. Italian seasoning
- 1 tbsp. avocado oil + a drizzle
- 2 tbsp. coconut milk
- 2 tbsp. fresh basil; chopped
- 2 tbsp. cheddar cheese; grated
- 2 cups mozzarella cheese; grated
- Salt and black pepper to taste

Directions:

1. Season eggplant slices with salt and pepper and set aside for 30 minutes. Then pat them dry them and brush with mayo and milk
2. In a bowl, combine the parsley, breadcrumbs, Italian seasoning, garlic powder, salt and black pepper; stir.
3. Next, dip the eggplant slices in this mix and place them on a lined baking sheet; drizzle with oil.
4. Place the baking sheet in your air fryer's basket and cook at 400°F for 15 minutes, flipping the eggplant slices halfway
5. Brush the bread slices with the remaining 1 tbsp. of the oil. Then arrange 2 of them on a working surface and add cheddar, mozzarella, baked eggplant slices, tomato paste and basil; top with the other 2 bread slices.
6. Grill sandwiches on your grill for 10 minutes, serve immediately

Chicken Omelet

(Prep + Cook Time: 31 minutes | Servings: 8)

Ingredients:

- 1/2 jalapeño pepper, seeded and chopped
- 3 eggs
- 1 onion; chopped
- 1/4 cup cooked chicken; shredded
- 1 tsp. butter
- Salt and freshly ground black pepper, as needed

Directions:

1. Take a frying pan, melt the butter over medium heat and sauté the onion for about 4 to 5 minutes.
2. Add in the jalapeño pepper and sauté for about 1 minute. Add the chicken and stir to combine. Remove from the heat and set aside.
3. Set the temperature of Air Fryer to 355°F. Grease an Air Fryer pan.

4. Meanwhile, in a bowl, mix together the eggs, salt and black pepper. Place the chicken mixture into the prepared pan.
5. Pour the egg mixture over chicken mixture. Air Fry for 10 minutes or until done completely. Serve hot.

Green Beans Omelet

(**Prep + Cook Time:** 15 minutes | **Servings:** 4)

Ingredients:
- 3 oz. green beans; trimmed and halved
- 4 eggs; whisked
- 4 garlic cloves; minced
- 1 tsp. soy sauce
- 1 tbsp. olive oil
- Salt and black pepper to taste

Directions:
1. In a bowl, mix all ingredients except the beans and oil; whisk well.
2. Heat up your air fryer at 320°F, then add the oil and heat it up
3. Add the beans, stir and sauté them for 3 minutes. Add the egg mixture over the beans, spread and cook for 7-8 minutes more. Slice the omelet and serve immediately

Banana Muffins

(Prep + Cook Time: 40 minutes | Servings: 12)

Ingredients:
- 4 ripe bananas, peeled and mashed
- 1/2 cup brown sugar
- 1/4 cup walnuts
- 2 eggs
- 1 2/3 cups plain flour
- 1 tsp. baking soda
- 1 tsp. baking powder
- 1 tsp. ground cinnamon
- 1 tsp. salt
- 3 tbsp. milk
- 1 tbsp. Nutella
- 1 tsp. vanilla essence

Directions:
1. In a large bowl, sift the flour, baking soda, baking powder, cinnamon and salt.
2. In another bowl, mix together the remaining Ingredients except walnuts.
3. Add the banana mixture into flour mixture and mix until just combined.
4. Fold in the walnuts. Set the temperature of Air Fryer to 248°F. Grease 12 muffin molds. Put the mixture evenly into the prepared muffin molds.
5. Arrange the molds into an Air Fryer basket. Air Fry for about 20 to 25 minutes or until a toothpick inserted in the center comes out clean.
6. Remove the muffin molds from Air Fryer and place onto a wire rack to cool for about 10 minutes.
7. Carefully, invert the muffins onto the wire rack to completely cool before serving. Serve.

Zucchini and Chicken Tortillas

(**Prep + Cook Time:** 12 minutes | **Servings:** 4)

Ingredients:
- 6 oz. rotisserie chicken; cooked and shredded
- 4 tortillas
- 1/3 cup mayonnaise
- 1 cup zucchini; shredded
- 1 cup parmesan cheese; grated
- 4 tbsp. butter; softened
- 2 tbsp. mustard

Directions:
1. Spread the butter on the tortillas, place them in your air fryer's basket and heat them up at 400°F for 3 minutes
2. In a bowl, mix the chicken, zucchini, mayo and mustard; stir. Divide the mixture between the tortillas, sprinkle with cheese, roll them and place in your air fryer's basket
3. Continue to cook at 400°F for 4 minutes more. Serve right away and enjoy!

Raisin and Oat Muffins

(Prep + Cook Time: 25 minutes | Servings: 4)

Ingredients:

- 1/2 cup flour
- 1/2 cup powdered sugar
- 1/4 cup raisins
- 1/4 cup rolled oats
- 1/2 cup butter; softened
- 2 eggs
- 1/8 tsp. baking powder
- 1/4 tsp. vanilla extract

Directions:

1. In a bowl, mix together the flour, oats and baking powder. In another bowl, add the sugar and butter. Beat until you get the creamy texture.
2. After that, add in the egg and vanilla extract and beat until well combined.
3. Add the egg mixture into oat mixture and mix until just combined. Fold in the raisins.
4. Set the temperature of Air Fryer to 355°F. Grease 4 muffin molds.
5. Place the mixture evenly into the prepared muffin molds. Arrange the molds into an Air Fryer basket. Air Fry for 10 minutes or until a toothpick inserted in the center comes out clean.
6. Remove the muffin molds from Air Fryer and place onto a wire rack to cool for about 10 minutes.
7. Carefully, invert the muffins onto the wire rack to completely cool before serving. Serve.

Fruity Casserole

(**Prep + Cook Time:** 30 minutes | **Servings:** 6)

Ingredients:

- 1 banana; peeled and mashed
- 2 eggs; whisked
- 2 cups milk
- 1 cup blueberries
- 2 cups old fashioned oats
- 1/3 cup sugar
- 1 tsp. cinnamon powder
- 1 tsp. vanilla extract
- 1 tsp. baking powder
- 2 tbsp. butter
- Cooking spray

Directions:

1. In a bowl, mix the sugar, baking powder, cinnamon, blueberries, banana, eggs, butter and vanilla; whisk.
2. Heat up your air fryer at 320°F and grease with cooking spray
3. Add the oats, the berries and banana mix; cover and cook for 20 minutes. Divide into bowls and serve.

Bread and Bacon Cups

(Prep + Cook Time: 20 minutes | Servings: 2)

Ingredients:

- 1 bacon slice; chopped
- 2 bread slices
- 4 tomato slices
- 2 eggs
- 1 tbsp. Mozzarella cheese, shredded
- 2 tbsp. mayonnaise
- 1/2 tsp. butter
- 1/4 tsp. fresh parsley; chopped
- 1/8 tsp. maple syrup
- 1/8 tsp. balsamic vinegar
- Salt and freshly ground pepper, to taste

Directions:

1. Set the temperature of Air Fryer to 320°F. Lightly, grease 2 ramekins.
2. Line each prepared ramekin with 1 bread slice. Divide evenly the bacon and tomato slices over bread slice in each ramekin.
3. Top evenly with the cheese. Crack 1 egg in each ramekin over cheese. Drizzle with maple syrup and vinegar and then sprinkle with parsley, salt and black pepper. Place the ramekins in an Air Fryer basket.
4. Air Fry for 10 minutes or until desired doneness. Top with mayonnaise and serve.

Apple and Zucchini Bread

(Prep + Cook Time: 45 minutes | Servings: 8)

Ingredients:
For Bread:

- 1 cup all-purpose flour
- 1/2 cup zucchini, shredded
- 1/2 cup apple, cored and shredded
- 1/3 cup vegetable oil
- 1/3 cup sugar
- 1 egg

- 5 tbsp. walnuts; chopped
- 3/4 tsp. baking powder
- 1 tsp. vanilla extract
- 1/4 tsp. baking soda
- 1¼ tsp. ground cinnamon
- 1/4 tsp. salt

For Topping:

- 1 tbsp. walnuts; chopped
- 1/4 tsp. ground cinnamon

- 2 tsp. brown sugar

Directions:

1. For bread: in a bowl, mix together the flour, baking powder, baking soda, cinnamon and salt.
2. In another large bowl, mix well the oil, sugar, egg and vanilla extract.
3. After that, add in the flour mixture and mix until just combined. Gently, fold in the zucchini, apple and walnuts.

For the topping: in a small bowl, add all the Ingredients and whisk them well.

4. Preheat the Air Fryer to 325°F. Grease and flour an 8 x 4-inch loaf pan.
5. Place the bread mixture evenly into the prepared pan and sprinkle with the topping mixture.
6. Arrange the loaf pan into an Air Fryer basket. Air Fry for about 30 minutes or until a toothpick inserted in the center comes out clean.
7. Remove from Air Fryer and place the pan onto a wire rack for about 10 to 15 minutes.
8. Carefully, take out the bread from pan and put onto a wire rack until it is completely cool before slicing. Cut the bread into desired size slices and serve.

Potato Rosti

(Prep + Cook Time: 30 minutes | Servings: 2)

Ingredients:

- 1/2 lb. russet potatoes, peeled and roughly grated
- 3½ oz. smoked salmon; cut into slices
- 1 tbsp. fresh chives; finely chopped

- 2 tbsp. sour cream
- 1 tsp. olive oil
- Salt and ground black pepper; as your liking

Directions:

1. Set the temperature of Air Fryer to 355°F. Grease a pizza pan with the olive oil.
2. In a large bowl, mix together the potatoes, chives, salt and black pepper.
3. Place the potato mixture into the prepared pizza pan.
4. Arrange the pan in an Air Fryer basket. Air Fry for about 15 minutes or until the top becomes golden brown. Cut the potato rosti into wedges.
5. Top with the sour cream and smoked salmon slices and serve immediately.

Trout Frittata

(Prep + Cook Time: 40 minutes | Servings: 4)

Ingredients:

- 2 hot smoked trout fillets; chopped
- 1 onion, sliced
- 6 eggs
- 1/4 cup fresh dill; chopped

- 2 tbsp. crème fraiche
- 2 tbsp. olive oil
- 1/2 tbsp. horseradish sauce

Directions:

1. Set the temperature of air fryer to 320°F. Take a frying pan, heat the oil over medium heat and sauté the onion for about 4 to 5 minutes.
2. Meanwhile, in a bowl, mix together the eggs, horseradish sauce and crème fraiche.
3. transfer the onion mixture into a baking dish.
4. Top with the egg mixture, followed by trout. Arrange the baking dish into an air fryer basket. Air fry for about 20 minutes. Serve hot.

Butter Banana Bread

(Prep + Cook Time: 55 minutes | Servings: 6)

Ingredients:

- 2 medium ripe bananas, peeled and mashed
- 1/3 cup granulated sugar
- 1/4 cup canola oil
- 3/4 cup walnuts, roughly chopped
- 1 cup plus 1 tbsp. all-purpose flour
- 1 large egg
- 2 tbsp. creamy peanut butter
- 2 tbsp. sour cream
- 1 tsp. vanilla extract
- 1 tsp. baking powder
- 1/4 tsp. baking soda
- 1/4 tsp. salt

Directions:

1. Take a bowl and mix together the flour, baking powder, baking soda and salt.
2. In another large bowl, add the egg, sugar, oil, peanut butter, sour cream and vanilla extract. Beat until well combined. Add in the bananas and beat until well combined.
3. Add the flour mixture and mix until just combined. Gently, fold in the walnuts. Set the temperature of Air Fryer to 330°F. Grease a non stick baking dish.
4. Transfer the mixture evenly into the prepared baking dish. Arrange the baking dish in an Air Fryer basket.
5. Air Fry for about 30 to40 minutes or until a toothpick inserted in the center comes out clean.
6. Remove the dish from Air Fryer and place onto a wire rack for about 10 to 15 minutes.
7. Carefully, take out the bread from dish and place onto a wire rack until it is completely cool before slicing. Cut the bread into desired size slices and serve.

Dates Bread

(Prep + Cook Time: 37 minutes | Servings: 10)

Ingredients:

- 1½ cups flour
- 1 cup hot water
- 1/2 cup brown sugar
- 1 egg
- 2½ cup dates, pitted and chopped
- 1/4 cup butter
- 1 tsp. baking powder
- 1 tsp. baking soda
- 1/2 tsp. salt

Directions:

1. In a large bowl, add the dates, butter and top with the hot water. Set aside for about 5 minutes.
2. In a separate bowl, mix together the flour, brown sugar, baking powder, baking soda and salt.
3. In the same bowl of dates, mix well the flour mixture and egg. Set the temperature of air fryer to 340°F. Grease an air fryer non stick pan.
4. Place the mixture into the prepared pan. Arrange the pan into an air fryer basket. Air fry for about 22 minutes or until a toothpick inserted in the center comes out clean.
5. Remove from air fryer and place the pan onto a wire rack for about 10 to 15 minutes.
6. Carefully, take out the bread from pan and put onto a wire rack until it is completely cool before slicing. Cut the bread into desired size slices and serve.

Jalapeño Cornbread

(Prep + Cook Time: 33 minutes | Servings: 10)

Ingredients:
- 1/4 cup pepper jack cheese; grated
- 1/2 of jalapeño pepper; finely chopped
- 2 large eggs
- 1 cup yellow cornmeal
- 1/2 cup white sugar
- 3/4 cup sour cream
- 1/2 cup buttermilk
- 1 cup flour
- 3 tbsp. butter, melted
- 2 tbsp. vegetable oil
- 2 tsp. baking powder
- 1/2 tsp. baking soda
- 1 tsp. salt

Directions:
1. In a bowl, mix together the flour, cornmeal, sugar, baking powder, baking soda and salt.
2. In another large bowl, mix well the eggs, sour cream, buttermilk, butter and oil.
3. After that, add in the flour mixture and mix until well combined. Add the cheese and jalapeño and stir to combine.
4. Set the temperature of Air Fryer to 300°F. Grease a round cake pan. Put the mixture evenly into the prepared pan. Arrange the cake pan into an Air Fryer basket.
5. Air Fry for about 18 minutes or until a toothpick inserted in the center comes out clean, turning the pan once halfway through.
6. Remove from Air Fryer and place the pan onto a wire rack for about 10 to 15 minutes.
7. Carefully, take out the bread from pan and put onto a wire rack until it is completely cool before slicing. Cut the bread into desired size slices and serve.

Easy Cornbread

(Prep + Cook Time: 40 minutes | Servings: 8)

Ingredients:
- 3/4 cup all-purpose flour
- 2 large eggs, lightly beaten
- 1½ cups buttermilk
- 1 cup cornmeal
- 6 tbsp. unsalted butter, melted
- 1 tbsp. sugar
- 1½ tsp. baking powder
- 1/2 tsp. baking soda
- 1/4 tsp. salt

Directions:
1. In a bowl, mix together the cornmeal, flour, sugar, baking soda, baking powder and salt.
2. Take a separate bowl, mix well the buttermilk, butter and eggs. After that, add in the flour mixture and mix until just combined.
3. Set the temperature of Air Fryer to 360°F. Lightly, grease an 8-inch baking dish. Transfer the flour mixture evenly into the prepared baking dish.
4. Place the dish into an Air Fryer basket. Air Fry for about 25 minutes or until a toothpick inserted in the center comes out clean, turning the dish once halfway through.
5. Remove from Air Fryer and place the dish onto a wire rack for about 10 to 15 minutes.
6. Carefully, take out the bread from dish and put onto a wire rack until it is completely cool before slicing. Cut the bread into desired size slices and serve.

Chocolatey Banana Bread

(Prep + Cook Time: 26 minutes | Servings: 10)

Ingredients:

- 1/2 cup bananas, peeled and mashed
- 1 cup chocolate chips
- 3/4 cup sugar
- 1/3 cup butter; softened
- 3 eggs
- 2 cups flour
- 1 cup milk
- 1/2 tsp. baking soda
- 1/2 tsp. baking powder
- 1/2 tsp. salt
- 1 tbsp. vanilla extract

Directions:

1. Take a bowl and mix together the flour, baking soda, baking powder and salt.
2. In another large bowl, add the butter and sugar. Beat until light and fluffy.
3. add in the eggs and vanilla extract. Beat until well combined.
4. Add the flour mixture and mix until well combined. Add in the milk and mashed bananas and mix them well.
5. Gently, fold in the chocolate chips. Set the temperature of Air Fryer to 360°F. Grease a loaf pan.
6. Place the mixture evenly into the prepared pan. Arrange the loaf pan into an Air Fryer basket.
7. Air Fry for about 20 minutes or until a toothpick inserted in the center comes out clean.
8. Remove from Air Fryer and place the pan onto a wire rack for about 10 to 15 minutes.
9. Carefully, take out the bread from pan and put onto a wire rack until it is completely cool before slicing. Cut the bread into desired size slices and serve.

Spinach and Egg Cups

(Prep + Cook Time: 38 minutes | Servings: 4)

Ingredients:

- 1 lb. fresh baby spinach
- 4 eggs
- 7 oz. ham, sliced
- 1 tbsp. olive oil
- 1 tbsp. unsalted butter, melted
- 4 tsp. milk
- Salt and freshly ground black pepper

Directions:

1. Set the temperature of Air Fryer to 355°F. Grease 4 ramekins with butter.
2. Take a skillet, heat the oil over medium heat and sauté the spinach for about 2 to 3 minutes or until just wilted.
3. Drain the liquid completely from the spinach. Divide the spinach into the prepared ramekins, followed by the ham slices. Crack 1 egg into each ramekin over ham slices.
4. Drizzle evenly with milk and sprinkle with salt and black pepper. Air Fry for about 16 to 20 minutes or until the desired doneness of eggs. Serve hot.

Eggs and Mushroom Scramble

(Prep + Cook Time: 25 minutes | Servings: 2)

Ingredients:

- 1/2 cup fresh mushrooms; finely chopped
- 4 eggs
- 2 tbsp. unsalted butter
- 2 tbsp. Parmesan cheese, shredded
- Salt and freshly ground black pepper, as needed

Directions:

1. Set the temperature of Air Fryer to 285°F. In a bowl, mix together the eggs, salt and black pepper.
2. In a baking pan, melt the butter and tilt the pan to spread the butter in the bottom.
3. Add the beaten eggs and Air Fry for about 4 to 5 minutes. Add in the mushrooms and cheese and cook for 5 minutes, stirring occasionally. Serve hot.

Eggs and Tomatoes Scramble

(Prep + Cook Time: 24 minutes | Servings: 4)

Ingredients:

- 1/2 cup Parmesan cheese; grated
- 8 grape tomatoes, halved
- 3/4 cup milk
- 4 eggs
- Salt and freshly ground black pepper

Directions:

1. Set the temperature of Air Fryer to 355°F. Grease an Air Fryer pan with cooking spray.
2. In a bowl, mix together the milk, eggs, salt and black pepper. Transfer the egg mixture into the prepared pan.
3. Air Fry for about 6 minutes until the edges begin to set. With a wooden spatula, stir the egg mixture.
4. Top with the tomatoes and Air Fry for about 3 minutes or until the eggs are done. Serve warm with the topping of cheese.

Zucchini Fritters

(Prep + Cook Time: 22 minutes | Servings: 4)

Ingredients:

- 7 oz. Halloumi cheese
- 10½ oz. zucchini; grated and squeezed
- 2 eggs
- 1/4 cup all-purpose flour
- 1 tsp. fresh dill; minced
- Salt and freshly ground black pepper, as needed

Directions:

1. In a large bowl and mix together all the listed ingredients. Make a small sized fritters from the mixture.
2. Set the temperature of Air Fryer to 355°F. Grease a baking dish.
3. Place the fritters into the prepared baking dish. Arrange the dish in an Air Fryer basket. Air Fry for about 6 to 7 minutes. Serve warm.

Mustard Toasts

(Prep + Cook Time: 30 minutes | Servings: 4)

Ingredients:

- 4 bread slices
- 2 eggs, whites and yolks, separated
- 1 tbsp. mustard
- 1 tbsp. paprika
- 2 tbsp. cheddar cheese; shredded

Directions:

1. Set the temperature of Air Fryer to 355°F. Place the bread slices in an Air fryer basket. Air Fry for about 5 minutes or until toasted.
2. Add the egg whites in a clean glass bowl and beat until they form soft peaks.
3. In another bowl, mix together the cheese, egg yolks, mustard and paprika.
4. Gently, fold in the egg whites. Spread the mustard mixture over the toasted bread slices. Air Fry for about 10 minutes. Serve warm!

Vanilla Cinnamon Toasts

(Prep + Cook Time: 20 minutes | Servings: 6)

Ingredients:

- 1/2 cup salted butter; softened
- 12 whole wheat bread slices
- 1/2 cup sugar
- 1½ tsp. vanilla extract
- 1/4 tsp. freshly ground black pepper
- 1½ tsp. ground cinnamon

Directions:

1. Set the temperature of Air Fryer to 400°F. Grease an Air Fryer pan and insert in the Air Fryer while heating.
2. In a bowl, add the sugar, vanilla, cinnamon, pepper and butter. Mix until smooth.
3. Spread the butter mixture evenly over each bread slice. Arrange the bread slices in the prepared pan.
4. Air Fry for about 5 minutes or until crispy. Cut the bread slices diagonally and serve.

Breakfast Potatoes

(Prep + Cook Time: 25 minutes | **Servings:** 4)

Ingredients:

- 1½ lbs. gold potatoes; cubed
- 4 oz. Greek yogurt
- 2 tbsp. olive oil
- 1 tbsp. sweet paprika
- 1 tbsp. cilantro; chopped.
- Salt and black pepper to taste

Directions:

1. Put the potatoes in your air fryer and then add the oil, salt, pepper and paprika.
2. Stir and cook at 360°F for 20 minutes. Transfer the potatoes to a bowl and add the yogurt and cilantro. Toss, serve and enjoy

Scrambled Eggs

(Prep + Cook Time: 15 minutes | **Servings:** 4)

Ingredients:

- 4 eggs; whisked
- 1 red onion; chopped.
- 2 tsp. sweet paprika
- A drizzle of olive oil
- Salt and black pepper to taste

Directions:

1. In a bowl, mix all ingredients and whisk. Heat up your air fryer with the oil at 240°F, add the eggs mixture, stir again and cook for 10 minutes. Serve right away

Breakfast Biscuits

(Prep + Cook Time: 18 minutes | **Servings:** 12)

Ingredients:

- 2 cups white flour
- 1 cup buttermilk
- 5 tbsp. butter
- 1/4 tsp. baking soda
- 1/2 tsp. baking powder
- 1 tsp. sugar

Directions:

1. In a bowl, mix the flour, baking soda, baking powder, sugar, 4 tbsp. of the butter and the buttermilk; stir until you obtain a dough
2. Transfer the dough to a floured working surface, roll and cut 12 pieces with a cookie cutter
3. Melt the remaining 1 tbsp. of butter, brush the biscuits with it and place them in your air fryer's cake pan. Cook at 400°F for 8 minutes, serve.

Tomato and Eggs

(Prep + Cook Time: 35 minutes | **Servings:** 2)

Ingredients:

- 1/2 cup cheddar cheese; shredded
- 1/4 cup milk
- 1/2 cup tomatoes; chopped.
- 2 eggs
- 2 tbsp. red onion; chopped.
- A pinch of salt and black pepper

Directions:

1. In a bowl, mix all ingredients except for the cheese; stir well. Pour mixture into a pan that fits your air fryer, sprinkle the cheese on top and place the pan in the fryer
2. Cook at 350°F for 30 minutes. Divide the mix between plates, serve and enjoy!

Roasted Peppers Frittata

(Prep + Cook Time: 30 minutes | **Servings:** 6)

Ingredients:

- 6 oz. jarred roasted red bell peppers; chopped.
- 1/2 cup parmesan cheese; grated
- 12 eggs; whisked
- 3 garlic cloves; minced
- 2 tbsp. parsley; chopped.
- 2 tbsp. chives; chopped.
- 6 tbsp. ricotta cheese
- A drizzle of olive oil
- Salt and black pepper to taste

Directions:

1. In a bowl, mix the bell peppers with the eggs, garlic, parsley, salt, pepper, chives and ricotta; whisk well.
2. Heat up your air fryer at 300°F, add the oil and spread
3. Add the egg mixture, spread, sprinkle the parmesan on top and cook for 20 minutes. Divide between plates and serve.

Bacon and Egg Cups

(Prep + Cook Time: 38 minutes | Servings: 2)

Ingredients:

- 2 bread slices, toasted and buttered
- 1 bacon slice
- 2 eggs
- 2 tbsp. milk
- 1 tbsp. Parmesan cheese; grated
- 1 tbsp. fresh parsley; chopped
- 1 tsp. marinara sauce
- Freshly ground black pepper, to taste

Directions:

1. Set the temperature of Air Fryer to 355°F. Place the bacon in an Air Fryer basket and Air Fry for about 10 to 15 minutes or until tender.
2. Remove from the Air Fryer and cut into small pieces. Divide the bacon into 2 ramekins.
3. Crack 1 egg in each ramekin over the bacon. Pour the milk evenly over eggs and sprinkle with black pepper.
4. Top with marinara sauce, followed by the Parmesan cheese.
5. Place the ramekins in an Air Fryer basket and air fryer for 8 minutes or until desired doneness. Sprinkle with parsley and serve alongside the toasts.

Chicken and Spinach Casserole

(Prep + Cook Time: 30 minutes | **Servings:** 4)

Ingredients:

- 1 lb. chicken meat; ground
- 12 eggs; whisked
- 1 cup baby spinach
- 1 tbsp. olive oil
- 1/2 tsp. sweet paprika
- Salt and black pepper to taste

Directions:

1. In a bowl, whisk the eggs with the salt, pepper and paprika. Then add the spinach and chicken and mix well.
2. Heat up your air fryer at 350°F; add the oil and allow it to heat up
3. Add the chicken and spinach mix, cover and cook for 25 minutes. Divide between plates and serve hot

Leek and Potato Frittata

(**Prep + Cook Time:** 28 Minutes | **Servings:** 4)

Ingredients:

- 2 gold potatoes; boiled, peeled and chopped
- 1/4 cup whole milk
- 5-ounce fromage blanc; crumbled
- 2 tbsp. butter
- 2 leeks; sliced
- 10 eggs; whisked
- Salt and black pepper to the taste

Directions:

1. Heat up a pan that fits your air fryer with the butter over medium heat, add leeks; stir and cook for 4 minutes.
2. Add potatoes, salt, pepper, eggs, cheese and milk, whisk well; cook for 1 minute more, introduce in your air fryer and cook at 350°F, for 13 minutes. Slice frittata, divide among plates and serve

Chicken and Broccoli Quiche

(Prep + Cook Time: 27 minutes | Servings: 8)

Ingredients:

- 1 frozen ready made pie crust
- 1 egg
- 1/3 cup cheddar cheese; grated
- 1/4 cup boiled broccoli; chopped
- 1/4 cup cooked chicken; chopped
- 3 tbsp. whipping cream
- 1/2 tbsp. olive oil
- Salt and freshly ground black pepper, as needed

Directions:

1. Set the temperature of Air Fryer to 390°F. Lightly, grease 2 small pie pans with olive oil.
2. Cut 2 (5-inch) rounds from the pie crust. Arrange 1 pie crust round in each pie pan and gently, press in the bottom and sides.
3. In a bowl, mix together the egg, cheese, cream, salt and black pepper.
4. Pour the egg mixture over dough base. Evenly top with the broccoli and chicken. Arrange the pie pans into an Air Fryer basket. Air Fry for about 12 minutes. Serve hot.

Creamy Peas Omelet

(**Prep + Cook Time:** 15 minutes | **Servings:** 8)

Ingredients:

- 1/2 lb. baby peas
- 8 eggs; whisked
- 1½ cups yogurt
- 1/2 cup mint; chopped.
- 3 tbsp. avocado oil
- Salt and black pepper to taste

Directions:

1. Heat up the oil in a pan that fits your air fryer over medium heat. Add the peas, stir and cook for 3-4 minutes. In a bowl, mix the yogurt, salt, pepper, eggs and mint; whisk
2. Pour yogurt mixture over the peas, toss and cook at 350°F for 7 minutes. Slice the omelet and serve right away.

Easy Onion Frittata

(**Prep + Cook Time:** 30 Minutes | **Servings:** 6)

Ingredients:

- 10 eggs; whisked
- 1/2 cup sour cream
- 2 yellow onions; chopped
- 1 tbsp. olive oil
- 1-pound small potatoes; chopped
- 1-ounce cheddar cheese; grated
- Salt and black pepper to the taste

Directions:

1. In a large bowl; mix eggs with potatoes, onions, salt, pepper, cheese and sour cream and whisk well.
2. Grease your air fryer's pan with the oil, add eggs mix; place in air fryer and cook for 20 minutes at 320 degrees F. Slice frittata, divide among plates and serve for breakfast

Hash Browns Breakfast

(Prep + Cook Time: 30 minutes | **Servings:** 4)

Ingredients:

- 1½ lbs. hash browns
- 2 eggs
- 1 red bell pepper; chopped.
- 1 red onion; chopped
- 2 tsp. vegetable oil
- 1 tsp. thyme; chopped.
- Salt and black pepper to taste

Directions:

1. Heat up your air fryer at 350°F. Then add the oil and heat it up
2. Add all other ingredients and cook for 25 minutes. Divide between plates and serve

Squash Breakfast

(Prep + Cook Time: 15 minutes | **Servings:** 4)

Ingredients:

- 1 red bell pepper; roughly chopped.
- 1 cup white mushrooms; sliced
- 1/2 cup feta cheese; crumbled
- 1 yellow squash; cubed
- 2 green onions; sliced
- 2 tbsp. butter; softened

Directions:

1. In a bowl, mix all ingredients except the feta cheese. Transfer to your air fryer and cook at 350°F for 10 minutes, shaking the fryer once
2. Divide the mixture between plates and serve with feta cheese sprinkled on top.

Chili and Parsley Soufflé

(Prep + Cook Time: 14 minutes | **Servings:** 3)

Ingredients:

- 3 eggs
- 1 red chili pepper; chopped.
- 2 tbsp. heavy cream
- 2 tbsp. parsley; finely chopped.
- Salt and white pepper to taste

Directions:

1. In a bowl, mix all ingredients, whisk and pour into 3 ramekins
2. Place ramekins in your air fryer's basket and cook at 400°F for 9 minutes. Serve the soufflés immediately and enjoy!

Sausage Bake

(Prep + Cook Time: 25 minutes | **Servings:** 4)

Ingredients:

- 1 lb. breakfast sausage; chopped.
- 4 bacon slices; cooked and crumbled
- A drizzle of olive oil
- 2 cups coconut milk
- 2½ cups cheddar cheese; shredded
- 3 tbsp. cilantro; chopped.
- 2 eggs
- Salt and black pepper to taste

Directions:

1. In a bowl, mix the eggs with milk, cheese, salt, pepper and the cilantro and whisk well
2. Grease your air fryer with the drizzle of oil and heat it up at 320°F. Add the bacon, sausage and the egg mixture, spread and cook for 20 minutes. Serve hot and enjoy!

Breakfast Sausage Rolls

(**Prep + Cook Time:** 16 minutes | **Servings:** 4)

Ingredients:
- 8 crescent roll dough pieces; separated
- 8 cheddar cheese slices
- 8 small sausages

Directions:
1. Unroll the crescent roll pieces on a working surface and place one sausage and one slice of cheese on each.
2. Wrap the sausage and cheese with each roll and seal the edges
3. Place 4 wraps in your air fryer, cook at 380°F for 3 minutes and transfer to a plate. Repeat with the remaining 4 sausage rolls and serve.

Vanilla Toast

(**Prep + Cook Time:** 10 minutes | **Servings:** 6)

Ingredients:
- 12 bread slices
- 1/2 cup brown sugar
- 1 stick butter; softened
- 2 tsp. vanilla extract

Directions:
1. In a bowl, mix the butter, sugar and vanilla; stir. Spread mixture over bread slices, put them in your air fryer and cook at 400°F for 5 minutes. Serve immediately and enjoy

Herbed Tomatoes Breakfast

(**Prep + Cook Time:** 25 minutes | **Servings:** 2)

Ingredients:
- 1 lb. cherry tomatoes; halved
- A drizzle of olive oil
- 1 cucumber; chopped.
- 1 spring onion; chopped
- 1 tsp. cilantro; chopped
- 1 tsp. basil; chopped
- 1 tsp. oregano; chopped
- 1 tsp. rosemary; chopped.
- Salt and black pepper to taste

Directions:
1. Grease the tomatoes with the oil, season with salt and pepper and place them in your air fryer's basket.
2. Cook the tomatoes at 320°F for 20 minutes and then transfer them to a bowl. Add all remaining ingredients, toss and serve

Sausage Omelet

(**Prep + Cook Time:** 16 minutes | **Servings:** 2)

Ingredients:
- 1 sausage link; sliced
- 2 eggs; whisked
- 4 cherry tomatoes; halved
- 1 tbsp. olive oil
- 1 tbsp. cheddar cheese; grated
- 1 tbsp. cilantro; chopped.
- Salt and black pepper to taste

Directions:
1. Put the tomatoes and sausage in the air fryer's basket and cook at 360°F for 5 minutes
2. Take a pan that fits your air fryer, grease it with the oil and then transfer the tomatoes and sausage to the pan
3. In a bowl, mix all remaining ingredients and stir. Pour this over the sausage and tomato mixture, spread and place the pan in the air fryer; cook at 360°F for 6 minutes more. Serve immediately and enjoy.

Parmesan Muffins

(Prep + Cook Time: 20 minutes | **Servings:** 4)

Ingredients:

- 3 oz. almond milk
- 4 oz. white flour
- 2 oz. parmesan cheese; grated
- 2 eggs
- 2 tbsp. olive oil
- 1 tbsp. baking powder
- A splash of Worcestershire sauce

Directions:

1. In a bowl, mix the eggs with 1 tbsp. of the oil, milk, baking powder, flour, Worcestershire sauce and the parmesan; stir well
2. Grease a muffin pan that fits your air fryer with the remaining 1 tbsp. of oil, divide the cheesy mix evenly and place the pan in the air fryer. Cook at 320°F for 15 minutes. Enjoy

Polenta Cakes

(Prep + Cook Time: 35 minutes | **Servings:** 4)

Ingredients:

- 1/4 cup potato starch
- 1 cup cornmeal
- 3 cups water
- A drizzle of vegetable oil
- Maple syrup for serving
- 1 tbsp. butter; softened
- Salt and black pepper to taste

Directions:

1. Put the water in a pot, heat up over medium heat, add the cornmeal, whisk and cook for 10 minutes.
2. Add the butter, whisk well again, then take off the heat and allow to cool down
3. Take spoonfuls of polenta and shape into balls; flatten them, dredge in potato starch and place them on a lined baking sheet that fits your air fryer. Drizzle with oil
4. Place the baking sheet in the fryer and cook at 380°F for 15 minutes, flipping them halfway. Serve with maple syrup drizzled on top.

Breakfast Potatoes

(Prep + Cook Time: 45 Minutes | **Servings:** 4)

Ingredients:

- 3 potatoes; cubed
- 2 tbsp. olive oil
- 1 tsp. garlic powder
- 1 tsp. sweet paprika
- 1 tsp. onion powder
- 1 yellow onion; chopped
- 1 red bell pepper; chopped
- Salt and black pepper to the taste

Directions:

1. Grease your air fryer's basket with olive oil; add potatoes, toss and season with salt and pepper
2. Add onion, bell pepper, garlic powder, paprika and onion powder, toss well, cover and cook at 370°F, for 30 minutes. Divide potatoes mix on plates and serve for breakfast

Pumpkin Oatmeal

(Prep + Cook Time: 25 minutes | **Servings:** 4)

Ingredients:

- 1/2 cup steel cut oats
- 1½ cups milk
- 1/2 cup pumpkin puree
- 1 tsp. pumpkin pie spice
- 3 tbsp. sugar

Directions:

1. In your air fryer's pan, mix all ingredients. Stir, cover and cook at 360°F for 20 minutes. Divide into bowls and serve

Apple Oatmeal

(Prep + Cook Time: 20 minutes | **Servings:** 6)

Ingredients:
- 1¼ cups steel cut oats
- 3 cups almond milk
- 2 apples; cored, peeled and chopped.
- 2 tsp. vanilla extract
- 2 tsp. sugar
- 1/2 tsp. cinnamon powder
- 1/4 tsp. nutmeg; ground
- 1/4 tsp. allspice; ground
- 1/4 tsp. ginger powder
- 1/4 tsp. cardamom; ground
- Cooking spray

Directions:
1. Spray your air fryer with cooking spray, add all ingredients and stir. Cover and cook at 360°F for 15 minutes. Divide into bowls and serve

Corn Pudding

(Prep + Cook Time: 1 hour 25 minutes | **Servings:** 6)

Ingredients:
- 4 bacon slices; cooked and chopped.
- 3 eggs
- 3 cups bread; cubed
- 1/2 cup heavy cream
- 1½ cups whole milk
- 1 cup cheddar cheese; grated
- 2 cups corn
- 1/2 cup green bell pepper; chopped
- 1 yellow onion; chopped.
- 1/4 cup celery; chopped.
- 1 tsp. thyme; chopped.
- 2 tsp. garlic; grated
- 3 tbsp. parmesan cheese; grated
- 1 tbsp. olive oil
- Salt and black pepper

Directions:
1. Heat up the oil in a pan over medium heat. Add the corn, celery, onion, bell pepper, salt, pepper, garlic and thyme to the pan; stir, sauté for 15 minutes and transfer to a bowl
2. To the same bowl, add the bacon, milk, cream, eggs, salt, pepper, bread and the cheddar cheese. Stir well, then pour into a casserole dish that fits your air fryer
3. Place the dish in the fryer and cook at 350°F for 30 minutes
4. Sprinkle the pudding with parmesan cheese and cook for 30 minutes more. Slice, divide between plates and serve.

Delicious Doughnuts

(Prep + Cook Time: 28 Minutes | **Servings:** 6)

Ingredients:
- 1/2 cup sugar
- 2 ¼ cups white flour
- 1 tsp. cinnamon powder
- 2 egg yolks
- 1/3 cup caster sugar
- 4 tbsp. butter; soft
- 1 ½ tsp. baking powder
- 1/2 cup sour cream

Directions:
1. In a bowl; mix 2 tablespoon butter with simple sugar and egg yolks and whisk well
2. Add half of the sour cream and stir.
3. In another bowls; mix flour with baking powder, stir and also add to eggs mix
4. Stir well until you obtain a dough, transfer it to a floured working surface; roll it out and cut big circles with smaller ones in the middle.
5. Brush doughnuts with the rest of the butter; heat up your air fryer at 360 degrees F; place doughnuts inside and cook them for 8 minutes
6. In a bowl; mix cinnamon with caster sugar and stir. Arrange doughnuts on plates and dip them in cinnamon and sugar before serving.

Blackberries and Cornflakes

(Prep + Cook Time: 15 minutes | Servings: 4)

Ingredients:

- 3 cups milk
- 1/4 cup blackberries
- 2 eggs; whisked
- 1 tbsp. sugar
- 1/4 tsp. nutmeg; ground
- 4 tbsp. cream cheese; whipped
- 1½ cups corn flakes

Directions:

1. In a bowl, mix all ingredients and stir well.
2. Heat up your air fryer at 350°F, add the corn flakes mixture, spread and cook for 10 minutes. Divide between plates, serve and enjoy

Fried Mushroom

(Prep + Cook Time: 25 minutes | Servings: 4)

Ingredients:

- 7 oz. spinach; torn
- 8 cherry tomatoes; halved
- 4 slices bacon; chopped.
- 4 eggs
- 8 white mushrooms; sliced
- 1 garlic clove; minced
- A drizzle of olive oil
- Salt and black pepper to taste

Directions:

1. In a pan greased with oil and that fits your air fryer, mix all ingredients except for the spinach; stir.
2. Put the pan in your air fryer and cook at 400°F for 15 minutes. Add the spinach, toss and cook for 5 minutes more. Divide between plates and serve

Smoked Bacon and Bread

(Prep + Cook Time: 40 minutes | Servings: 6)

Ingredients:

- 1 lb. white bread; cubed
- 1 lb. smoked bacon; cooked and chopped.
- 1/2 lb. cheddar cheese; shredded
- 1/2 lb. Monterey jack cheese; shredded
- 30 oz. canned tomatoes; chopped.
- 1/4 cup avocado oil
- 1 red onion; chopped.
- 2 tbsp. chicken stock
- 2 tbsp. chives; chopped.
- 8 eggs; whisked
- Salt and black pepper to taste

Directions:

1. Add the oil to your air fryer and heat it up at 350°F
2. Add all other ingredients except the chives and cook for 30 minutes, shaking halfway. Divide between plates and serve with chives sprinkled on top

Pancakes

(Prep + Cook Time: 30 minutes | Servings: 4)

Ingredients:

- 1¾ cups white flour
- 1 cup apple; peeled, cored and chopped.
- 1¼ cups milk
- 1 egg; whisked
- 2 tbsp. sugar
- 2 tsp. baking powder
- 1/4 tsp. vanilla extract
- 2 tsp. cinnamon powder
- Cooking spray

Directions:

1. In a bowl, mix all ingredients (except cooking spray) and stir until you obtain a smooth batter
2. Grease your air fryer's pan with the cooking spray and pour in 1/4 of the batter; spread it into the pan.
3. Cover and cook at 360°F for 5 minutes, flipping it halfway

4. Repeat steps 2 and 3 with 1/4 of the batter 3 more times and then serve the pancakes right away.

Creamy Mushroom Pie

(Prep + Cook Time: 20 minutes | Servings: 4)

Ingredients:
- 6 white mushrooms; chopped.
- 3 eggs
- 1 red onion; chopped.
- 9-inch pie dough
- 1/4 cup cheddar cheese; grated
- 1/2 cup heavy cream
- 2 tbsp. bacon; cooked and crumbled
- 1 tbsp. olive oil
- 1/2 tsp. thyme; dried
- Salt and black pepper to taste

Directions:
1. Roll the dough on a working surface, then press it on the bottom of a pie pan that fits your air fryer and grease with the oil
2. In a bowl, mix all other ingredients except the cheese, stir well and pour mixture into the pie pan
3. Sprinkle the cheese on top, put the pan in the air fryer and cook at 400°F for 10 minutes. Slice and serve.

Cheesy Hash Brown

(Prep + Cook Time: 30 minutes | Servings: 6)

Ingredients:
- 1½ lbs. hash browns
- 6 bacon slices; chopped.
- 8 oz. cream cheese; softened
- 1 yellow onion; chopped.
- 6 eggs
- 6 spring onions; chopped.
- 1 cup cheddar cheese; shredded
- 1 cup almond milk
- A drizzle of olive oil
- Salt and black pepper to taste

Directions:
1. Heat up your air fryer with the oil at 350°F. In a bowl, mix all other ingredients except the spring onions and whisk well
2. Add this mixture to your air fryer, cover and cook for 20 minutes
3. Divide between plates, sprinkle the spring onions on top and serve.

Pear Oatmeal

(Prep + Cook Time: 17 minutes | Servings: 4)

Ingredients:
- 1 cup milk
- 1/4 cups brown sugar
- 1/2 cup walnuts; chopped.
- 2 cups pear; peeled and chopped.
- 1 cup old fashioned oats
- 1/2 tsp. cinnamon powder
- 1 tbsp. butter; softened

Directions:
1. In a heat-proof bowl that fits your air fryer, mix all ingredients and stir well. Place in your fryer and cook at 360°F for 12 minutes. Divide into bowls and serve

Ham and Cheese Patties

(Prep + Cook Time: 20 minutes | Servings: 4)

Ingredients:
- 8 ham slices; chopped.
- 4 handfuls mozzarella cheese; grated
- 1 puff pastry sheet
- 4 tsp. mustard

Directions:
1. Roll out puff pastry on a working surface and cut it in 12 squares. Divide cheese, ham and mustard on half of them, top with the other halves and seal the edges

2. Place all the patties in your air fryer's basket and cook at 370°F for 10 minutes. Divide the patties between plates and serve

Peppers and Lettuce Salad

(Prep + Cook Time: 15 minutes | Servings: 4)

Ingredients:
- 2 oz. rocket leaves
- 4 red bell peppers
- 1 lettuce head; torn
- 2 tbsp. olive oil
- 1 tbsp. lime juice
- 3 tbsp. heavy cream
- Salt and black pepper to taste

Directions:
1. Place the bell peppers in your air fryer's basket and cook at 400°F for 10 minutes
2. Remove the peppers, peel, cut them into strips and put them in a bowl. Add all remaining ingredients, toss and serve

Cod Tortilla

(Prep + Cook Time: 27 minutes | Servings: 4)

Ingredients:
- 4 cod fillets; skinless and boneless
- 4 tortillas
- 1 green bell pepper; chopped.
- 1 red onion; chopped.
- A drizzle of olive oil
- 1 cup corn
- 1/2 cup salsa
- 4 tbsp. parmesan cheese; grated
- A handful of baby spinach

Directions:
1. Put the fish fillets in your air fryer's basket, cook at 350°F for 6 minutes and transfer to a plate.
2. Heat up a pan with the oil over medium heat, add the bell peppers, onions and corn and stir
3. Sauté for 5 minutes and take off the heat. Arrange all the tortillas on a working surface and divide the cod, salsa, sautéed veggies, spinach and parmesan evenly between the 4 tortillas; then wrap / roll them
4. Place the tortillas in your air fryer's basket and cook at 350°F for 6 minutes. Divide between plates, serve.

Artichoke Omelet

(Prep + Cook Time: 20 minutes | Servings:)

Ingredients:
- 3 artichoke hearts; canned, drained and chopped.
- 6 eggs; whisked
- 2 tbsp. avocado oil
- 1/2 tsp. oregano; dried
- Salt and black pepper to taste

Directions:
1. In a bowl, mix all ingredients except the oil; stir well. Add the oil to your air fryer's pan and heat it up at 320°F.
2. Add the egg mixture, cook for 15 minutes, divide between plates and serve

Carrot Oatmeal

(Prep + Cook Time: 20 minutes | Servings: 4)

Ingredients:
- 1/2 cup steel cut oats
- 2 cups almond milk
- 1 cup carrots; shredded
- 2 tsp. sugar
- 1 tsp. cardamom; ground
- Cooking spray

Directions:
1. Spray your air fryer with cooking spray, add all ingredients, toss and cover. Cook at 365°F for 15 minutes. Divide into bowls and serve

Chicken Burrito

(Prep + Cook Time: 15 minutes | **Servings:** 2)

Ingredients:

- 4 chicken breast slices; cooked and shredded
- 2 tortillas
- 1 avocado; peeled, pitted and sliced
- 1 green bell pepper; sliced
- 2 eggs; whisked
- 2 tbsp. mild salsa
- 2 tbsp. cheddar cheese; grated
- Salt and black pepper to taste

Directions:

1. In a bowl, whisk the eggs with the salt and pepper and pour them into a pan that fits your air fryer. Put the pan in the air fryer's basket, cook for 5 minutes at 400°F and transfer the mix to a plate
2. Place the tortillas on a working surface and between them divide the eggs, chicken, bell peppers, avocado and the cheese; roll the burritos
3. Line your air fryer with tin foil, add the burritos and cook them at 300°F for 3-4 minutes. Serve for breakfast-or lunch, or dinner!

Potato Frittata

(Prep + Cook Time: 25 minutes | **Servings:** 6)

Ingredients:

- 1 lb. small potatoes; chopped.
- 1 oz. parmesan cheese; grated
- 1/2 cup heavy cream
- 2 red onions; chopped.
- 8 eggs; whisked
- 1 tbsp. olive oil
- Salt and black pepper to taste

Directions:

1. In a bowl, mix all ingredients except the potatoes and oil; stir well.
2. Heat up your air fryer's pan with the oil at 320°F. Add the potatoes, stir and cook for 5 minutes
3. Add the egg mixture, spread and cook for 15 minutes more. Divide the frittata between plates and serve

Herbed Omelet

(Prep + Cook Time: 20 minutes | **Servings:** 4)

Ingredients:

- 6 eggs; whisked
- 2 tbsp. parmesan cheese; grated
- 4 tbsp. heavy cream
- 1 tbsp. parsley; chopped.
- 1 tbsp. tarragon; chopped.
- 2 tbsp. chives; chopped.
- Salt and black pepper to taste

Directions:

1. In a bowl, mix all ingredients except for the parmesan and whisk well. Pour this into a pan that fits your air fryer, place it in preheated fryer and cook at 350°F for 15 minutes
2. Divide the omelet between plates and serve with the parmesan sprinkled on top

Cheese Toast

(Prep + Cook Time: 13 minutes | **Servings:**2)

Ingredients:

- 4 bread slices
- 4 cheddar cheese slices
- 4 tsp. butter; softened

Directions:

1. Spread the butter on each slice of bread. Place 2 cheese slices each on 2 bread slices, then top with the other 2 bread slices; cut each in half
2. Arrange the sandwiches in your air fryer's basket and cook at 370°F for 8 minutes. Serve hot and enjoy!

Carrots and Cauliflower Mix

(Prep + Cook Time: 30 minutes | Servings: 4)

Ingredients:

- 1 cauliflower head; stems removed, florets separated and steamed
- 2 oz. milk
- 2 oz. cheddar cheese; grated
- 3 carrots; chopped and steamed
- 3 eggs
- 2 tsp. cilantro; chopped.
- Salt and black pepper to taste

Directions:

1. In a bowl, mix the eggs with the milk, parsley, salt and pepper; whisk. Put the cauliflower and the carrots in your air fryer, add the egg mixture and spread. Then sprinkle the cheese on top
2. Cook at 350°F for 20 minutes, divide between plates and serve

Vanilla Oatmeal

(Prep + Cook Time: 22 minutes | Servings: 4)

Ingredients:

- 1 cup steel cut oats
- 1 cup milk
- 2½ cups water
- 2 tsp. vanilla extract
- 2 tbsp. brown sugar

Directions:

1. In a pan that fits your air fryer, mix all ingredients and stir well. Place the pan in your air fryer and cook at 360°F for 17 minutes. Divide into bowls and serve

Fish Tacos Breakfast

(Prep + Cook Time: 23 Minutes | Servings: 4)

Ingredients:

- 4 big tortillas
- 1 yellow onion; chopped
- 1 cup corn
- 1 red bell pepper; chopped
- 1/2 cup salsa
- 4 white fish fillets; skinless and boneless
- A handful mixed romaine lettuce; spinach and radicchio
- 4 tbsp. parmesan; grated

Directions:

1. Put fish fillets in your air fryer and cook at 350°F, for 6 minutes
2. Meanwhile; heat up a pan over medium high heat, add bell pepper, onion and corn; stir and cook for 1 - 2 minutes
3. Arrange tortillas on a working surface, divide fish fillets, spread salsa over them; divide mixed veggies and mixed greens and spread parmesan on each at the end.
4. Roll your tacos; place them in preheated air fryer and cook at 350°F, for 6 minutes more. Divide fish tacos on plates and serve for breakfast

Tuna Sandwiches

(Prep + Cook Time: 14 minutes | Servings: 4)

Ingredients:

- 16 oz. canned tuna; drained
- 6 bread slices
- 6 provolone cheese slices
- 2 spring onions; chopped.
- 1/4 cup mayonnaise
- 2 tbsp. mustard
- 1 tbsp. lime juice
- 3 tbsp. butter; melted

Directions:

1. In a bowl, mix the tuna, mayo, lime juice, mustard and spring onions; stir until combined.
2. Spread the bread slices with the butter, place them in preheated air fryer and bake them at 350°F for 5 minutes

3. Spread tuna mix on half of the bread slices and top with the cheese and the other bread slices
4. Place the sandwiches in your air fryer's basket and cook for 4 minutes more. Divide between plates and serve.

Tofu and Bell Peppers

(Prep + Cook Time: 15 minutes | **Servings:** 8)

Ingredients:

- 3 oz. firm tofu; crumbled
- 1 green onion; chopped.
- 1 yellow bell pepper; cut into strips
- 1 orange bell pepper; cut into strips
- 1 green bell pepper; cut into strips
- 2 tbsp. parsley; chopped.
- Salt and black pepper to taste

Directions:

1. In a pan that fits your air fryer, place the bell pepper strips and mix
2. Then add all remaining ingredients, toss and place the pan in the air fryer. Cook at 400°F for 10 minutes. Divide between plates and serve

Chicken & Poultry

Chicken with Potatoes

(Prep + Cook Time: 1 hour 15 minutes | Servings: 2)

Ingredients:

- 1 (1½-pounds) whole chicken
- 1/2 lb. small potatoes
- 1 tbsp. olive oil
- Salt and ground black pepper, as required

Directions:

1. Set the temperature of Air Fryer to 390°F. Grease an Air Fryer basket.
2. Season the chicken with salt and black pepper. Place chicken into the prepared Air Fryer basket. Air Fry for about 35 to 40 minutes or until done completely.
3. Transfer the chicken onto a platter and cover with a piece of foil to keep warm.
4. In a bowl, add the potatoes, oil, salt and black pepper and toss to coat well.
5. Again, set the temperature of Air Fryer to 390°F. Grease an Air Fryer basket.
6. Place potatoes into the prepared Air Fryer basket. Air Fry for about 20 minutes or until golden brown.
7. Remove from the Air Fryer and transfer potatoes into a bowl. Cut the chicken into desired size pieces using a sharp knife and serve alongside the potatoes.

Cinnamon Chicken

(**Prep + Cook Time:** 45 minutes | **Servings:** 8)

Ingredients:

- 1 cup chicken stock
- 1 whole chicken; cut into pieces
- 1½ tbsp. lemon zest
- 1 tbsp. coriander powder
- 1½ tsp. cinnamon powder
- 2 tsp. garlic powder
- 1 tbsp. olive oil
- Salt and black pepper to taste

Directions:

1. Place all of the ingredients in a bowl and mix well
2. Transfer the chicken to your air fryer's basket and cook at 370°F for 35 minutes, shaking the fryer from time to time
3. Divide the chicken between plates and serve with a side salad.

Chicken Wings and Endives

(**Prep + Cook Time:** 40 minutes | **Servings:** 4)

Ingredients:

- 8 chicken wings; halved
- 6 endives; shaved
- 1/4 cup white wine
- 2 garlic cloves; minced
- 1 tbsp. olive oil
- 1 tsp. cumin; ground
- 1 tbsp. rosemary; chopped.
- Salt and black pepper to taste

Directions:

1. Season the chicken wings with the salt, pepper, cumin and rosemary.
2. Place the wings in your air fryer's basket and cook at 360°F for 10 minutes on each side; divide between plates
3. Heat up a pan with the oil over medium heat and then add the garlic, endives, salt, pepper and the wine; bring to a simmer. Cook for 8 minutes, spread over the chicken and serve

Cheese Stuffed Chicken Breasts

(Prep + Cook Time: 30 minutes | Servings: 4)

Ingredients:

- 2 (8-oz.) skinless, boneless chicken breast fillets
- 4 cured ham slices
- 4 Brie cheese slices
- 1 tbsp. fresh chive; minced
- Salt and ground black pepper; as your liking

Directions:

1. Cut each chicken fillet in 2 equal-sized pieces. Carefully, make a slit in each chicken piece horizontally about 1/4-inch from the edge.
2. Open each chicken piece and season with the salt and black pepper.
3. Place 1 cheese slice in the open area of each chicken piece and sprinkle with chives. Close the chicken pieces and wrap each one with a ham slice.
4. Set the temperature of Air Fryer to 355°F. Grease an Air Fryer basket. Arrange the wrapped chicken pieces into the prepared Air Fryer basket. Air Fry for about 15 minutes.
5. Remove from Air Fryer and transfer the chicken fillets onto a serving platter. Serve hot.

Sweet and Spicy Chicken Drumsticks

(Prep + Cook Time: 35 minutes | Servings: 4)

Ingredients:

- 4 (6-oz.) chicken drumsticks
- 1 garlic clove; crushed
- 1 tbsp. vegetable oil
- 1 tbsp. mustard
- 1 tsp. red chili powder
- 2 tsp. brown sugar
- 1 tsp. cayenne pepper
- Salt and ground black pepper; as your liking

Directions:

1. In a bowl, mix together garlic, mustard, brown sugar, oil and spices
2. Rub the chicken drumsticks with marinade and refrigerate to marinate for about 20 to 30 minutes.
3. Set the temperature of Air Fryer to 390°F. Grease an Air Fryer basket.
4. Arrange drumsticks into the prepared Air Fryer basket in a single layer. Air Fry for about 10 minutes and then 10 more minutes at 300°F.
5. Remove from Air Fryer and transfer the chicken drumsticks onto a serving platter. Serve hot.

Herbed Chicken

(**Prep + Cook Time:** 35 minutes | **Servings:** 8)

Ingredients:

- 8 chicken thighs
- 3 garlic cloves; minced
- 1 cup chicken stock
- 1/4 cup cheddar cheese; grated
- 1/2 tsp. thyme; dried
- 1/2 tsp. oregano; dried
- 1/4 cup heavy cream
- 3 tbsp. butter; melted
- 1 tbsp. mustard
- 1/2 tsp. basil; dried
- Salt and black pepper to taste

Directions:

1. In a baking dish that fits your air fryer, place all ingredients except the cheddar cheese; mix well
2. Transfer the dish to your air fryer and cook at 370°F for 25 minutes
3. Sprinkle the cheese on top and cook for 5 more minutes. Divide everything between plates and serve.

Parmesan Chicken

(Prep + Cook Time: 40 minutes | **Servings:** 4)

Ingredients:

- 4 chicken breasts; boneless and skinless
- 1/2 cup parmesan cheese; grated
- 1/4 cup butter; melted
- 1 cup corn flakes; crushed
- 1 tbsp. olive oil
- Salt and black pepper to taste

Directions:

1. In a bowl, mix all the ingredients and toss
2. Place the chicken in your air fryer's basket and cook at 360°F for 15 minutes on each side. Divide between plates and serve.

Lemon and Garlic Chicken

(Prep + Cook Time: 25 minutes | **Servings:** 4)

Ingredients:

- 4 chicken breasts; skinless and boneless
- 4 garlic heads; peeled, cloves separated and cut into quarters
- 1½ tbsp. avocado oil
- 2 tbsp. lemon juice
- 1/2 tsp. lemon pepper
- Salt and black pepper to taste

Directions:

1. In a bowl, mix all of the ingredients and toss well.
2. Transfer the chicken mixture to your air fryer and cook at 360°F for 15 minutes. Divide between plates and serve with a side salad

Buffalo Chicken Tenders

(Prep + Cook Time: 32 minutes | Servings: 3)

Ingredients:

- 16 oz. boneless, skinless chicken breasts, sliced into tenders
- 1 large egg
- 1/2 cup pork rinds; crushed
- 1/4 cup buffalo wing sauce
- 1/2 cup unflavored whey protein powder
- 2 tbsp. butter, melted
- 1 tbsp. water
- 1/2 tsp. garlic powder
- Salt and ground black pepper; as your liking

Directions:

1. In a large bowl, add the water and egg. Beat until well combined.
2. Add the chicken and generously coat with egg mixture. Place the chicken in a colander to drain completely.
3. In a shallow bowl, mix together the pork rinds, protein powder, garlic powder, salt and black pepper.
4. Coat chicken tenders with the pork rinds mixture. Set the temperature of Air Fryer to 400°F. Grease an Air Fryer basket.
5. Arrange chicken tenders into the prepared Air Fryer basket and drizzle with the melted butter. Air Fry for about 10 to 12 minutes.
6. Remove from Air Fryer and transfer the chicken tenders into a bowl. Place with the buffalo sauce and toss to coat well.

Fried Chicken Wings

(Prep + Cook Time: 55 minutes | **Servings:** 4)

Ingredients:
- 16 chicken wings
- 1/4 cup butter; melted
- 4 tbsp. garlic; minced
- 1/4 cup clover honey
- Salt and black pepper to taste

Directions:
1. Put the chicken wings in your air fryer's basket and season with salt and pepper.
2. Cook at 380°F for 25 minutes, then at 400°F for 5 minutes and put it in a bowl
3. Melt the butter in a pan over medium-high heat; then add the garlic, stir and sauté for 5 minutes
4. Add salt, pepper, the air fried chicken and the honey; stir and simmer for 10 minutes more over medium heat. Divide the chicken wings and the sauce between plates and serve.

Ginger Chicken Drumsticks

(Prep + Cook Time: 35 minutes | Servings: 3)

Ingredients:
- 1/4 cup full-fat coconut milk
- 3 (6-oz.) chicken drumsticks
- 2 tsp. fresh ginger; minced
- 2 tsp. galangal; minced
- 2 tsp. ground turmeric
- Salt, to taste

Directions:
1. In a bowl, mix together the coconut milk, galangal, ginger and spices.
2. Add the chicken drumsticks and generously coat with the marinade. Refrigerate to marinate for at least 6 to 8 hours.
3. Set the temperature of Air Fryer to 375°F. Grease an Air Fryer basket.
4. Place chicken drumsticks into the prepared Air Fryer basket in a single layer. Air Fry for about 20 to 25 minutes.
5. Remove from Air Fryer and transfer the chicken drumsticks onto a serving platter. Serve hot.

Duck Breast with Figs

(Prep + Cook Time: 65 minutes | Servings: 2)

Ingredients:
- 1 lb. boneless duck breast
- 6 fresh figs, halved
- 2 cups fresh pomegranate juice
- 1 tbsp. fresh thyme; chopped
- 2 tbsp. lemon juice
- 3 tbsp. brown sugar
- 1 tsp. olive oil
- Salt and ground black pepper; as your liking

Directions:
1. In a medium saucepan, add the pomegranate juice, lemon juice and brown sugar over medium heat and bring to a boil.
2. lower the heat to low and cook for about 25 minutes until the mixture becomes thick. Remove the pan from heat and let it cool slightly.
3. Set the temperature of Air Fryer to 400°F. Grease an Air Fryer basket.
4. Score the fat of duck breasts several times using a sharp knife. Sprinkle the duck breast with salt and black pepper.
5. Arrange duck breast into the prepared Air Fryer basket, skin side up. Air Fry for about 14 minutes, flipping once halfway through.
6. Remove from Air Fryer and place the duck breast onto a cutting board for about 5 to 10 minutes.
7. Meanwhile, in a bowl, add the figs, oil, salt and black pepper and toss to coat well.
8. Once again, set the temperature of Air Fryer to 400°F. Grease the Air Fryer basket.
9. Arrange figs into the prepared basket in a single layer. Air Fry for about 5 minutes.

10. Using a sharp knife; cut the duck breast into desired size slices and transfer onto serving plates alongside the roasted figs.
11. Drizzle with warm pomegranate juice mixture and serve with the garnishing of fresh thyme.

Lemon Chicken and Asparagus

(Prep + Cook Time: 20 minutes | **Servings:** 4)

Ingredients:
- 1/2 lb. asparagus; trimmed and halved
- 1 lb. chicken thighs
- 1 zucchini; roughly cubed
- 1 lemon; sliced
- 2 tbsp. olive oil
- 1 tsp. oregano; dried
- 3 garlic cloves; minced
- Juice of 1 lemon
- Salt and black pepper to taste

Directions:
1. In a pan that fits your air fryer, mix all of the ingredients
2. Place the pan in your air fryer and cook at 380°F for 15 minutes. Divide between plates and serve.

Crispy Chicken Tenders

(Prep + Cook Time: 50 minutes | Servings: 3)

Ingredients:
- 2 (6-oz.) boneless, skinless chicken breasts, pounded into 1/2-inch thickness and cut into tenders
- 2 large eggs
- 1/2 cup all-purpose flour
- 1½ cups panko breadcrumbs
- 1/4 cup Parmesan cheese; finely grated
- 3/4 cup buttermilk
- 2 tbsp. butter, melted
- 1½ tsp. Worcestershire sauce; divided
- 1/2 tsp. smoked paprika; divided
- Salt and ground black pepper; as your liking

Directions:
1. In a large bowl, mix together buttermilk, 3/4 tsp. of Worcestershire sauce, ¼ tsp. of paprika, salt and black pepper.
2. Add in the chicken tenders and refrigerate overnight.
3. In another bowl, mix together the flour, remaining paprika, salt and black pepper.
4. Place the remaining Worcestershire sauce and eggs in a third bowl and beat until well combined.
5. Mix well the panko, Parmesan and butter in a fourth bowl. Remove the chicken tenders from bowl and discard the buttermilk.
6. Coat the chicken tenders with flour mixture, then dip into egg mixture and finally coat with the panko mixture.
7. Set the temperature of air fryer to 400°F. Grease an air fryer basket.
8. Arrange chicken tenders into the prepared air fryer basket in 2 batches in a single layer. Air fry for about 13 to 15 minutes, flipping once halfway through.
9. Remove from air fryer and transfer the chicken tenders onto a serving platter. Serve hot.

Crispy Chicken Burgers

(Prep + Cook Time: 50 minutes | Servings: 4)

Ingredients:

- 6 boneless, skinless chicken breasts
- 4 hamburger buns, split and toasted
- 4 lettuce leaves
- 1¾ oz. plain flour
- 1 small egg
- 4 mozzarella cheese slices
- 6¾ tbsp. breadcrumbs
- 1/4 tsp. dried oregano
- 1 tsp. dried garlic
- 1 tsp. chicken seasoning
- 1/2 tsp. cayenne pepper
- 1 tsp. mustard powder
- 1/2 tsp. paprika
- 1 tsp. Worcestershire sauce
- 1/4 tsp. dried parsley
- 1/4 tsp. dried tarragon
- Salt and ground black pepper; as your liking

Directions:

1. In a food processor, add the chicken breasts and pulse until minced. Add the mustard, paprika, Worcester sauce, salt and black pepper and pulse until well combined.
2. Make 4 equal-sized patties from the mixture. In a shallow bowl, place the flour.
3. In a second bowl, crack the egg and beat well. In a third bowl, mix well breadcrumbs, dried herbs and spices.
4. Coat each chicken patty with flour, then dip into egg and finally, coat with breadcrumb mixture.
5. Set the temperature of air fryer to 355°F. Grease an air fryer basket.
6. Arrange chicken patties into the prepared air fryer basket in a single layer. Air fry for about 15 minutes per side. Remove from air fryer and place the patties onto a plate.
7. Place one lettuce leaf over bottom half of each bun, followed by one patty and cheese slice. Cover with bun top and serve.

Chicken with Carrots

(Prep + Cook Time: 40 minutes | Servings: 2)

Ingredients:

- 2 (4-oz.) chicken breast halves
- 1 carrot, peeled and thinly sliced
- 1 tbsp. fresh rosemary; chopped
- 2 tbsp. fresh lemon juice
- 2 tbsp. butter
- Salt and ground black pepper; as your liking

Directions:

1. Arrange 2 square-shaped parchment papers onto a smooth surface. Place carrot slices evenly in the center of each parchment paper.
2. Place 1/2 tbsp. of butter over carrot slices and sprinkle with salt and black pepper.
3. Arrange 1 chicken breast over carrot slices in each parcel.
4. Top each chicken breast evenly with rosemary and drizzle with lemon juice.
5. Top with the remaining butter. Seal each parchment paper by folding all four corners.
6. Set the temperature of Air Fryer to 375°F. Arrange the chicken parcels into an Air Fryer basket.
7. Air Fry for about 20 to 25 minutes. Remove from Air Fryer and transfer the chicken mixture onto a serving platter. Serve hot.

Salsa Verde Chicken Breast.

(**Prep + Cook Time:** 30 minutes | **Servings:** 4)

Ingredients:
- 16 oz. salsa Verde
- 1 lb. chicken breast; boneless and skinless
- 1½ cups cheddar cheese; grated
- 1/4 cup parsley; chopped.
- 1 tsp. sweet paprika
- 1 tbsp. avocado oil
- Salt and black pepper to taste

Directions:
1. In a baking dish that fits your air fryer, place all ingredients except the cheese; toss well
2. Put the pan into the fryer and cook at 380°F for 17 minutes
3. Sprinkle with the cheese and cook for 3-4 minutes more. Divide between plates and serve.

Chinese Chicken Drumsticks

(Prep + Cook Time: 35 minutes | Servings: 4)

Ingredients:
- 4 (6-oz.) chicken drumsticks
- 1 cup corn flour
- 1 tbsp. oyster sauce
- 1/2 tsp. sesame oil
- 1 tsp. Chinese five spice powder
- 1 tsp. light soy sauce
- Salt and ground white pepper; as your liking

Directions:
1. In a bowl, mix together the sauces, oil, five spice powder, salt and black pepper. Add the chicken drumsticks and generously coat with the marinade. Refrigerate for at least 30 to 40 minutes.
2. In a shallow dish, place the corn flour. Remove the chicken from marinade and lightly coat with corn flour.
3. Set the temperature of Air Fryer to 390°F. Grease an Air Fryer basket. Arrange chicken drumsticks into the prepared Air Fryer basket in a single layer. Air Fry for about 20 minutes.
4. Remove from Air Fryer and transfer the chicken drumsticks onto a serving platter. Serve hot.

Sausage Stuffed Chicken Breasts

(Prep + Cook Time: 30 minutes | Servings: 4)

Ingredients:
- 4 sausages, casing removed
- 4 (4-oz.) skinless, boneless chicken breasts

Directions:
1. Place the chicken breasts onto a smooth surface and with a meat mallet, lb. each into an even thickness.
2. Place 1 sausage over each chicken breast. Roll each breast around the sausage and secure with toothpicks.
3. Set the temperature of Air Fryer to 375°F. Grease an Air Fryer basket. Arrange chicken breasts into the prepared Air Fryer basket. Air Fry for about 15 minutes.
4. Remove from Air Fryer and transfer the chicken breasts onto a serving platter. Serve hot.

Spinach Stuffed Chicken Breasts

(Prep + Cook Time: 45 minutes | Servings: 2)

Ingredients:
- 1/4 cup ricotta cheese; shredded
- 2 (4-oz.) skinless, boneless chicken breasts
- 1¾ oz. fresh spinach
- 2 tbsp. cheddar cheese; grated
- 1 tbsp. olive oil
- 1/4 tsp. paprika
- Salt and ground black pepper; as your liking

Directions:
1. In a medium skillet, add the oil over medium heat and cook until heated.
2. Add the spinach and cook for about 3 to 4 minutes. Stir in the ricotta and cook for about 40 to 60 seconds. Remove the skillet from heat and set aside to cool.
3. Cut slits into the chicken breasts about ¼-inch apart but not all the way through.
4. Stuff each chicken breast with the spinach mixture. Sprinkle each chicken breast evenly with salt and black pepper and then with cheddar cheese and paprika.
5. Set the temperature of Air Fryer to 390°F. Grease an Air Fryer basket. Arrange chicken breasts into the prepared basket in a single layer. Air Fry for about 20 to 25 minutes.
6. Remove from Air Fryer and transfer the chicken breasts onto a serving platter. Serve hot.

Awesome Oregano Chicken Thighs

(Prep + Cook Time: 35 minutes | **Servings:** 4)

Ingredients:
- 8 chicken thighs
- 2 garlic cloves; minced
- 4 tsp. oregano; chopped.
- 1/2 tsp. sweet paprika
- 2 tbsp. olive oil
- 1 red onion; chopped.
- Salt and black pepper to taste

Directions:
1. In a baking dish that fits your air fryer, place all of the ingredients and mix well.
2. Transfer the dish to your air fryer and cook at 400°F for 30 minutes, shaking halfway. Divide between plates and serve

Turkey Meatloaf

(Prep + Cook Time: 40 minutes | Servings: 4)

Ingredients:
- 1 lb. ground turkey
- 1 (4-oz.) can chopped green chilies
- 2 garlic cloves; minced
- 1 egg, beaten
- 1/2 cup fresh breadcrumbs
- 1 cup kale leaves, trimmed and finely chopped
- 1 cup onion; chopped
- 1 cup Monterey Jack cheese; grated
- 1/4 cup salsa verde
- 3 tbsp. chopped fresh cilantro
- 1/2 tsp. ground cumin
- 1/2 tsp. dried oregano; crushed
- 1 tsp. red chili powder
- Salt and ground black pepper; as your liking

Directions:
1. In a deep bowl, put all the Ingredients and with your hands, mix until well combined.
2. Divide the turkey mixture into 4 equal-sized portions and shape each into a mini loaf.
3. Set the temperature of air fryer to 400°F. Grease an air fryer basket.
4. Arrange loaves into the prepared air fryer basket. Air fry for about 20 minutes.
5. Remove from air fryer and place the loaves onto plates for about 5 minutes before serving. Serve warm.

Crispy Chicken Thighs

(Prep + Cook Time: 40 minutes | Servings: 4)

Ingredients:
- 4 (4-oz.) skin-on chicken thighs
- 1 egg
- 1/2 cup all-purpose flour
- 1½ tbsp. Cajun seasoning
- 1 tsp. seasoning salt

Directions:
1. Mix together the flour, Cajun seasoning and salt in a shallow bowl.
2. In another bowl, crack the egg and beat well. Coat each chicken thigh with the flour mixture, then dip into beaten egg and finally, coat with the flour mixture again.

3. Shake off the excess flour thoroughly. Set the temperature of Air Fryer to 390°F. Grease an Air Fryer basket.
4. Arrange chicken thighs into the prepared Air Fryer basket, skin side down. Air Fry for about 25 minutes.
5. Remove from Air Fryer and transfer the chicken thighs onto a serving platter. Serve hot.

Turkey Legs

(Prep + Cook Time: 45 minutes | Servings: 2)

Ingredients:
- 2 turkey legs
- 2 garlic cloves; minced
- 1 tbsp. fresh lime juice
- 2 tbsp. olive oil
- 1 tbsp. fresh rosemary; minced
- 1 tsp. fresh lime zest; finely grated
- Salt and ground black pepper; as your liking

Directions:
1. Mix together the garlic, rosemary, lime zest, oil, lime juice, salt and black pepper in a large bowl.
2. Add the turkey legs and generously coat with marinade. Refrigerate to marinate for about 6 to 8 hours.
3. Set the temperature of Air Fryer to 350°F. Grease an Air Fryer basket.
4. Place turkey legs into the prepared Air Fryer basket.
5. Air Fry for about 30 minutes, flipping once halfway through. Remove from Air Fryer and place the turkey legs onto the serving plates. Serve hot.

Chicken Cutlets

(Prep + Cook Time: 45 minutes | Servings: 4)

Ingredients:
- 4 (6-oz.) (¼-inch thick) skinless, boneless chicken cutlets
- 1½ cups panko breadcrumbs
- 1/4 cup Parmesan cheese; grated
- 1 lemon; cut into slices
- 3/4 cup all-purpose flour
- 2 large eggs
- 1 tbsp. mustard powder
- Salt and ground black pepper; as your liking

Directions:
1. In a shallow bowl, add the flour. In a second bowl, crack the eggs and beat well.
2. In a third bowl, mix together the breadcrumbs, cheese, mustard powder, salt and black pepper. Season the chicken with salt and black pepper.
3. Coat the chicken with flour, then dip into beaten eggs and finally coat with the breadcrumbs mixture.
4. Set the temperature of Air Fryer to 355°F. Grease an Air Fryer basket. Arrange chicken cutlets into the prepared Air Fryer basket in a single layer. Air Fry for about 30 minutes.
5. Remove from Air Fryer and transfer the chicken cutlets onto a serving platter. Serve hot with the topping of lemon slices.

Crispy Chicken Wings

(Prep + Cook Time: 45 minutes | Servings: 2)

Ingredients:
- 1 lb. chicken wings, rinsed and trimmed
- 1 onion; finely chopped
- 1/2 cup cornstarch
- 2 lemongrass stalk (white portion); minced
- 1 tbsp. soy sauce
- 1½ tbsp. honey
- Salt and ground white pepper, as required

Directions:
1. In a bowl, mix together the lemongrass, onion, soy sauce, honey, salt and white pepper.
2. Add the wings and generously coat with marinade. Cover and refrigerate to marinate overnight.
3. Set the temperature of Air Fryer to 355°F. Grease an Air Fryer basket.

4. Remove the chicken wings from marinade and coat with the cornstarch.
5. Arrange chicken wings into the prepared Air Fryer basket in a single layer. Air Fry for about 25 minutes, flipping once halfway through.
6. Remove from Air Fryer and transfer the chicken wings onto a serving platter. Serve hot.

Chicken Breasts and Veggies.

(Prep + Cook Time: 30 minutes | **Servings:** 4)

Ingredients:
- 2 lbs. chicken breasts; skinless and boneless
- 12 brown mushrooms; halved
- 1 green bell pepper; roughly chopped.
- 2 garlic cloves; minced
- 2 tbsp. olive oil
- 1 red onion; chopped.
- 1 red bell pepper; chopped.
- 2 tbsp. cheddar cheese; shredded
- Salt and black pepper to taste

Directions:
1. Season the chicken breasts with salt and pepper and then rub with the garlic and 1 tbsp. of the oil
2. Place the chicken breasts in your preheated air fryer's basket, cook at 390°F for 6 minutes on each side and divide between plates.
3. Heat up a pan with the remaining 1 tbsp. of the oil over medium heat; add the onions, stir and cook for 2 minutes
4. Add the mushrooms and bell peppers, stir and cook for 5-6 minutes more
5. Divide this next to the chicken, sprinkle the cheese all over and serve.

Chicken with Broccoli and Rice

(Prep + Cook Time: 35 minutes | Servings: 6)

Ingredients:
- 2 lbs. boneless, skinless chicken breasts, sliced
- 3 cups instant white rice
- 3/4 cup cream soup
- 3 cups small broccoli florets
- 1/3 cup butter
- 3 cups water
- 1 tbsp. onion powder
- 1 tbsp. garlic powder
- 3 tbsp. dried parsley; crushed
- 1/2 tsp. paprika
- 1/2 tsp. red chili powder

Directions:
1. Mix together the parsley and spices in a large bowl. Add the chicken slices and generously coat with spice mixture. Arrange 6 large pieces of foil onto a smooth surface.
2. Place 1/2 cup of rice over each foil piece, followed by 1/6 of chicken, 2 tbsp. of cream soup, 1/2 cup of broccoli, 1 tbsp. of butter and 1/2 cup of water.
3. Fold the foil tightly to seal the rice mixture. Set the temperature of Air Fryer to 390°F. Arrange the foil packets into an Air Fryer basket. Air Fry for about 15 minutes.
4. Remove from Air Fryer and carefully, transfer the rice mixture onto serving plates. Serve hot.

Chicken and Dates

(Prep + Cook Time: 35 minutes | **Servings:** 6)

Ingredients:
- 1 whole chicken; cut into medium pieces
- 4 dates; chopped.
- 1/4 cup olive oil
- 3/4 cup water
- 1/3 cup honey
- Salt and black pepper to taste

Directions:
1. Put the water in a pot, bring to a simmer over medium heat.
2. Add the honey, whisk and take off the heat. Rub the chicken with the oil, season with salt and pepper and place in your air fryer's basket
3. Add the dates and cook at 350°F for 10 minutes

4. Brush the chicken with some of the honey mix, cook for 6 minutes more, flip again, brush one more time with the honey mix and cook for 7 minutes more
5. Divide the chicken and the dates between plates and serve.

Sweet Chicken Kabobs

(Prep + Cook Time: 34 minutes | Servings: 3)

Ingredients:
- 1 lb. chicken tenders
- 4 garlic cloves; minced
- 4 scallions; chopped
- 1/2 cup pineapple juice
- 1/2 cup soy sauce
- 1/4 cup sesame oil
- 1 tbsp. fresh ginger; finely grated
- 2 tsp. sesame seeds, toasted
- A pinch of black pepper

Directions:
1. In a large baking dish, mix together the scallion, ginger, garlic, pineapple juice, soy sauce, oil, sesame seeds and black pepper.
2. Thread chicken tenders onto the pre-soaked wooden skewers. Add the skewers into the baking dish and evenly coat with marinade. Cover and refrigerate for about 2 hours or overnight.
3. Set the temperature of Air Fryer to 390°F. Grease an Air Fryer basket.
4. Place chicken skewers into the prepared Air Fryer basket in 2 batches.
5. Air Fry for about 5 to 7 minutes. Remove from Air Fryer and transfer the chicken skewers onto a serving platter. Serve hot.

Turkey and Parsley Pesto

(**Prep + Cook Time:** 1 hour 5 minutes | **Servings:** 4)

Ingredients:
- 2 turkey breasts; boneless, skinless and halved
- 1 cup parsley; chopped.
- 1/4 cup red wine
- 4 garlic cloves
- 1/2 cup olive oil
- A drizzle of maple syrup
- A pinch of salt and black pepper

Directions:
1. In a blender, mix the parsley, garlic, salt, pepper, oil, wine and maple syrup; pulse to make a parsley pesto and then transfer to a bowl.
2. Add the turkey breasts to the bowl and toss well. Then place the bowl in the fridge for 30 minutes
3. Drain the turkey breasts (retaining the parsley pesto), put them in your air fryer's basket and cook at 380°F for 35 minutes, flipping the meat halfway
4. Divide the turkey between plates, drizzle the parsley pesto, all over and serve.

Chicken and Veggie Kabobs

(Prep + Cook Time: 50 minutes | Servings: 3)

Ingredients:
- 1 lb. skinless, boneless chicken thighs; cut into cubes
- 2 small bell peppers, seeded and cut into large chunks
- 1 large red onion; cut into large chunks
- 1/2 cup plain Greek yogurt
- 1 tbsp. olive oil
- 2 tsp. curry powder
- 1/2 tsp. smoked paprika
- 1/4 tsp. cayenne pepper
- Salt, to taste

Directions:
1. In a bowl, add the chicken, oil, yogurt and spices and mix until well combined Refrigerate to marinate for about 2 hours.
2. Thread the chicken cubes, bell pepper and onion onto pre-soaked wooden skewers.
3. Set the temperature of Air Fryer to 360°F. Grease an Air Fryer basket.

4. Arrange chicken skewers into the prepared Air Fryer basket in 2 batches. Air Fry for about 15 minutes.
5. Remove from Air Fryer and transfer the chicken skewers onto a serving platter. Serve hot.

Spicy Chicken Legs

(Prep + Cook Time: 40 minutes | Servings: 3)

Ingredients:
- 3 (8-oz.) chicken legs
- 2 cups white flour
- 1 cup buttermilk
- 1 tbsp. olive oil
- 1 tsp. garlic powder
- 1 tsp. ground cumin
- 1 tsp. paprika
- 1 tsp. onion powder
- Salt and ground black pepper; as your liking

Directions:
1. In a bowl, put the chicken legs and buttermilk. Refrigerate for about 2 hours.
2. In another bowl, mix together the flour and spices. Remove the chicken from buttermilk.
3. Coat the chicken legs with flour mixture, then dip into buttermilk and finally, coat with the flour mixture again.
4. Set the temperature of Air Fryer to 360°F. Grease an Air Fryer basket. Arrange chicken legs into the prepared Air Fryer basket and drizzle with the oil
5. Air Fry for about 20 to 25 minutes. Remove from the Air Fryer and transfer chicken legs onto a serving platter. Serve hot.

Chicken Tenderloins

(Prep + Cook Time: 30 minutes | Servings: 4)

Ingredients:
- 8 skinless, boneless chicken tenderloins
- 1/2 cup breadcrumbs
- 1 egg, beaten
- 2 tbsp. vegetable oil

Directions:
1. In a shallow dish, beat the egg. In another dish, add the oil and breadcrumbs and mix until a crumbly mixture forms.
2. Dip the chicken tenderloins into beaten egg and then coat with the breadcrumbs mixture. Shake off the excess coating.
3. Set the temperature of Air Fryer to 355°F. Grease an Air Fryer basket.
4. Arrange chicken tenderloins into the prepared Air Fryer basket in a single layer. Air Fry for about 12 to 15 minutes.
5. Remove from Air Fryer and transfer the chicken thighs onto a serving platter. Serve hot.

Bacon Wrapped Chicken Breasts

(Prep + Cook Time: 43 minutes | Servings: 4)

Ingredients:
- 2 (8-oz.) chicken breasts; cut each breast in half horizontally
- 6 to 7 Fresh basil leaves
- 12 bacon strips
- 2 tbsp. water
- 1 tbsp. palm sugar
- 2 tbsp. fish sauce
- 1½ tsp. honey
- Salt and ground black pepper; as your liking

Directions:
1. In a small heavy-bottomed pan, add palm sugar over medium-low heat and cook for about 2 to 3 minutes or until caramelized, stirring continuously.
2. Add the basil, fish sauce and water and stir to combine. Remove from heat and transfer the sugar mixture into a large bowl.
3. Sprinkle each chicken breast with salt and black pepper. Add the chicken pieces in sugar mixture and coat generously.

4. Refrigerate to marinate for about 4 to 6 hours. Set the temperature of Air Fryer to 365°F. Grease an Air Fryer basket. Wrap each chicken piece with 3 bacon strips. Coat each piece slightly with honey.
5. Arrange chicken pieces into the prepared Air Fryer basket. Air Fry for about 20 minutes, flipping once halfway through.
6. Remove from Air Fryer and transfer the chicken pieces onto a serving platter. Serve hot.

Glazed Chicken and Apples

(**Prep + Cook Time:** 30 minutes | **Servings:** 4)

Ingredients:
- 6 chicken thighs; skin-on
- 3 apples; cored and sliced
- 1 tbsp. mustard
- 2/3 cup apple cider
- 2 tbsp. olive oil
- 1 tbsp. rosemary; chopped
- 2 tbsp. honey
- Salt and black pepper to taste

Directions:
1. Heat up a pan that fits your air fryer with 1 tbsp. of the oil over medium heat.
2. Add the cider, honey and mustard; whisk
3. Bring to a simmer and take off the heat.
4. Add the chicken, apples, salt, pepper and rosemary; toss
5. Place the pan in your air fryer and cook at 390°F for 17 minutes. Divide between plates and serve.

Chicken and Scallion Kabobs

(Prep + Cook Time: 44 minutes | Servings: 4)

Ingredients:
- 4 (4-oz.) skinless, boneless chicken thighs, cubed into 1-inch size
- 5 scallions; cut into 1-inch pieces lengthwise
- 1/4 cup light soy sauce
- 1 tbsp. mirin
- 1 tsp. sugar
- 1 tsp. garlic salt

Directions:
1. In a baking dish, mix together the soy sauce, mirin, garlic salt and sugar. Thread chicken and scallions onto pre-soaked wooden skewers.
2. Place skewers into the baking dish and generously coat with marinade.
3. Cover and refrigerate for about 3 hours. Set the temperature of Air Fryer to 355°F. Grease an Air Fryer basket.
4. Arrange skewers into the prepared Air Fryer basket in 2 batches in a single layer. Air Fry for about 10 to 12 minutes.
5. Once done, remove from Air Fryer and transfer the chicken skewers onto a serving platter. Serve hot.

Chicken Wings

(Prep + Cook Time: 35 minutes | Servings: 2)

Ingredients:
- 1 lb. chicken wings
- Salt and ground black pepper; as your liking

Directions:
1. Set the temperature of Air Fryer to 380°F. Generously, grease an Air Fryer basket.
2. Sprinkle the chicken wings evenly with salt and black pepper.
3. Arrange chicken wings into the prepared Air Fryer basket in a single layer. Air Fry for about 25 minutes, flip the wings once halfway through.
4. Remove from Air Fryer and transfer the chicken wings onto a serving platter. Serve hot.

Herbed Roasted Chicken

(Prep + Cook Time: 1 hour 15 minutes | Servings: 7)

Ingredients:

- 1 (5-pounds) whole chicken
- 3 garlic cloves; minced
- 2 tbsp. fresh lemon juice
- 2 tbsp. olive oil
- 1 tsp. fresh lemon zest; finely grated
- 1 tsp. dried thyme; crushed
- 1 tsp. dried oregano; crushed
- 1 tsp. dried rosemary; crushed
- 1 tsp. smoked paprika
- Salt and ground black pepper; as your liking

Directions:

1. In a bowl, mix together the garlic, lemon zest, herbs and spices. Rub the chicken evenly with herb mixture.
2. Drizzle the chicken with lemon juice and oil. Set aside at the room temperature for about 2 hours.
3. Set the temperature of Air Fryer to 360°F. Grease an Air Fryer basket.
4. Place chicken into the prepared Air Fryer basket, breast side down. Air Fry for about 50 minutes. Flip the chicken and Air Fry for about 10 more minutes.
5. Remove from the Air Fryer and place chicken onto a cutting board for about 10 minutes before carving.
6. With a knife, slice the chicken into desired size pieces and serve.

Spicy Roasted Chicken

(Prep + Cook Time: 1 hour 15 minutes | Servings: 6)

Ingredients:

- 1 (5-pounds) whole chicken, necks and giblets removed
- 3 tbsp. oil
- 1 tsp. ground white pepper
- 1 tsp. onion powder
- 1 tsp. garlic powder
- 2 tsp. dried thyme
- 2 tsp. paprika
- 1 tsp. cayenne pepper
- Salt and ground black pepper; as your liking

Directions:

1. In a bowl, mix together the thyme and spices. Generously, coat the chicken with oil and then rub it with spice mixture.
2. Set the temperature of Air Fryer to 350°F. Grease an Air Fryer basket.
3. Place chicken into the prepared Air Fryer basket, breast side down. Air Fry for about 30 minutes. Flip the chicken and Air Fry for about 30 more minutes.
4. Remove from the Air Fryer and place chicken onto a cutting board for about 10 minutes before carving.
5. Slice the chicken into desired size pieces using a sharp knife and serve.

Oats Crusted Chicken Breasts

(Prep + Cook Time: 32 minutes | Servings: 2)

Ingredients:

- 2 (6-oz.) chicken breasts
- 3/4 cup oats
- 2 medium eggs
- 1 tbsp. fresh parsley
- 2 tbsp. mustard powder
- Salt and ground black pepper, as required

Directions:

1. Put the chicken breasts onto a cutting board and with a meat mallet, flatten each into even thickness. Then; cut each breast in half.
2. Sprinkle the chicken pieces with salt and black pepper and set aside.
3. In a blender, add the oats, mustard powder, parsley, salt and black pepper. Pulse until a coarse breadcrumb like mixture is formed.
4. Transfer the oat mixture into a shallow bowl. In another bowl, crack the eggs and beat well.

5. Coat the chicken with oats mixture and then, dip into beaten eggs and again, coat with the oats mixture.
6. Set the temperature of Air Fryer to 350 °F. Grease a grill pan of Air Fryer. Arrange chicken breasts into the prepared grill pan in a single layer.
7. Air Fry for about 12 minutes, flipping once halfway through.
8. Remove from Air Fryer and transfer the chicken breasts onto a serving platter. Serve hot.

Crispy Chicken Drumsticks

(Prep + Cook Time: 35 minutes | Servings: 2)

Ingredients:
- 4 (4-oz.) chicken drumsticks
- 1/2 cup all-purpose flour
- 1/2 cup panko breadcrumbs
- 1/2 cup buttermilk
- 3 tbsp. butter, melted
- 1/4 tsp. ground ginger
- 1/4 tsp. cayenne pepper
- 1/4 tsp. dried thyme
- 1/4 tsp. celery salt
- 1/4 tsp. garlic powder
- 1/4 tsp. paprika
- 1/4 tsp. baking powder
- 1/4 tsp. dried oregano
- Salt and ground black pepper; as your liking

Directions:
1. Place the chicken drumsticks and buttermilk in a resealable plastic bag. Squeeze the air out and seal the bag tightly. Refrigerate for about 2 to 3 hours.
2. In a shallow bowl, mix well flour, breadcrumbs, baking powder, herbs and spices.
3. Remove the chicken drumsticks from bag and shake off the excess buttermilk. Coat chicken drumsticks evenly with the seasoned flour mixture.
4. Set the temperature of air fryer to 390°F. Line an air fryer basket with a piece of foil. Arrange chicken drumsticks into the prepared air fryer basket.
5. Air fry for about 20 minutes, flipping once and coating with the melted butter.
6. Remove from air fryer and transfer the chicken drumsticks onto serving plates. Serve hot.

Chicken Thighs and Rice

(**Prep + Cook Time:** 35 minutes | **Servings:** 4)

Ingredients:
- 2 lbs. chicken thighs; boneless and skinless
- 1 cup white rice
- 1/4 cup red wine vinegar
- 2 cups chicken stock
- 3 carrots; chopped.
- 1 tbsp. Italian seasoning
- 1 tsp. turmeric powder
- 4 garlic cloves; minced
- 4 tbsp. olive oil
- 1 tbsp. garlic powder
- Salt and black pepper to taste

Directions:
1. In a pan that fits your air fryer, mix all of the ingredients and toss
2. Place the pan in the fryer and cook at 370°F for 30 minutes. Divide between plates and serve.

Glazed Turkey Breast

(Prep + Cook Time: 70 minutes | Servings: 8)

Ingredients:
- 1 (5-pounds) boneless turkey breast
- 1/4 cup maple syrup
- 2 tbsp. Dijon mustard
- 1 tbsp. butter; softened
- 1/2 tsp. smoked paprika
- 1/2 tsp. dried sage; crushed
- 2 tsp. olive oil
- 1 tsp. dried thyme; crushed
- Salt and ground black pepper; as your liking

Directions:

1. In a bowl, mix together the herbs, paprika, salt and black pepper. Coat the turkey breast evenly with oil.
2. coat the outer side of turkey breast with herb mixture. Set the temperature of Air Fryer to 350°F. Grease an Air Fryer basket.
3. Place turkey breast into the prepared Air Fryer basket. Air Fry for about 25 minutes.
4. Flip the side and Air Fry for another 12 minutes. Again flip the side and Air Fry for 13 more minutes.
5. Meanwhile, in a bowl, mix together the maple syrup, mustard and butter. Coat the turkey evenly with glaze. Air Fry for about 5 more minutes.
6. Remove from Air Fryer and place the turkey breast onto a cutting board for about 10 minutes before slicing.
7. With a sharp knife; cut the turkey breast into desired size slices and serve.

Fried Whole Chicken

(**Prep + Cook Time:** 30 minutes | **Servings:** 8)

Ingredients:

- 1 whole chicken; cut into medium pieces
- 3 tbsp. white wine
- 1 tbsp. ginger; grated
- 1 cup chicken stock
- 2 carrots; chopped.
- Salt and black pepper to taste

Directions:

1. In a pan that fits your air fryer, mix all of the ingredients
2. Put the pan in the air fryer and cook at 370°F for 20 minutes. Divide between plates and serve.

Chicken Breasts

(Prep + Cook Time: 42 minutes | Servings: 2)

Ingredients:

- 2 (6-oz.) chicken breasts
- 4 oz.' breadcrumbs
- 1/4 cup pasta sauce
- 1/4 cup Parmesan cheese, grated
- 1 egg, beaten
- 2 tbsp. vegetable oil
- 1 tbsp. fresh basil

Directions:

1. In a shallow bowl, beat the egg. In another bowl, add the oil, breadcrumbs and basil and mix until a crumbly mixture forms.
2. dip each chicken breast into the beaten egg and then, coat with the breadcrumb mixture. Set the temperature of Air Fryer to 350°F. Grease an Air Fryer basket.
3. Arrange chicken breasts into the prepared basket Air Fry for about 15 minutes.
4. Spoon the pasta sauce evenly over chicken breast and sprinkle with cheese.
5. Air Fry for about 5 to 7 more minutes. Remove from Air Fryer and transfer the chicken breasts onto a serving platter. Serve hot.

Chicken and Leeks

(**Prep + Cook Time:** 40 minutes | **Servings:** 4)

Ingredients:

- 4 chicken thighs; bone-in
- 3 leeks; sliced
- 2 tbsp. chives; chopped.
- 1 tbsp. olive oil
- 3 carrots; cut into thin sticks
- 1 cup chicken stock
- Salt and black pepper to taste

Directions:

1. Heat up a pan that fits your air fryer over medium heat, add the stock, leeks and carrots, cover and simmer for 20 minutes
2. Rub the chicken with olive oil, season with salt and pepper, put it in your air fryer and cook at 350°F for 4 minutes

3. Add the chicken to the leeks mix, place the pan in your air fryer and cook for 6 minutes more. Divide between plates, serve and enjoy!

Chicken and Pancetta

(Prep + Cook Time: 35 minutes | Servings: 4)

Ingredients:

- 2 chicken breasts; skinless, boneless, cubed
- 4 oz. smoked pancetta; chopped.
- 1/2 bunch thyme; chopped.
- 1/2bunch rosemary; chopped.
- 1/2 fennel bulb; cut into matchsticks
- 1/2 cup chicken stock
- 4 carrots; cut into thin matchsticks
- 2 scallions; chopped.
- Juice of 1 lemon
- A drizzle of olive oil
- Salt and black pepper to taste

Directions:

1. Heat up the oil in a pan that fits your air fryer over medium heat
2. Add the scallions, pancetta, thyme, rosemary, salt, pepper, fennel and carrots; toss and cook for 5 minutes.
3. Add the lemon juice and the chicken, toss and cook for 5 more minutes
4. Place the pan in the fryer and cook at 380°F for 15 minutes. Divide everything between plates and serve.

Turmeric Chicken Legs

(Prep + Cook Time: 25 minutes | Servings: 4)

Ingredients:

- 4 chicken legs
- 2 tbsp. ginger; grated
- 5 tsp. turmeric powder
- 4 tbsp. heavy cream
- Salt and black pepper to taste

Directions:

1. Place all ingredients in a bowl and mix well
2. Transfer the chicken to your air fryer and cook at 380°F for 20 minutes. Divide between plates and serve.

Spiced Chicken

(Prep + Cook Time: 35 minutes | Servings: 4)

Ingredients:

- 6 chicken thighs; boneless
- 2 yellow onions; chopped.
- 5 garlic cloves; chopped.
- 1/4 cup white wine
- 1 cup chicken stock
- 1/2 cup cilantro; chopped.
- 1/4 cup cranberries; dried
- 2 tbsp. olive oil
- 1/2 tsp. coriander; ground
- 1/2 tsp. cumin; ground
- 1/2 tsp. turmeric; ground
- 1/2 tsp. cinnamon; ground
- 1/2 tsp. ginger powder
- 1 tsp. sweet paprika
- Juice of 1 lemon

Directions:

1. Heat up the oil in a pan that fits your air fryer over medium heat
2. Add all other ingredients except the chicken, lemon juice and cilantro; stir and cook for 5 minutes.
3. Then add the chicken and toss
4. Place the pan in the fryer and cook at 380°F for 20 minutes
5. Add the lemon juice and the cilantro and toss. Divide between plates, serve and enjoy!

Herbed Turkey Breast

(Prep + Cook Time: 50 minutes | Servings: 3)

Ingredients:

- 1 (2½-pounds) bone-in, skin-on turkey breast
- 1 tbsp. olive oil
- 1/2 tsp. dark brown sugar
- 1/2 tsp. garlic powder
- 1/2 tsp. paprika
- 1 tsp. dried thyme; crushed
- 1 tsp. dried rosemary; crushed
- 1/2 tsp. dried sage; crushed

Directions:

1. In a bowl, mix together the herbs, brown sugar and spices.
2. Coat the turkey breast evenly with oil and then, generously rub with the herb mixture.
3. Set the temperature of Air Fryer to 360°F. Grease an Air Fryer basket. Arrange turkey breast into the prepared Air Fryer basket, skin-side down. Air Fry for about 35 minutes, flipping once halfway through.
4. Remove from Air Fryer and place the turkey breast onto a cutting board for about 10 minutes before slicing.
5. With a sharp knife; cut the turkey breast into desired size slices and serve.

Turkey Chili

(**Prep + Cook Time:** 35 minutes | **Servings:** 4)

Ingredients:

- 1 lb. turkey meat; cubed and browned
- 15 oz. canned lentils; drained
- 12 oz. veggie stock
- 3 garlic cloves; chopped.
- 2½ tbsp. chili powder
- 1½ tsp. cumin; ground
- 1 yellow onion; chopped.
- 1 green bell pepper; chopped.
- Salt and black pepper to taste

Directions:

1. Add all of the ingredients to a pan that fits your air fryer and mix well
2. Place the pan in the fryer and cook at 380°F for 25 minutes. Divide into bowls and serve hot.

Turkey Rolls

(Prep + Cook Time: 60 minutes | Servings: 3)

Ingredients:

- 1 lb. turkey breast fillet
- 1 small red onion; finely chopped
- 1 garlic clove; crushed
- 3 tbsp. fresh parsley; finely chopped
- 2 tbsp. olive oil
- 1 tsp. ground cinnamon
- 1½ tsp. ground cumin
- 1/2 tsp. red chili powder
- Salt, to taste

Directions:

1. Place the turkey fillet on a cutting board. Carefully; cut horizontally along the length about 1/3 of way from the top, stopping about ¼-inch from the edge.
2. Open this part to have a long piece of fillet. In a bowl, mix together the garlic, spices and oil.
3. In a small cup, reserve about 1 tbsp. of oil mixture. In the remaining oil mixture, add the parsley and onion and mix well.
4. Set the temperature of Air Fryer to 355°F. Grease an Air Fryer basket. Coat the open side of fillet with onion mixture.
5. Roll the fillet tightly from the short side. With a kitchen string, tie the roll at 1 to 1½-inch intervals. Coat the outer side of roll with the reserved oil mixture.
6. Arrange roll into the prepared Air Fryer basket. Air Fry for about 40 minutes.
7. Remove from Air Fryer and place the turkey roll onto a cutting board for about 5 to 10 minutes before slicing. With a sharp knife; cut the turkey roll into desired size slices and serve.

Sour and Sweet Chicken Thighs

(Prep + Cook Time: 35 minutes | Servings: 2)

Ingredients:

- 2 (4-oz.) skinless, boneless chicken thighs
- 1/2 cup corn flour
- 1 garlic clove; minced
- 1 scallion; finely chopped
- 1/2 tbsp. rice vinegar
- 1/2 tbsp. soy sauce
- 1 tsp. sugar
- Salt and ground black pepper, as required

Directions:

1. Mix together all the Ingredients except chicken and corn flour in a bowl. Add the chicken thighs and generously coat with marinade.
2. Add the corn flour in another bowl. Remove the chicken thighs from marinade and coat with corn flour.
3. Set the temperature of Air Fryer to 390°F. Grease an Air Fryer basket. Arrange chicken thighs into the prepared Air Fryer basket, skin side down.
4. Air Fry for about 10 minutes and then another 10 minutes at 355°F.
5. Remove from Air Fryer and transfer the chicken thighs onto a serving platter. Serve hot.

Beer Coated Duck Breast

(Prep + Cook Time: 35 minutes | Servings: 2)

Ingredients:

- 1 (10½-oz.) duck breast
- 6 cherry tomatoes
- 1 cup beer
- 1 tbsp. fresh thyme; chopped
- 1 tbsp. olive oil
- 1 tbsp. balsamic vinegar
- 1 tsp. mustard
- Salt and ground black pepper; as your liking

Directions:

1. In a bowl, mix together the oil, mustard, thyme, beer, salt and black pepper.
2. Add the duck breast and generously coat with marinade.
3. Cover and refrigerate for about 4 hours.
4. Set the temperature of Air Fryer to 390°F. With a piece of foil, cover the duck breast and arrange into an Air Fryer basket.
5. Air Fry for about 15 minutes. Remove the foil from breast. Now, set the temperature of Air Fryer to 355°F. Grease the Air Fryer basket.
6. Place duck breast and tomatoes into the prepared Air Fryer basket. Air Fry for about 5 minutes.
7. Remove from Air Fryer and place the duck breast onto a cutting board for about 5 minutes before slicing.
8. With a sharp knife; cut the duck breast into desired size slices and transfer onto serving plates.
9. Drizzle with vinegar and serve alongside the cherry tomatoes.

Jerk Chicken, Pineapple and Veggie Kabobs

(Prep + Cook Time: 38 minutes | Servings: 8)

Ingredients:

- 1 (20-oz.) can pineapple chunks, drained
- 2 large zucchinis, sliced
- 8 oz. white mushrooms; stems removed
- 8 (4-oz.) boneless, skinless chicken thigh fillets, trimmed and cut into cubes
- 1 tbsp. jerk seasoning
- 1 tbsp. jerk sauce
- Salt and ground black pepper; as your liking

Directions:

1. In a bowl, mix together the chicken cubes and jerk seasoning. Cover the bowl and refrigerate overnight.
2. Sprinkle the zucchini slices and mushrooms evenly with salt and black pepper. Thread the chicken, vegetables and pineapple onto greased metal skewers.

3. Set the temperature of Air Fryer to 370°F. Grease an Air Fryer basket. Arrange skewers into the prepared Air Fryer basket in 2 batches.
4. Air Fry for about 8 to 9 minutes, flipping and coating with jerk sauce once halfway through.
5. Remove from Air Fryer and transfer the chicken skewers onto a serving platter. Serve hot.

Tomato Chicken

(Prep + Cook Time: 30 minutes | Servings: 6)

Ingredients:
- 14 oz. tomato sauce
- 6 oz. mozzarella cheese; grated
- 4 medium chicken breasts; skinless and boneless
- 1 tbsp. olive oil
- 1 tsp. oregano; dried
- 1 tsp. garlic powder
- Salt and black pepper to taste

Directions:
1. Put the chicken in your air fryer and season with salt, pepper, garlic powder and the oregano.
2. Cook the chicken at 360°F for 5 minutes; then transfer to a pan that fits your air fryer, greased with the oil
3. Add the tomato sauce, sprinkle the mozzarella on top, place the pan in the fryer and cook at 350°F for 15 minutes more. Divide between plates and serve

Chinese Style Chicken Thighs

(Prep + Cook Time: 40 minutes | Servings: 4)

Ingredients:
- 4 chicken thighs
- 1 bunch spring onions; chopped.
- 14 oz. water
- 1 tbsp. rice wine
- 1 tbsp. olive oil
- 1 tbsp. ginger; grated
- 2 green chilies; chopped.
- 1 tbsp. fish sauce
- 1 tbsp. soy sauce
- 1 tsp. sesame oil

Directions:
1. Heat up a pan that fits your air fryer with the olive and sesame oil over medium heat.
2. Add the chilies, onions, ginger, fish sauce, soy sauce, rice wine and the water; whisk, bring to a simmer, cook for 3-4 minutes and then take off the heat
3. Add the chicken thighs and toss everything
4. Place the pan into the air fryer and cook at 370°F for 25 minutes. Divide between plates and serve.

Buttered Duck Breasts

(Prep + Cook Time: 37 minutes | Servings: 4)

Ingredients:
- 2 (12-oz.) duck breasts
- 3 tbsp. unsalted butter, melted
- 1/4 tsp. star anise powder
- 1/2 tsp. dried thyme; crushed
- Salt and ground black pepper; as your liking

Directions:
1. With a sharp knife, score the fat of duck breasts several times. Season the duck breasts generously with salt and black pepper.
2. Set the temperature of Air Fryer to 390°F. Grease an Air Fryer basket.
3. Arrange duck breasts into the prepared Air Fryer basket. Air Fry for about 10 minutes.
4. Remove duck breasts from the basket and coat with melted butter and sprinkle with thyme and star anise powder.
5. Place duck breasts into the Air Fryer basket for the second time. Air Fry for about 12 more minutes.
6. Remove from Air Fryer and place the duck breasts onto a cutting board for about 5 to 10 minutes before slicing.
7. Using a sharp knife; cut each duck breast into desired size slices and serve.

Honey Duck Breasts

(Prep + Cook Time: 30 minutes | **Servings:** 6)

Ingredients:

- 6 duck breasts; boneless
- 20 oz. chicken stock
- 1 tsp. olive oil
- 4 tbsp. hoisin sauce
- 4 tbsp. soy sauce
- 2 tbsp. honey
- 1 tbsp. ginger; grated
- Salt and black pepper to taste

Directions:

1. Place all of the ingredients in a bowl and toss well. Put the bowl in the fridge for 10 minutes
2. Transfer the duck breasts to your air fryer's basket and cook at 400°F for 10 minutes on each side.
3. Divide between plates and serve with a side salad.

Turkey Wings

(Prep + Cook Time: 36 minutes | Servings: 4)

Ingredients:

- 2 lbs. turkey wings
- 3 tbsp. olive oil
- 4 tbsp. chicken rub

Directions:

1. In a large bowl, mix together the turkey wings, chicken rub and oil using your hands. Set the temperature of Air Fryer to 380°F. Grease an Air Fryer basket.
2. Arrange turkey wings into the prepared Air Fryer basket.
3. Air Fry for about 26 minutes, flipping once halfway through. Remove from Air Fryer and place the turkey wings onto the serving plates. Serve hot.

Turkey Breast

(Prep + Cook Time: 60 minutes | **Servings:** 4)

Ingredients:

- 2 turkey breasts; skinless, boneless and halved
- 1 tbsp. lemon juice
- 2 tbsp. olive oil
- 1 tsp. garlic powder
- 1 tsp. rosemary; dried
- 1 tsp. onion powder
- 1/2 tsp. thyme; dried
- Salt and black pepper to taste

Directions:

1. In a bowl, mix all the ingredients and rub the turkey well
2. Transfer to your air fryer's basket and cook at 370°F for 25 minutes on each side. Serve hot with a side salad.

Japanese Style Chicken Thighs

(Prep + Cook Time: 40 minutes | **Servings:** 5)

Ingredients:

- 2 lbs. chicken thighs
- 5 spring onions; chopped.
- 1/2 tsp. white vinegar
- 1/4 tsp. sugar
- 2 tbsp. olive oil
- 1 tbsp. soy sauce
- 1 tbsp. sherry wine
- Salt and black pepper to taste

Directions:

1. Season the chicken with salt and pepper, rub with 1 tbsp. of the oil and put it in the air fryer's basket.
2. Cook at 360°F for 10 minutes on each side and divide between plates
3. Heat up a pan with the remaining tbsp. of oil over medium-high heat and add the spring onions, sherry wine, vinegar, soy sauce and sugar; whisk
4. Cook for 10 minutes, drizzle over the chicken and serve.

Blue Cheese Chicken

(Prep + Cook Time: 30 minutes | **Servings:** 4)

Ingredients:
- 1 lb. chicken breasts; skinless, boneless and cut into thin strips
- 1/2 cup buffalo sauce
- 1/2 cup chicken stock
- 1/4 cup bleu cheese; crumbled
- 1 small yellow onion; sliced

Directions:
1. In a pan that fits your air fryer, mix the chicken with the onions, buffalo sauce and the stock.
2. Toss everything and then place the pan in the fryer; cook at 370°F for 20 minutes
3. Sprinkle the cheese on top, divide everything between plates and serve

Herbed Duck Legs

(Prep + Cook Time: 40 minutes | Servings: 2)

Ingredients:
- 2 duck legs
- 1 garlic clove; minced
- 1/2 tbsp. fresh parsley; chopped
- 1/2 tbsp. fresh thyme; chopped
- 1 tsp. five spice powder
- Salt and ground black pepper; as your liking

Directions:
1. Set the temperature of air fryer to 340°F. Grease an air fryer basket.
2. In a bowl, mix together the garlic, herbs, five spice powder, salt and black pepper. Generously rub the duck legs with garlic mixture.
3. Arrange duck legs into the prepared air fryer basket.
4. Air fry for about 25 minutes and then 5 more minutes at 390°F.
5. Remove from air fryer and place the duck legs onto the serving platter. Serve hot.

Curried Chicken

(Prep + Cook Time: 33 minutes | Servings: 3)

Ingredients:
- 1 lb. boneless chicken, cubed
- 1 egg
- 1/2 cup evaporated milk
- 1 medium yellow onion, thinly sliced
- 1 green chili; chopped
- 5 curry leaves
- 1 tbsp. chili sauce
- 1 tbsp. light soy sauce
- 1/2 tbsp. cornstarch
- 2 tbsp. olive oil
- 1 tsp. fresh ginger; grated
- 1 tsp. curry powder
- 1 tsp. sugar
- 3 tsp. garlic; minced
- Salt and ground black pepper; as your liking

Directions:
1. In a bowl, add the chicken cubes, soy sauce, cornstarch and egg and mix until well combined.
2. Cover the bowl and place at room temperature for about 1 hour.
3. Remove chicken cubes from the bowl and with paper towels, pat them dry. Set the temperature of Air Fryer to 390°F. Grease an Air Fryer basket.
4. Arrange chicken cubes into the prepared Air Fryer basket. Air Fry for about 10 minutes. Remove chicken cubes from the Air fryer and set aside.
5. In a medium skillet, add the oil over medium heat and cook until heated. Add the onion, green chili, garlic, ginger and curry leaves. Sauté for about 3 to 4 minutes.
6. Add the chicken cubes, curry powder, chili sauce, sugar, salt and black pepper and mix until well combined.
7. Stir in the evaporated milk and cook for about 3 to 4 minutes. Remove from heat and transfer the chicken mixture into a serving bowl. Serve hot.

Chicken and Pear Sauce

(**Prep + Cook Time:** 30 minutes | **Servings:** 6)

Ingredients:

- 6 chicken breasts; skinless and boneless
- 3 cups ketchup
- 1 tsp. chili powder
- 1 tsp. garlic powder
- 1 cup pear jelly
- 1/4 cup honey
- 1/2 tsp. smoked paprika
- 1 tsp. mustard powder
- Salt and black pepper to taste

Directions:

1. Season the chicken with salt and pepper; put it in preheated air fryer and cook at 350°F for 10 minutes
2. Heat up a pan with the ketchup over medium heat, add the pear jelly, honey, smoked paprika, chili powder, mustard powder, garlic powder, salt and pepper; whisk and cook for 5-6 minutes
3. Add the chicken, toss and cook for 4 minutes more. Divide everything between plates and serve.

Mexican Style Turkey

(**Prep + Cook Time:** 25 minutes | **Servings:** 4)

Ingredients:

- 1 lb. turkey meat; ground
- 10 oz. tomato sauce
- 4 oz. mushrooms; sliced
- 1 cup cheddar cheese; grated
- 1 yellow onion; chopped.
- 1 tbsp. oregano; dried
- 1 tsp. garlic; minced
- 1 tsp. basil; dried
- 2 tbsp. olive oil
- Salt and black pepper to taste

Directions:

1. Heat up the oil in a pan that fits your air fryer over medium heat.
2. Add the turkey, oregano, garlic, basil and the onions; toss and cook for 2-3 minutes
3. Then add the mushrooms and tomato sauce, toss and cook for 2 minutes more
4. Place the pan in the fryer and cook at 370°F for 16 minutes
5. Sprinkle the cheese all over, divide the mix between plates and serve.

Easy Chicken Thighs

(**Prep + Cook Time:** 21 minutes | **Servings:** 6)

Ingredients:

- 8 chicken thighs
- 1 tbsp. ginger; grated
- 1 tbsp. sweet paprika
- 1 tbsp. lime juice
- 2 tbsp. olive oil
- 1 tbsp. turmeric powder
- 1 tbsp. coriander; ground
- Salt and black pepper to taste

Directions:

1. Place all the ingredients in a bowl and toss well
2. Transfer the chicken thighs to your air fryer's basket and cook at 370°F for 8 minutes on each side
3. Divide between plates and serve with a side salad.

Chicken and Green Coconut Sauce.

(**Prep + Cook Time:** 26 minutes | **Servings:** 4)

Ingredients:

- 10 green onions; roughly chopped
- 10 chicken drumsticks
- 1 cup coconut milk
- 1/4 cup parsley; chopped.
- 4 garlic cloves; minced
- 2 tbsp. oyster sauce
- 3 tbsp. soy sauce
- 1 tbsp. ginger; grated
- 1 tsp. Chinese five spice
- 1 tsp. olive oil
- 1 tbsp. lemon juice
- Salt and black pepper to taste

Directions:
1. In a blender, mix the green onions with the ginger, garlic, soy sauce, oyster sauce, five spice, salt, pepper, oil and coconut milk; pulse well
2. In a baking dish that fits your air fryer, mix the chicken with the green sauce, toss and then place the dish in the air fryer
3. Cook at 370°F for 16 minutes, shaking the fryer once
4. Divide between plates, sprinkle the parsley on top, drizzle the lemon juice all over and serve.

Chicken Breasts Delight

(Prep + Cook Time: 30 minutes | **Servings:** 6)

Ingredients:
- 3½ lbs. chicken breasts
- 1¼ cups yellow onion; chopped.
- 1 cup chicken stock
- 1 tbsp. lime juice
- 1 tbsp. olive oil
- 1 tsp. red pepper flakes
- 2 tsp. sweet paprika
- 2 tbsp. green onions; chopped.
- Salt and black pepper to taste

Directions:
1. Heat the oil up in a pan that fits your air fryer over medium heat.
2. Add the onions, lime juice, paprika, green onions, pepper flakes, salt and pepper
3. Stir the onion mixture and cook for 8 minutes.
4. Add the chicken and the stock, toss and simmer for 1 more minute
5. Transfer the pan to your air fryer and cook at 370°F for 12 minutes. Divide between plates and serve.

Honey Glazed Chicken Drumsticks

(Prep + Cook Time: 37 minutes | Servings: 4)

Ingredients:
- 4 (6-oz.) boneless chicken drumsticks
- 1/4 cup Dijon mustard
- 1/2 tbsp. fresh rosemary; minced
- 2 tbsp. olive oil
- 1 tbsp. fresh thyme; minced
- 1 tbsp. honey
- Salt and ground black pepper; as your liking

Directions:
1. In a bowl, mix well the mustard, honey, oil, herbs, salt and black pepper. Add the drumsticks and generously coat with the mixture.
2. Cover and refrigerate to marinate overnight. Set the temperature of Air Fryer to 320°F. Grease an Air Fryer basket.
3. Arrange the chicken drumsticks into the prepared Air Fryer basket in a single layer. Air Fry for about 12 minutes.
4. Set the temperature of Air Fryer to 355°F. Air Fry for 5 to 10 more minutes. Remove from Air Fryer and transfer the chicken drumsticks onto a serving platter. Serve hot.

Tarragon Chicken Breasts

(Prep + Cook Time: 25 minutes | **Servings:** 2)

Ingredients:
- 2 chicken breasts; skinless and boneless
- 2 garlic cloves; minced
- 1/4 cup soy sauce
- 1 tbsp. butter; melted
- 8 tarragon sprigs; chopped.
- 1 cup white wine
- Salt and black pepper to taste

Directions:
1. In a bowl, mix the chicken with the wine, soy sauce, garlic, tarragon, salt, pepper and the butter; toss well and set aside for 10 minutes

2. Transfer the chicken and its marinade to a baking dish that fits your air fryer and cook at 370°F for 15 minutes, shaking the fryer halfway. Divide everything between plates and serve.

Chicken Thighs

(**Prep + Cook Time:** 30 minutes | **Servings:** 4)

Ingredients:
- 5 chicken thighs
- 2 garlic cloves; minced
- 1/4 cup cheddar cheese; grated
- 1/2 cup heavy cream
- 1 tbsp. olive oil
- 1 tbsp. rosemary
- 3/4 cup chicken stock
- 1/2 cup tomatoes; chopped
- 2 tbsp. basil; chopped.
- 1 tsp. chili powder
- Salt and black pepper to taste

Directions:
1. Season the chicken with salt and pepper and rub it with 1/2 tbsp. of the oil.
2. Put the chicken in your air fryer's basket and cook at 350°F for 4 minutes.
3. Heat up a pan that fits your air fryer with the remaining 1/2 tbsp. of oil over medium heat
4. Add rosemary, garlic, chili powder, tomatoes, cream, stock, cheese, salt and pepper; stir / combine.
5. Bring the mixture to a simmer, take off the heat and then add the chicken thighs and toss everything
6. Place the pan in the air fryer and cook at 340°F for 12 minutes. Divide between plates, sprinkle the basil on top, serve and enjoy.

Chicken with Apple

(Prep + Cook Time: 40 minutes | Servings: 2)

Ingredients:
- 2 (4-oz.) boneless, skinless chicken thighs, sliced into chunks
- 1/2 cup apple cider
- 1 large apple, cored and cubed
- 1 shallot, thinly sliced
- 2 tbsp. maple syrup
- 1 tbsp. fresh ginger; finely grated
- 1 tsp. fresh thyme; minced
- Salt and ground black pepper; as your liking

Directions:
1. In a bowl, mix together the shallot, ginger, thyme, apple cider, maple syrup, salt and black pepper.
2. Add the chicken pieces and generously mix with the marinade. Refrigerate to marinate for about 6 to 8 hours.
3. Set the temperature of Air Fryer to 390°F. Grease an Air Fryer basket.
4. Place the chicken pieces and cubed apple into the prepared Air Fryer basket. Air Fry for about 20 minutes, flipping once halfway.
5. Remove from Air Fryer and transfer the chicken mixture onto a serving platter. Serve hot.

Marinara Chicken

(**Prep + Cook Time:** 35 minutes | **Servings:** 6)

Ingredients:
- 2 lbs. chicken breasts; skinless, boneless and cubed
- 1 cup green bell pepper; chopped.
- 3/4 cup marinara sauce
- 1/2 cup cheddar cheese; grated
- 3/4 cup yellow onion; diced
- 1 tbsp. olive oil
- Salt and black pepper to taste

Directions:
1. Heat up a pan that fits your air fryer with the oil over medium heat.
2. Add the chicken, toss and brown for 3 minutes
3. Add the salt, pepper, onions, bell peppers and the marinara sauce; stir and cook for 3 minutes more.
4. Place the pan in the air fryer and cook at 370°F for 15 minutes
5. Sprinkle the cheese on top, divide the mix between plates and serve.

Tomato Duck Breast

(Prep + Cook Time: 25 minutes | Servings: 2)

Ingredients:
- 1 smoked duck breast
- 1/2 tsp. apple vinegar
- 1 tsp. honey
- 1 tbsp. tomato paste

Directions:
1. In a bowl, mix the duck with the other ingredients and toss
2. Transfer the contents to your air fryer and cook at 370°F for 10 minutes on each side. Cut the meat into halves, divide between plates and serve.

Chicken with Veggies and Rice

(Prep + Cook Time: 35 minutes | Servings: 3)

Ingredients:
- 3 cups cold boiled white rice
- 1 cup cooked chicken, diced
- 1/2 cup frozen carrots
- 1/2 cup frozen peas
- 1/2 cup onion; chopped
- 1 tbsp. vegetable oil
- 6 tbsp. soy sauce

Directions:
1. In a large bowl, add the rice, soy sauce and oil and mix thoroughly.
2. Add the remaining Ingredients and mix until well combined. Transfer the rice mixture into a 7" nonstick pan.
3. Arrange the pan into an Air Fryer basket. Set the temperature of Air Fryer to 360°F. Air Fry for about 20 minutes.
4. Remove the pan from Air Fryer and transfer the rice mixture onto serving plates. Serve immediately.

Turkey Wings Orange Sauce

(Prep + Cook Time: 45 minutes | Servings: 4)

Ingredients:
- 2 turkey wings
- 1½ cups cranberries
- 1 cup orange juice
- 2 tbsp. butter; melted
- 1 yellow onion; sliced
- 1 bunch thyme; roughly chopped.
- Salt and black pepper to taste

Directions:
1. Place the butter in a pan that fits your air fryer and heat up over medium-high heat.
2. Add the cranberries, salt, pepper, onions and orange juice; whisk and cook for 3 minutes
3. Add the turkey wings, toss and cook for 3-4 minutes more
4. Transfer the pan to your air fryer and cook at 380°F for 25 minutes
5. Add the thyme, toss and divide everything between plates. Serve and enjoy!

Chicken and Yogurt

(Prep + Cook Time: 1 hour 15 minutes | Servings: 4)

Ingredients:
- 17 oz. chicken meat; boneless and cubed
- 14 oz. yogurt
- 3½ oz. cherry tomatoes; halved
- 1 red bell pepper; deseeded and cubed
- 1 yellow bell pepper; deseeded and cubed
- 2 tbsp. coriander powder
- 2 tsp. olive oil
- 1 tsp. turmeric powder
- 3 mint leaves; torn
- 1 green bell pepper; deseeded and cubed
- 1 tbsp. ginger; grated
- 2 tbsp. red chili powder
- 2 tbsp. cumin powder
- Salt and black pepper to taste

Directions:
1. In a bowl, mix all of the ingredients, toss well and place in the fridge for 1 hour
2. Transfer the whole mix to a pan that fits your air fryer and cook at 400°F for 15 minutes, shaking the pan halfway. Divide everything between plates and serve

Chicken and Peppercorns

(Prep + Cook Time: 25 minutes | **Servings:** 4)

Ingredients:
- 8 chicken thighs; boneless
- 1 tsp. black peppercorns
- 4 garlic cloves; minced
- 1/2 cup soy sauce
- 1/2 cup balsamic vinegar
- Salt and black pepper to taste

Directions:
1. In a pan that fits your air fryer; mix the chicken with all the other ingredients and toss
2. Place the pan in the fryer and cook at 380°F for 20 minutes. Divide everything between plates and serve.

Duck and Sauce

(Prep + Cook Time: 30 minutes | **Servings:** 4)

Ingredients:
- 2 duck breasts; skin scored
- 8 oz. white wine
- 1 tbsp. garlic; minced
- 2 tbsp. heavy cream
- 1 tbsp. sugar
- 2 tbsp. cranberries
- 1 tbsp. olive oil
- Salt and black pepper to taste

Directions:
1. Season the duck breasts with salt and pepper and put them in preheated air fryer
2. Cook at 350°F for 10 minutes on each side and divide between plates
3. Heat up a pan with the oil over medium heat and add the cranberries, sugar, wine, garlic and the cream; whisk well. Cook for 3-4 minutes, drizzle over the duck and serve.

Barbeque Chicken Wings

(Prep + Cook Time: 40 minutes | Servings: 4)

Ingredients:
- 1/2 cup BBQ sauce
- 2 lbs. chicken wings; cut into drumettes and flats

Directions:
1. Set the temperature of Air Fryer to 380°F. Grease an Air Fryer basket. Arrange chicken wings into the prepared Air Fryer basket in a single layer.
2. Air Fry for about 24 minutes, flipping once halfway through. Now, set the temperature of Air Fryer to 400°F.
3. Air Fry for about 6 minutes. Remove from Air Fryer and transfer the chicken wings into a bowl. Drizzle with the BBQ sauce and toss to coat well. Serve immediately.

Turkey and Spring Onions

(Prep + Cook Time: 40 minutes | **Servings:** 2)

Ingredients:
- 2 small turkey breasts; boneless and skinless
- 1 bunch spring onions; chopped.
- 2 red chilies; chopped.
- 1 tbsp. Chinese rice wine
- 1 tbsp. oyster sauce
- 1 cup chicken stock
- 1 tbsp. olive oil
- 1 tbsp. soy sauce

Directions:

1. Add the oil to a pan that fits your air fryer and place it over medium heat
2. Then add the chilies, spring onions, oyster sauce, soy sauce, stock and rice wine; whisk and simmer for 3-4 minutes
3. Add the turkey, toss and place the pan in the air fryer and cook at 380°F for 30 minutes. Divide everything between plates and serve.

Chicken and Squash

(Prep + Cook Time: 35 minutes | **Servings:** 4)

Ingredients:

- 14 oz. coconut milk
- 6 cups squash; cubed
- 8 chicken drumsticks
- 1/2 cup cilantro; chopped.
- 2 tbsp. olive oil
- 2 tbsp. green curry paste
- 1/4 tsp. coriander; ground
- 1/2 cup basil; chopped.
- 2 red chilies; minced
- 3 garlic cloves; minced
- A pinch of cumin; ground
- Salt and black pepper to taste

Directions:

1. Heat up a pan that fits your air fryer with the oil over medium heat.
2. Add the garlic, chilies, curry paste, cumin, coriander, salt and pepper; stir and cook for 3-4 minutes.
3. Add the chicken pieces and the coconut milk and stir
4. Place the pan in the fryer and cook at 380°F for 15 minutes
5. Add the squash, cilantro and basil; toss and cook for 5-6 minutes more. Divide into bowls and serve. Enjoy!

Soy Sauce Chicken

(Prep + Cook Time: 50 minutes | **Servings:** 6)

Ingredients:

- 1 whole chicken; cut into pieces
- 1 tsp. sesame oil
- 2 tsp. soy sauce
- 1 chili pepper; minced
- 1 tbsp. ginger; grated
- Salt and black pepper to taste

Directions:

1. In a bowl, mix the chicken with all the other ingredients and rub well
2. Transfer the chicken pieces to your air fryer's basket
3. Cook at 400°F for 30 minutes and then at 380°F for 10 minutes more. Divide everything between plates and serve

Chicken and Veggies

(Prep + Cook Time: 35 minutes | **Servings:** 4)

Ingredients:

- 4 chicken breasts; boneless and skinless
- 3 garlic cloves; minced
- 1 celery stalk; chopped.
- 1 red onion; chopped.
- 2 tbsp. olive oil
- 1 tsp. sage; dried
- 1 carrot; chopped.
- 1 cup chicken stock
- 1/2 tsp. rosemary; dried
- Salt and black pepper to taste

Directions:

1. In a pan that fits your air fryer, place all ingredients and toss well
2. Put the pan in the fryer and cook at 360°F for 25 minutes. Divide everything between plates, serve and enjoy!

Rosemary Chicken Breasts

(Prep + Cook Time: 35 minutes | Servings: 4)

Ingredients:

- 2 chicken breasts; skinless, boneless and halved
- 1 yellow onion; sliced
- 1 cup chicken stock
- 4 garlic cloves; chopped.
- 2 tbsp. cornstarch mixed with 2½ tbsp. water
- 2 tbsp. butter; melted
- 1 tbsp. soy sauce
- 1 tsp. rosemary; dried
- 1 tbsp. fresh rosemary; chopped.
- Salt and black pepper to taste

Directions:

1. Heat up the butter in a pan that fits your air fryer over medium heat.
2. Add the onions, garlic, dried and fresh rosemary, stock, soy sauce, salt and pepper; stir and simmer for 2-3 minutes
3. Add the cornstarch mixture, whisk, cook for 2 minutes more and take off the heat
4. Add the chicken, toss gently and place the pan in the fryer; cook at 370°F for 20 minutes. Divide between plates and serve hot.

Sesame Chicken

(Prep + Cook Time: 30 minutes | Servings: 4)

Ingredients:

- 2 lbs. chicken breasts; skinless, boneless and cubed
- 1/2 cup soy sauce
- 1/2 cup honey
- 1 tbsp. olive oil
- 2 tsp. sesame oil
- 1/4 tsp. red pepper flakes
- 1/2 cup yellow onion; chopped.
- 2 garlic cloves; minced
- 1 tbsp. sesame seeds; toasted
- Salt and black pepper to taste

Directions:

1. Heat up the oil in a pan that fits your air fryer oil over medium heat.
2. Add the chicken, toss and brown for 3 minutes
3. Add the onions, garlic, salt and pepper; stir and cook for 2 minutes more.
4. Add the soy sauce, sesame oil, honey and pepper flakes; toss well
5. Place the pan in the fryer and cook at 380°F for 15 minutes
6. Top with the sesame seeds and toss. Divide between plates and serve.

Turkey with Fig Sauce

(Prep + Cook Time: 40 minutes | Servings: 4)

Ingredients:

- 2 turkey breasts; halved
- 1 shallot; chopped.
- 1 cup chicken stock
- 1/2 cup red wine
- 1 tbsp. olive oil
- 3 tbsp. butter; melted
- 1 tbsp. white flour
- 1/2 tsp. garlic powder
- 1/4 tsp. sweet paprika
- 4 tbsp. figs; chopped.
- Salt and black pepper to taste

Directions:

1. Heat up a pan with the olive oil and 1½ tbsp. of the butter over medium-high heat.
2. Add the shallots, stir and cook for 2 minutes
3. Add the garlic powder, paprika, stock, salt, pepper, wine and the figs; stir and cook for 7-8 minutes.
4. Next add the flour, stir well and cook the sauce for 1-2 minutes more; take off heat
5. Season the turkey with salt and pepper and drizzle the remaining 1½ tbsp. of butter over them

6. Place the turkey in your air fryer's basket and cook at 380°F for 15 minutes, flipping them halfway. Divide between plates, drizzle the sauce all over and serve.

Duck Breast and Potatoes

(Prep + Cook Time: 40 minutes | **Servings:** 2)

Ingredients:
- 1 duck breast; halved and scored
- 1 oz. red wine
- 2 tbsp. butter; melted
- 2 gold potatoes; cubed
- Salt and black pepper to taste

Directions:
1. Season the duck pieces with salt and pepper, put them in a pan and heat up over medium-high heat.
2. Cook for 4 minutes on each side, transfer to your air fryer's basket and cook at 360°F for 8 minutes
3. Put the butter in a pan and heat it up over medium heat; then add the potatoes, salt, pepper and the wine and cook for 8 minutes
4. Add the duck pieces, toss and cook everything for 3-4 minutes more. Divide all between plates and serve.

Cajun Chicken and Okra

(Prep + Cook Time: 40 minutes | **Servings:** 4)

Ingredients:
- 1 lb. chicken thighs; halved
- 1/2 lb. okra
- 1 red bell pepper; chopped.
- 1 yellow onion; chopped.
- 1 cup chicken stock
- 1 tbsp. Cajun spice
- 4 garlic cloves; minced
- 1 tbsp. olive oil
- Salt and black pepper to taste

Directions:
1. Add the oil to a pan that fits your air fryer and heat up over medium heat.
2. Then add the chicken and brown for 2-3 minutes
3. Next, add all remaining ingredients, toss and cook for 3-4 minutes more
4. Place the pan into the air fryer and cook at 380°F for 22 minutes. Divide everything between plates and serve.

Chicken and Beer

(Prep + Cook Time: 40 minutes | **Servings:** 4)

Ingredients:
- 15 oz. beer
- 1 yellow onion; minced
- 1 chili pepper; chopped.
- 2 tbsp. olive oil
- 4 chicken drumsticks
- 1 tbsp. balsamic vinegar
- Salt and black pepper to taste

Directions:
1. Put the oil in a pan that fits your air fryer and heat up over medium heat.
2. Add the onion and the chili pepper, stir and cook for 2 minutes
3. Add the vinegar, beer, salt and pepper; stir and cook for 3 more minutes
4. Add the chicken, toss and put the pan in the fryer and cook at 370°F for 20 minutes. Divide everything between plates and serve.

Turkey Meatballs

(Prep + Cook Time: 25 minutes | **Servings:** 8)

Ingredients:

- 1 lb. turkey meat; ground
- 1/4 cup parsley; chopped.
- 1/4 cup milk
- 1/2 cup panko breadcrumbs
- 1 tsp. fish sauce
- 1 tsp. oregano; dried
- 1 egg; whisked
- 1/4 cup parmesan cheese; grated
- 1 yellow onion; minced
- 4 garlic cloves; minced
- 2 tsp. soy sauce
- Cooking spray
- Salt and black pepper to taste

Directions:

1. In a bowl, mix together all of the ingredients (except the cooking spray), stir well and then shape into medium-sized meatballs
2. Place the meatballs in your air fryer's basket, grease them with cooking spray and cook at 380°F for 15 minutes. Serve the meatballs with a side salad

Chicken and Baby Carrots

(Prep + Cook Time: 35 minutes | **Servings:** 4)

Ingredients:

- 6 chicken thighs
- 1/2 lb. baby carrots; halved
- 15 oz. canned tomatoes; chopped.
- 1 cup chicken stock
- 1 yellow onion; chopped.
- 1 tsp. olive oil
- 1/2 tsp. thyme; dried
- 1/2 cup white wine
- 2 tbsp. tomato paste
- Salt and black pepper to taste

Directions:

1. Put the oil into a pan that fits your air fryer and heat up over medium heat.
2. Add the chicken thighs and brown them for 1-2 minutes on each side
3. Add all the remaining ingredients, toss and cook for 4-5 minutes more
4. Place the pan in the air fryer and cook at 380°F for 22 minutes. Divide the chicken and carrots mix between plates and serve.

Balsamic Chicken

(Prep + Cook Time: 30 minutes | **Servings:** 4)

Ingredients:

- 4 chicken breasts; skinless and boneless
- 1 yellow onion; minced
- 1/4 cup cheddar cheese; grated
- 1/4 tsp. garlic powder
- 1/4 cup balsamic vinegar
- 12 oz. canned tomatoes; chopped.
- Salt and black pepper to taste

Directions:

1. In a baking dish that fits your air fryer, mix the chicken with the onions, vinegar, tomatoes, salt, pepper and garlic powder
2. Sprinkle the cheese on top and place the pan in the air fryer; cook at 400°F for 20 minutes. Divide between plates and serve.

Chicken Curry

(Prep + Cook Time: 40 minutes | **Servings:** 4)

Ingredients:

- 15 oz. chicken breast; skinless, boneless, cubed
- 6 potatoes; peeled and cubed
- 5 oz. heavy cream
- 1/2 bunch coriander; chopped
- 1 yellow onion; sliced
- 1 tbsp. olive oil
- 1 tsp. curry powder
- Salt and black pepper to taste

Directions:

1. Heat up the oil in a pan that fits your air fryer over medium heat.
2. Add the chicken, toss and brown for 2 minutes
3. Then add the onions, curry powder, salt and pepper; toss and cook for 3 minutes.
4. Next add the potatoes and the cream; toss well
5. Place the pan in the air fryer and cook at 370°F for 20 minutes
6. Add the coriander and stir. Divide the curry into bowls and serve.

Asian Atyle Chicken

(Prep + Cook Time: 40 minutes | **Servings:** 4)

Ingredients:

- 1 lb. spinach; chopped.
- 1½ lbs. chicken drumsticks
- 15 oz. canned tomatoes; crushed
- 1/4 cup lemon juice
- 1/2 cup chicken stock
- 1/2 cup heavy cream
- 1/2 cup cilantro; chopped.
- 4 garlic cloves; minced
- 1 yellow onion; chopped.
- 2 tbsp. butter; melted
- 1 tbsp. ginger; grated
- 1½ tsp. coriander; ground
- 1½ tsp. paprika
- 1 tsp. turmeric powder
- Salt and black pepper to taste

Directions:

1. Place the butter in a pan that fits your air fryer and heat over medium heat.
2. Add the onions and the garlic, stir and cook for 3 minutes
3. Add the ginger, paprika, coriander, turmeric, salt, pepper and the chicken; toss and cook for 4 minutes more.
4. Add the tomatoes and the stock and stir
5. Place the pan in the fryer and cook at 370°F for 15 minutes
6. Add the spinach, lemon juice, cilantro and the cream; stir and cook for 5-6 minutes more. Divide everything into bowls and serve.

Lemongrass Chicken

(Prep + Cook Time: 40 minutes | **Servings:** 4)

Ingredients:
- 10 chicken drumsticks
- 1 cup coconut milk
- 1 bunch lemongrass; trimmed
- 1/4 cup parsley; chopped.
- 1 yellow onion; chopped.
- 2 tbsp. fish sauce
- 3 tbsp. soy sauce
- 1 tsp. butter; melted
- 1 tbsp. ginger; chopped.
- 4 garlic cloves; minced
- 1 tbsp. lemon juice
- Salt and black pepper to taste

Directions:
1. In a blender, combine the lemongrass, ginger, garlic, soy sauce, fish sauce and coconut milk; pulse well.
2. Put the butter in a pan that fits your air fryer and heat it up over medium heat; add the onions, stir and cook for 2-3 minutes
3. Add the chicken, salt, pepper and the lemongrass mix; toss well
4. Place the pan in the fryer and cook at 380°F for 25 minutes
5. Add the lemon juice and the parsley and toss. Divide everything between plates and serve.

Chicken and Chickpeas

(Prep + Cook Time: 35 minutes | **Servings:** 4)

Ingredients:
- 2 lbs. chicken thighs; boneless
- 8 oz. canned chickpeas; drained
- 5 oz. bacon; cooked and crumbled
- 1 cup chicken stock
- 1 tsp. balsamic vinegar
- 2 tbsp. olive oil
- 1 cup yellow onion; chopped.
- 2 carrots; chopped.
- 1 tbsp. parsley; chopped.
- Salt and black pepper to taste

Directions:
1. Heat up a pan that fits your air fryer with the oil over medium heat.
2. Add the onions, carrots, salt and pepper; stir and sauté for 3-4 minutes.
3. Add the chicken, stock, vinegar and chickpeas; then toss
4. Place the pan in the fryer and cook at 380°F for 20 minutes
5. Add the bacon and the parsley and toss again. Divide everything between plates and serve.

Beef, Pork & Lamb

Buttered Filet Mignon

(Prep + Cook Time: 24 minutes | Servings: 4)

Ingredients:

- 2 (6-oz.) filet mignon steaks
- Salt and ground black pepper; as your liking
- 1 tbsp. butter; softened

Directions:

1. Coat each steak evenly with butter and then, season with salt and black pepper. Set the temperature of air fryer to 390°F. Grease an air fryer basket.
2. Arrange steaks into the prepared air fryer basket.
3. Air fry for about 14 minutes, flipping once halfway through. Remove from the air fryer and transfer onto serving plates. Serve hot.

Beef and Mushroom Meatloaf

(Prep + Cook Time: 40 minutes | Servings: 4)

Ingredients:

- 1 lb. lean ground beef
- 2 mushrooms; thickly sliced
- 1 small onion; finely chopped
- 1 egg, lightly beaten
- 1 tbsp. olive oil
- 1 tbsp. fresh thyme; finely chopped
- 3 tbsp. dry breadcrumbs
- Salt and ground black pepper, as required

Directions:

1. In a bowl, add the beef, onion, thyme, breadcrumbs, egg, salt and black pepper. With your hands, mix until well combined.
2. Put the beef mixture into a lightly greased baking pan and with the back of spoon, smooth the top surface.
3. Arrange the mushroom slices on top and gently, press each inside the meatloaf. Coat the meatloaf with oil.
4. Set the temperature of Air Fryer to 392°F. Arrange the pan of meatloaf into the Air Fryer basket.
5. Air Fry for about 25 minutes or until meatloaf becomes golden brown.
6. Remove from Air Fryer and place the pan onto a wire rack for about 10 minutes before serving. Cut into desired size wedges and serve.

Pork Meatloaf

(**Prep + Cook Time:** 25 minutes | **Servings:** 4)

Ingredients:

- 1 lb. ground pork meat
- 3 tbsp. breadcrumbs
- 1 tbsp. thyme; chopped.
- 1 oz. chorizo; chopped.
- 1 egg; whisked
- 1 yellow onion; chopped.
- Cooking spray
- Salt and black pepper to taste

Directions:

1. Place all of the ingredients (except the cooking spray) in a bowl and stir / combine well.
2. Transfer the mixture to a loaf pan, greased with cooking spray, that fits your air fryer
3. Place the pan in the fryer and cook at 390°F for 20 minutes. Slice and serve

Herbed Beef Roast

(Prep + Cook Time: 55 minutes | Servings: 5)

Ingredients:
- 2 lbs. beef roast
- 1 tsp. dried rosemary; crushed
- 1 tbsp. olive oil
- 1 tsp. dried thyme; crushed
- Salt; as your liking

Directions:
1. In a bowl, mix together the oil, herbs and salt. Generously coat the roast with herb mixture. Set the temperature of air fryer to 360°F. Grease an air fryer basket.
2. Arrange roast into the prepared air fryer basket. Air fry for about 45 minutes.
3. Remove from air fryer and transfer the roast onto a platter.
4. With a piece of foil, cover the roast for about 10 minutes before slicing.
5. Cut the roast into desired size slices and serve.

Buttered Rib Eye Steak

(Prep + Cook Time: 34 minutes | Servings: 2)

Ingredients:
- 2 (8-oz.) rib eye steak
- 1/2 cup unsalted butter; softened
- 2 tbsp. fresh parsley; chopped
- 1 tbsp. olive oil
- 2 tsp. garlic; minced
- 1 tsp. Worcestershire sauce
- Ground black pepper; as your liking
- Salt; as your liking

Directions:
1. In a bowl, add the butter, parsley, garlic, Worcestershire sauce and salt. Mix until well combined. Place the butter mixture onto a parchment paper and roll into a log. Refrigerate until using.
2. Coat the steak evenly with oil and then, sprinkle with salt and black pepper.
3. Set the temperature of air fryer to 400°F. Grease an air fryer basket. Arrange steaks into the prepared air fryer basket. Air fry for about 14 minutes, flipping once halfway through.
4. Remove from air fryer and place the steaks onto a platter for about 5 minutes.
5. Cut each steak into desired size slices and divide onto serving plates.
6. Now; cut the butter log into slices. Top each steak with butter slices and serve.

Pork and Cauliflower

(**Prep + Cook Time:** 28 minutes | **Servings:** 4)

Ingredients:
- 1 lb. pork stew meat; cubed
- 1 garlic clove; minced
- 2 tbsp. olive oil
- 1 cauliflower head; florets separated
- 1/3 cup balsamic vinegar
- 1 tsp. soy sauce
- 1 tsp. sugar

Directions:
1. Place all the ingredients in a pan that fits your air fryer and mix well.
2. Put the pan into the fryer and cook at 390°F for 22 minutes. Divide into bowls, serve and enjoy

Pork Rolls

(Prep + Cook Time: 35 minutes | Servings: 4)

Ingredients:
- 4 (6-oz.) pork cutlets, pounded slightly
- 1 scallion; chopped
- 1/4 cup sun dried tomatoes; finely chopped
- 1/2 tbsp. olive oil
- 2 tbsp. fresh parsley; chopped
- 2 tsp. paprika
- Salt and ground black pepper; as your liking

Directions:

1. In a bowl, mix well scallion, tomatoes, parsley, salt and black pepper. Spread the tomato mixture over each pork cutlet.
2. Roll each cutlet and secure with cocktail sticks. Rub the outer part of rolls with paprika, salt and black pepper.
3. Coat the rolls evenly with oil. Set the temperature of air fryer to 390°F. Grease an air fryer basket. Arrange pork rolls into the prepared air fryer basket in a single layer. Air fry for about 15 minutes.
4. Remove from air fryer and transfer the pork rolls onto serving plates. Serve hot.

Beef and Veggie Kebabs

(Prep + Cook Time: 32 minutes | Servings: 4)

Ingredients:

- 1 lb. sirloin steak; cut into-inch chunks
- 8 oz. baby Bella mushrooms; stems removed
- 1 large bell pepper, seeded and cut into 1-inch pieces
- 1 red onion; cut into 1-inch pieces
- 1/4 cup olive oil
- 1/4 cup soy sauce
- 1 tbsp. garlic; minced
- 1/2 tsp. ground cumin
- 1 tsp. brown sugar
- Salt and ground black pepper; as your liking

Directions:

1. In a bowl, mix together the soy sauce, oil, garlic, brown sugar, cumin, salt and black pepper.
2. Add the steak cubes and generously coat with marinade. Refrigerate to marinate for about 30 minutes.
3. Thread the steak cubes, mushrooms, bell pepper and onion onto metal skewers.
4. Set the temperature of Air Fryer to 390°F. Grease an Air Fryer basket. Arrange skewers into the prepared Air Fryer basket. Air Fry for about 10 to 12 minutes, flipping once halfway through.
5. Remove from Air Fryer and transfer the kebabs onto a platter. Serve hot.

Beef Cheeseburgers

(Prep + Cook Time: 27 minutes | Servings: 2)

Ingredients:

- 1/2 lb. ground beef
- 2 slices cheddar cheese
- 1 garlic clove; minced
- 2 salad leaves
- 2 dinner rolls; cut into half
- 2 tbsp. fresh cilantro; minced
- Salt and ground black pepper; as your liking

Directions:

1. In a bowl, mix together the beef, garlic, cilantro, salt and black pepper. Make 2 (4-inches) patties from the mixture. Set the temperature of air fryer to 390°F. Grease an air fryer pan.
2. Arrange patties into the prepared pan in a single layer. Air fry for about 10 to 11 minutes. Place 1 cheese slice over each patty and air fry for about 1 more minute. Remove patties from the air fryer. Arrange salad leaf between each dinner roll and top with 1 patty. Serve immediately.

Pork Chops and Mushrooms Mix

(Prep + Cook Time: 50 Minutes | **Servings:** 3)

Ingredients:

- 3 pork chops; boneless
- 8-ounce mushrooms; sliced
- 1 tsp. nutmeg
- 1 tbsp. balsamic vinegar
- 1 cup mayonnaise
- 1 tsp. garlic powder
- 1 yellow onion; chopped.
- 1/2 cup olive oil

Directions:

1. Heat up a pan that fits your air fryer with the oil over medium heat, add mushrooms and onions; stir and cook for 4 minutes
2. Add pork chops, nutmeg and garlic powder and brown on both sides.
3. Introduce pan your air fryer at 330°F and cook for 30 minutes. Add vinegar and mayo; stir, divide everything on plates and serve

Spiced and Herbed Skirt Steak

(Prep + Cook Time: 25 minutes | Servings: 4)

Ingredients:

- 3 garlic cloves; minced
- 2 (8-oz.) skirt steaks
- 3/4 cup olive oil
- 1 cup fresh parsley leaves; finely chopped
- 1 tbsp. ground cumin
- 3 tbsp. red wine vinegar
- 3 tbsp. fresh oregano; finely chopped
- 3 tbsp. fresh mint leaves; finely chopped
- 1 tsp. cayenne pepper
- 1 tsp. red pepper flakes; crushed
- 2 tsp. smoked paprika
- Salt and ground black pepper; as your liking

Directions:

1. In a bowl, mix together the garlic, herbs, spices, oil and vinegar. In a resealable bag, place ¼ cup of the herb mixture and steaks.
2. Seal the bag and shake to coat well. Refrigerate for about 24 hours. Reserve the remaining herb mixture in refrigerator.
3. Take out the steaks from fridge and place at room temperature for about 30 minutes. Set the temperature of air fryer to 390°F. Grease an air fryer basket.
4. Arrange steaks into the prepared air fryer basket. Air fry for about 8 to 10 minutes.
5. Remove from air fryer and place the steaks onto a cutting board for about 10 minutes before slicing. Cut each steak into desired size slices and transfer onto serving platter. Top with reserved herb mixture and serve.

Pork Chops with Peanut Sauce

(Prep + Cook Time: 32 minutes | Servings: 4)

Ingredients:

For Chops:

- 1-lb. boneless pork chop, cubed into 1-inch size
- 1 garlic clove, minced
- 2 tbsp. soy sauce
- 1 tbsp. olive oil
- 1 tsp. fresh ginger, minced
- 1 tsp. hot pepper sauce

For Peanut Sauce:

- 1 shallot; finely chopped
- 1 garlic clove; minced
- 3/4 cup coconut milk
- 3/4 cup ground peanuts
- 1 tbsp. olive oil
- 1 tsp. ground coriander
- 1 tsp. hot pepper sauce

Directions:

1. **For the pork:** in a bowl, mix together the ginger, garlic, soy sauce, oil and hot pepper sauce.
2. Add the pork chops and generously coat with mixture. Place at the room temperature for about 15 minutes.
3. Set the temperature of air fryer to 390°F. Grease an air fryer basket.
4. Arrange chops into the prepared air fryer basket in a single layer. Air fry for about 12 minutes.
5. Meanwhile, for the sauce: in a pan, heat oil over medium heat and sauté the shallot and garlic for about 2 to 3 minutes.

6. Add the coriander and sauté for about 1 minute. Stir in the remaining Ingredients and cook for about 5 minutes, stirring continuously.
7. Remove the pan of sauce from heat and let it cool slightly.
8. Remove the chops from air fryer and transfer onto serving plates. Serve immediately with the topping of peanut sauce.

Pork Spare Ribs

(Prep + Cook Time: 35 minutes | Servings: 6)

Ingredients:
- 12 (1-inch) pork spare ribs
- 1/2 cup cornstarch
- 5 to 6 garlic cloves; minced
- 1/2 cup rice vinegar
- 2 tbsp. soy sauce
- 2 tbsp. olive oil
- Salt and ground black pepper; as your liking

Directions:
1. In a large bowl, mix together the garlic, vinegar, soy sauce, salt and black pepper.
2. Add the ribs and generously coat with mixture. Refrigerate to marinate overnight.
3. In a shallow bowl, place the cornstarch. Coat the ribs evenly with cornstarch and then, drizzle with oil.
4. Set the temperature of air fryer to 390°F. Grease an air fryer basket.
5. Arrange ribs into the prepared air fryer basket in a single layer. Air fry for about 10 minutes per side.
6. Remove from air fryer and transfer the ribs onto serving plates. Serve immediately.

Beef Stuffed Bell Peppers

(Prep + Cook Time: 46 minutes | Servings: 4)

Ingredients:
- 1 lb. lean ground beef
- 8 oz. tomato sauce; divided
- 1/2 medium onion; chopped
- 2 garlic cloves; minced
- 1/2 cup cooked jasmine rice
- 2/3 cup light Mexican cheese; shredded and divided
- 2 tsp. Worcestershire sauce
- 4 bell peppers, tops removed and seeded
- 1 tsp. olive oil
- 1 tsp. dried basil; crushed
- 1 tsp. garlic salt
- 1/2 tsp. red chili powder
- Ground black pepper; as your liking

Directions:
1. In a medium-sized skillet, heat oil over medium heat and sauté the onion and garlic for about 3 to 5 minutes or until cooked thoroughly. Add the ground beef, basil and spices. Cook for about 8 to 10 minutes.
2. Remove the skillet from heat and drain off the excess grease from skillet. Add the rice, half of the cheese, 2/3 of the tomato sauce and Worcestershire sauce and mix until well combined.
3. Stuff each bell pepper evenly with beef mixture. Set the temperature of air fryer to 400°F. Grease an air fryer basket.
4. Arrange bell peppers into the prepared air fryer basket. Air fry for about 7 minutes.
5. Remove from air fryer and top each bell pepper with the remaining tomato sauce and cheese.
6. Air fry for about 4 more minutes. Remove from air fryer and transfer the bell peppers onto a platter. Serve warm.

Bacon Wrapped Filet Mignon

(Prep + Cook Time: 30 minutes | Servings: 2)

Ingredients:

- 2 (6-oz.) filet mignon steaks
- 2 bacon slices
- 1 tsp. avocado oil
- Salt and ground black pepper; as your liking

Directions:

1. Wrap one bacon slice around each mignon steak and secure with a toothpick.
2. Season the steak evenly with salt and black pepper. After that, coat each steak with avocado oil.
3. Set the temperature of air fryer to 375°F. Grease an air fryer basket. Arrange steaks into the prepared air fryer basket. Air fry for about 15 minutes, flipping once halfway through.
4. Remove from air fryer and transfer the steaks onto serving plates. Serve hot.

Beef Tips with Onion

(Prep + Cook Time: 25 minutes | Servings: 2)

Ingredients:

- 1 lb. top round beef; cut into 1½-inch cubes
- 1/2 yellow onion; chopped
- 1 tbsp. avocado oil
- 2 tbsp. Worcestershire sauce
- 1 tsp. garlic powder
- 1 tsp. onion powder
- Salt and ground black pepper; as your liking

Directions:

1. In a bowl, mix together the beef tips, onion, Worcestershire sauce, oil and spices. Set the temperature of Air Fryer to 360°F. Grease an Air Fryer basket.
2. Arrange beef mixture into the prepared Air Fryer basket. Air Fry for about 8 to 10 minutes. Remove from Air Fryer and transfer the steak mixture onto serving plates. Serve hot.

Beef Taco Wraps

(Prep + Cook Time: 19 minutes | Servings: 6)

Ingredients:

- 2 lbs. cooked ground beef
- 12 oz. nacho cheese
- 2 cups Mexican blend cheese; shredded
- 2 cups sour cream
- 2 cups Bibb lettuce, shredded
- 6 (12-inch) flour tortillas
- 6 tostadas
- 3 Roma tomatoes, sliced
- Olive oil cooking spray

Directions:

1. Arrange the tortillas onto a smooth surface. Divide each ingredient into 6 portions.
2. Place 1 portion of beef in the center of each tortilla, followed by the nacho cheese, tostada, sour cream, lettuce, tomato slices and Mexican cheese.
3. Bring the edges of each tortilla up, over the center to look like a pinwheel. Set the temperature of Air Fryer to 400°F. Grease an Air Fryer basket.
4. Arrange taco wraps into the prepared Air Fryer basket, seam side down and spray each with cooking spray. Air Fry for about 2 minutes.
5. Carefully flip the wraps and spray each with cooking spray again. Air Fry for about 2 more minutes.
6. Remove from Air Fryer and transfer the wraps onto a platter. Serve warm.

Herbs Crumbed Rack of Lamb

(Prep + Cook Time: 50 minutes | Servings: 5)

Ingredients:

- 1¾ lbs. rack of lamb
- 1 garlic clove; finely chopped
- 1 egg
- 1/2 cup panko breadcrumbs
- 1 tbsp. butter, melted
- 1 tbsp. fresh thyme; minced
- 1 tbsp. fresh rosemary; minced
- Salt and ground black pepper; as your liking

Directions:

1. In a bowl, mix together the butter, garlic, salt and black pepper. Coat the rack of lamb evenly with garlic mixture.
2. In a shallow dish, beat the egg. In another dish, mix together the breadcrumbs and herbs.
3. Dip the rack of lamb in beaten egg and then, coat with breadcrumbs mixture.
4. Set the temperature of air fryer to 212°F. Grease an air fryer basket. Place rack of lamb into the prepared air fryer basket. Air Fry for about 25 minutes and then 5 more minutes at 390°F.
5. Remove from air fryer and place the rack of lamb onto a cutting board for about 5 minutes
6. With a sharp knife; cut the rack of lamb into individual chops and serve.

Buttered Striploin Steak

(Prep + Cook Time: 22 minutes | Servings: 2)

Ingredients:

- 2 (7-oz.) striploin steak
- 1½ tbsp. butter; softened
- Salt and ground black pepper; as your liking

Directions:

1. Coat each steak evenly with butter and then, season with salt and black pepper.
2. Set the temperature of air fryer to 392°F. Grease an air fryer basket.
3. Arrange steaks into the prepared air fryer basket. Air fry for about 8 to 12 minutes.
4. Remove from air fryer and transfer the steaks onto serving plates. Serve hot.

Skirt Steak with Veggies

(Prep + Cook Time: 21 minutes | Servings: 4)

Ingredients:

- 1/2 lb. fresh mushrooms, quartered
- 1 (12-oz.) skirt steak; cut into thin strips
- 6 oz. snow peas
- 1 onion; cut into half rings
- ¼ cup olive oil, divided
- 2 tbsp. honey
- 2 tbsp. soy sauce
- Salt and ground black pepper; as your liking

Directions:

1. In a bowl, mix together 2 tbsp. of oil, soy sauce and honey. Add the steak strips and generously coat with the oil mixture.
2. In another bowl, add the vegetables, remaining oil, salt and black pepper. Toss to coat well.
3. Set the temperature of air fryer to 390°F. Grease an air fryer basket. Arrange steak strips and vegetables into the prepared air fryer basket.
4. Air fry for about 5 to 6 minutes or until desired doneness.
5. Remove from air fryer and place the steak onto a cutting board for about 10 minutes before slicing.
6. Cut each steak into desired size slices and transfer onto serving plates. Serve immediately alongside the veggies.

Simple New York Strip Steak

(Prep + Cook Time: 18 minutes | Servings: 2)

Ingredients:

- 1 (9½-oz.) New York strip steak
- 1 tsp. olive oil
- Kosher salt and ground black pepper; as your liking

Directions:

1. Set the temperature of air fryer to 400°F. Grease an air fryer basket.
2. Coat the steak with oil and then, generously season with salt and black pepper.
3. Place steak into the prepared air fryer basket. Air fry for about 7 to 8 minutes or until desired doneness.
4. Remove from air fryer and place the steak onto a cutting board for about 10 minutes before slicing.
5. Cut the steak into desired size slices and transfer onto serving plates. Serve immediately.

Pork Chops

(**Prep + Cook Time:** 20 minutes | **Servings:** 4)

Ingredients:

- 4 medium pork chops
- 1 tbsp. olive oil
- 2 tbsp. sweet paprika
- 2 tbsp. onion powder
- 2 tbsp. garlic powder
- 1 tbsp. cumin; ground
- 1 tbsp. rosemary; dried
- 2 tbsp. oregano; dried
- Salt and black pepper to taste

Directions:

1. In a bowl, mix all of the ingredients and rub the pork chops well.
2. Put the pork chops in your air fryer's basket and cook at 400°F for 15 minutes, flipping them halfway. Divide between plates, serve and enjoy

Herbed Pork Chops

(Prep + Cook Time: 27 minutes | Servings: 4)

Ingredients:

- 2 (6-oz.) (1-inch thick) pork chops
- 2 garlic cloves; minced
- 1/2 tbsp. fresh cilantro; chopped
- 1/2 tbsp. fresh rosemary; chopped
- 1/2 tbsp. fresh parsley; chopped
- 2 tbsp. olive oil
- 3/4 tbsp. Dijon mustard
- 1 tbsp. ground coriander
- 1 tsp. sugar
- Salt, to taste

Directions:

1. In a bowl, mix together the garlic, herbs, oil, mustard, coriander, sugar and salt.
2. Add the pork chops and generously coat with marinade. Cover and refrigerate for about 2 to 3 hours.
3. Remove chops from the refrigerator and set aside at room temperature for about 30 minutes.
4. Set the temperature of air fryer to 390°F. Grease an air fryer basket. Arrange chops into the prepared air fryer basket in a single layer.
5. Air fry for about 10 to 12 minutes. Remove from air fryer and transfer the chops onto plates. Serve hot.

Crispy Sirloin Steak

(Prep + Cook Time: 25 minutes | Servings: 2)

Ingredients:
- 2 (6-oz.) sirloin steaks, pounded
- 1 cup white flour
- 2 eggs
- 1 cup panko breadcrumbs
- 1 tsp. onion powder
- 1 tsp. garlic powder
- Salt and ground black pepper; as your liking

Directions:
1. In a shallow bowl, place the flour. Crack the eggs in a second bowl and beat well. In a third bowl, mix together the panko and spices.
2. Coat each steak with the white flour, then dip into beaten eggs and finally, coat with panko mixture.
3. Set the temperature of air fryer to 360°F. Grease an air fryer basket. Arrange steaks into the prepared air fryer basket. Air fry for about 10 minutes.
4. Remove from air fryer and transfer the steaks onto the serving plates. Serve immediately.

Beef Jerky

(Prep + Cook Time: 1 hour 20 minutes | Servings: 3)

Ingredients:
- 1 lb. bottom round beef; cut into thin strips
- 1/4 cup Worcestershire sauce
- 1/2 cup dark brown sugar
- 1/2 cup soy sauce
- 1 tbsp. hickory liquid smoke
- 1 tbsp. chili pepper sauce
- 1 tsp. cayenne pepper
- 1/2 tsp. smoked paprika
- 1/2 tsp. ground black pepper
- 1 tsp. garlic powder
- 1 tsp. onion powder

Directions:
1. In a large bowl, mix together the brown sugar, all sauces, liquid smoke and spices. Add the beef strips and generously coat with marinade. Cover the bowl and marinate overnight.
2. Set the temperature of Air Fryer to 180°F. Lightly, grease an Air Fryer basket. Remove the beef strips from fridge and with paper towels, pat them dry.
3. Arrange half of the beef strips in the bottom of prepared Air Fryer basket in a single layer. Now, arrange a cooking rack over the strips.
4. Place the remaining beef strips on top of the rack in a single layer.
5. Air Fry for about 1 hour. Remove from Air Fryer and arrange the strips onto a paper towel-lined baking sheet to cool completely before serving.

Beef Short Ribs

(Prep + Cook Time: 31 minutes | Servings: 8)

Ingredients:
- 4 lbs. bone in beef short ribs
- 1 cup low-sodium soy sauce
- 1/2 cup rice vinegar
- 1/3 cup scallions; chopped
- 1 tbsp. Sriracha
- 2 tbsp. brown sugar
- 1 tbsp. fresh ginger; finely grated
- 1 tsp. ground black pepper

Directions:
1. In a resealable bag, put the ribs and all the above ingredients. Seal the bag and shake to coat well.
2. Refrigerate overnight. Set the temperature of air fryer to 380°F. Grease an air fryer basket.
3. Take out the short ribs from resealable bag and arrange into the prepared air fryer basket in 2 batches in a single layer.
4. Air Fry for about 8 minutes, flipping once halfway through.
5. Remove from air fryer and transfer onto a serving platter. Serve hot.

Steak with Bell Peppers

(Prep + Cook Time: 42 minutes | Servings: 4)

Ingredients:
- 1¼ lbs. beef steak; cut into thin strips
- 2 green bell peppers, seeded and cubed
- 1 red bell pepper, seeded and cubed
- 1 red onion, sliced
- 2 tbsp. olive oil
- 1 tsp. red chili powder
- 1 tsp. paprika
- 1 tsp. dried oregano; crushed
- 1 tsp. onion powder
- 1 tsp. garlic powder
- Salt, to taste

Directions:
1. In a large bowl, mix together the oregano and spices. Add the beef strips, bell peppers, onion and oil. Mix until well combined.
2. Set the temperature of air fryer to 390°F. Grease an air fryer basket. Arrange steak strips mixture into the prepared Air Fryer basket in 2 batches. Air Fry for about 10 to 11 minutes or until done completely.
3. Remove from air fryer and transfer the steak mixture onto serving plates. Serve immediately.

Glazed Ham

(Prep + Cook Time: 55 minutes | Servings: 4)

Ingredients:
- 1 lb. 10½ oz. ham
- 2 tbsp. French mustard
- 1 cup whiskey
- 2 tbsp. honey

Directions:
1. Place the ham at room temperature for about 30 minutes before cooking.
2. In a bowl, mix together the whiskey, mustard and honey. Place the ham in a baking dish that fits in the air fryer.
3. Top with half of the honey mixture and coat well. Set the temperature of air fryer to 320°F. Place the baking dish into the air fryer. Air fry for about 15 minutes.
4. Flip the side of ham and top with the remaining honey mixture. Air fry for about 25 more minutes.
5. Remove from air fryer and place the ham onto a platter for about 10 minutes before slicing. Cut the ham into desired size slices and serve.

Beef Roast

(Prep + Cook Time: 60 minutes | Servings: 6)

Ingredients:
- 2½ lbs. beef eye of round roast, trimmed
- 2 tbsp. olive oil
- 1/2 tsp. cayenne pepper
- 1/2 tsp. ground black pepper
- 1/2 tsp. onion powder
- 1/2 tsp. garlic powder
- Salt, to taste

Directions:
1. In a bowl, mix together the oil and spices. Generously coat the roast with spice mixture. Set the temperature of air fryer to 360°F. Grease an air fryer basket.
2. Arrange roast into the prepared air fryer basket. Air fry for about 50 minutes.
3. Remove from air fryer and transfer the roast onto a platter.
4. With a piece of foil, cover the roast for about 10 minutes before slicing. Cut the roast into desired size slices and serve.

Pork and Bell Pepper

(Prep + Cook Time: 25 minutes | **Servings:** 4)

Ingredients:
- 1 lb. pork; cut into strips
- 1/2 cup beef stock
- 4 shallots; chopped.
- 2 tbsp. olive oil
- 2 red bell peppers; cut in strips
- 4 garlic cloves; minced
- A pinch of salt and black pepper
- 2 tbsp. fish sauce

Directions:
1. In a pan that fits your air fryer, place all the ingredients and toss
2. Place the pan in the fryer and cook at 400°F for 20 minutes, shaking the fryer halfway. Divide everything between plates and serve

Cheesy Beef Meatballs

(Prep + Cook Time: 54 minutes | Servings: 8)

Ingredients:
- 2 lbs. ground beef
- 1/4 cup fresh parsley; chopped
- 2 large eggs
- 1 small garlic clove; chopped
- 1¼ cups breadcrumbs
- 1/4 cup Parmigiana-Reggiano cheese; grated
- 1 tsp. dried oregano; crushed
- Salt and ground black pepper; as your liking

Directions:
1. Add all the Ingredients in a bowl and with your hands, mix until well combined. Gently shape the mixture into 2-inches balls.
2. Set the temperature of Air Fryer to 350°F. Line an Air Fryer basket with greased paper towels. Arrange meatballs into the prepared Air Fryer basket in a single layer in 2 batches.
3. Air Fry for about 10 to 12 minutes. Flip the side and Air Fry for extra 4 to 5 minutes.
4. Remove from Air Fryer and transfer the meatballs onto a serving platter. Serve warm.

Pork Neck Salad

(Prep + Cook Time: 32 minutes | Servings: 2)

Ingredients:
For Pork:
- 1/2 lb. pork neck
- 1/2 tbsp. oyster sauce
- 1 tbsp. soy sauce
- 1 tbsp. fish sauce

For Salad:
- 1 red onion, sliced
- 1 ripe tomato; thickly sliced
- 1 bunch fresh basil leaves
- 1 bunch fresh cilantro leaves
- 1 scallion; chopped

For Dressing:
- 1 bird eye chili
- 1 tbsp. garlic; minced
- 1 tbsp. palm sugar
- 3 tbsp. fish sauce
- 2 tbsp. olive oil
- 1 tsp. apple cider vinegar

Directions:
1. **For the pork:** in a bowl, mix together all the sauces.
2. Add the pork neck and generously coat with marinade. Refrigerate for about 2 to 3 hours.
3. Set the temperature of air fryer to 340°F. Grease an air fryer basket. Place pork neck into the prepared basket.
4. Air fry for about 12 minutes. Meanwhile, for the salad: in a serving bowl, mix together all the ingredients.
5. **For the dressing:** in another bowl, add all the Ingredients and beat until well combined.

6. Remove pork neck from air fryer and cut into desired size slices.
7. Place the pork slices over salad. Add the dressing and toss to coat well. Serve.

Lamb Loin Chops with Lemon

(Prep + Cook Time: 45 minutes | Servings: 4)

Ingredients:
- 8 (4-oz.) lamb loin chops
- 1 tbsp. fresh lemon juice
- 2 tbsp. Dijon mustard
- 1 tsp. dried tarragon
- 1/2 tsp. olive oil
- Salt and ground black pepper; as your liking

Directions:
1. In a large bowl, mix together the mustard, lemon juice, oil, tarragon, salt and black pepper. Add chops and generously coat with the mixture.
2. Set the temperature of air fryer to 390°F. Grease an air fryer basket. Arrange chops into the prepared air fryer basket in a single layer in 2 batches.
3. Air fry for about 15 minutes, flipping once halfway through. Remove the chops from air fryer and transfer onto serving plates.

Sweet and Sour Pork Chops

(Prep + Cook Time: 31 minutes | Servings: 6)

Ingredients:
- 6 pork loin chops
- 2 garlic cloves; minced
- 2 tbsp. soy sauce
- 1 tbsp. balsamic vinegar
- 2 tbsp. honey
- 1/4 tsp. ground ginger
- Salt and ground black pepper; as your liking

Directions:
1. With a meat tenderizer, tenderize the chops completely and then, sprinkle each with salt and black pepper.
2. In a large bowl, mix the remaining ingredients. Add the chops and generously coat with marinade.
3. Cover and refrigerate for about 2 to 8 hours. Set the temperature of air fryer to 355°F. Grease an air fryer basket.
4. Arrange chops into the prepared air fryer basket in a single layer.
5. Air fry for about 6 to 8 minutes per side. Remove from air fryer and transfer the chops onto plates. Serve hot.

Bacon Wrapped Pork tenderloin

(Prep + Cook Time: 45 minutes | Servings: 4)

Ingredients:
- 4 bacon strips
- 1 (1½ pound) pork tenderloins
- 2 tbsp. Dijon mustard

Directions:
1. Coat the tenderloin evenly with mustard. Wrap the tenderloin with bacon strips.
2. Set the temperature of air fryer to 360°F. Grease an air fryer basket.
3. Arrange pork tenderloin into the prepared air fryer basket. Air fry for about 15 minutes. Flip and air fry for another 10 to 15 minutes.
4. Remove from air fryer and transfer the pork tenderloin onto a platter, wait for about 5 minutes before slicing.
5. Cut the tenderloin into desired size slices and serve.

Pork Loin with Potatoes

(Prep + Cook Time: 40 minutes | Servings: 2)

Ingredients:

- 2 lbs. pork loin
- 3 large red potatoes; chopped
- 3 tbsp. olive oil; divided
- 1/2 tsp. garlic powder
- 1/2 tsp. red pepper flakes; crushed
- 1 tsp. fresh parsley; chopped
- Salt and ground black pepper, as required

Directions:

1. Coat the pork loin with oil and then, season evenly with parsley, salt and black pepper.
2. In a large bowl, add the potatoes, remaining oil, garlic powder, red pepper flakes, salt and black pepper and toss to coat well.
3. Set the temperature of air fryer to 325°F. Grease an air fryer basket. Place loin into the prepared air fryer basket. Arrange potato pieces around the pork loin.
4. Air fry for about 25 minutes.
5. Remove from air fryer and transfer the pork loin onto a platter, wait for about 5 minutes before slicing.
6. Cut the pork loin into desired size slices and serve alongside the potatoes.

Beef and Chives Marinade

(**Prep + Cook Time:** 60 minutes | **Servings:** 6)

Ingredients:

- 2 lbs. beef roast
- 3 garlic cloves; minced
- 1 cup balsamic vinegar
- 2 tbsp. chives; minced
- 2 tbsp. olive oil
- Salt and black pepper to taste

Directions:

1. In a bowl, mix the oil, vinegar and spices (all ingredients except for the roast); whisk well.
2. Add the roast and coat with the mixture
3. Transfer the roast to your air fryer's basket and cook at 390°F for 55 minutes, flipping the roast halfway. Carve and serve right away

Herbed Lamb Chops

(Prep + Cook Time: 17 minutes | Servings: 2)

Ingredients:

- 4 (4-oz.) lamb chops
- 1 tbsp. olive oil
- 1 tbsp. fresh lemon juice
- 1/2 tsp. ground cumin
- 1/2 tsp. ground coriander
- 1 tsp. dried rosemary
- 1 tsp. dried thyme
- 1 tsp. dried oregano
- Salt and ground black pepper; as your liking

Directions:

1. In a large bowl, mix together the lemon juice, oil, herbs and spices.
2. Add the chops and coat evenly with the herb mixture. Refrigerate to marinate for about 1 hour Set the temperature of air fryer to 390°F. Grease an air fryer basket.
3. Arrange chops into the prepared air fryer basket in a single layer. Air fry for about 7 minutes, flipping once halfway through.
4. Remove from air fryer and transfer the chops onto plates. Serve hot.

French Beef

(**Prep + Cook Time:** 20 minutes | **Servings:** 2)

Ingredients:

- 7 oz. beef fillets; cut into strips
- 1 green bell pepper; cut in strips
- 1/2 tbsp. mustard
- 1 tbsp. olive oil
- 1 red onion; sliced
- 2 tsp. Provencal herbs
- Salt and black pepper to taste

Directions:

1. Place all the ingredients in a baking dish that fits your air fryer and mix well.
2. Put the pan in the fryer and cook at 400°F for 15 minutes. Divide the mixture between bowls and serve

Pork and Peanuts

(**Prep + Cook Time:** 20 minutes | **Servings:** 4)

Ingredients:

- 14 oz. pork chops; cubed
- 3 oz. peanuts; chopped.
- 2 tsp. chili paste
- 1 tsp. coriander; ground
- 2 tbsp. olive oil
- 7 oz. coconut milk
- 2 garlic cloves; minced
- 1 shallot; chopped.
- Salt and black pepper to taste

Directions:

1. Place all of the ingredients into a pan that fits your air fryer; mix well
2. Put the pan in the fryer and cook at 400°F for 15 minutes. Divide into bowls and serve.

Breaded Pork Chops

(Prep + Cook Time: 30 minutes | Servings: 2)

Ingredients:

- 2 (6-oz.) pork chops
- 4 oz. breadcrumbs
- 1/4 cup plain flour
- 1 egg
- 1 tbsp. vegetable oil
- Salt and ground black pepper; as your liking

Directions:

1. Season each pork chop evenly with salt and pepper. In a shallow bowl, place the flour Crack the egg in a second bowl and beat well.
2. Add the breadcrumbs and oil in a third bowl and mix until a crumbly mixture forms.
3. Coat the pork chop with flour, then dip into beaten egg and finally, coat with the breadcrumbs mixture.
4. Set the temperature of air fryer to 400°F. Grease an air fryer basket.
5. Arrange chops into the prepared air fryer basket in a single layer. Air fry for about 15 minutes, flipping once halfway through.
6. Remove from air fryer and transfer the chops onto plates. Serve hot.

Pesto Coated Rack of Lamb

(Prep + Cook Time: 30 minutes | Servings: 4)

Ingredients:

- 1/2 bunch fresh mint
- 1/4 cup extra-virgin olive oil
- 1 (1½-pounds) rack of lamb
- 1 garlic clove
- 1/2 tbsp. honey
- Salt and ground black pepper; as your liking

Directions:
1. For pesto: in a blender, add the mint, garlic, oil, honey, salt and black pepper and pulse until smooth.
2. Coat the rack of lamb evenly with some pesto. Set the temperature of air fryer to 200°F. Grease an air fryer basket.
3. Place rack of lamb into the prepared air fryer basket. Air fry for about 15 minutes, coating with the remaining pesto after every 5 minutes.
4. Remove from air fryer and place the rack of lamb onto a cutting board for about 5 minutes Cut the rack into individual chops and serve.

Glazed Pork Shoulder

(Prep + Cook Time: 33 minutes | Servings: 5)

Ingredients:
- 2 lbs. pork shoulder; cut into 1½-inch thick slices
- 1/3 cup soy sauce
- 1 tbsp. honey
- 2 tbsp. sugar

Directions:
1. In a bowl, mix together all the soy sauce, sugar and honey. Add the pork and generously coat with marinade.
2. Cover and refrigerate to marinate for about 4 to 6 hours.
3. Set the temperature of air fryer to 335°F. Grease an air fryer basket. Place pork shoulder into the prepared air fryer basket.
4. Air fry for about 10 minutes and then, another 6 to 8 minutes at 390°F.
5. Remove from air fryer and transfer the pork shoulder onto a platter.
6. With a piece of foil, cover the pork for about 10 minutes before serving.

Pork Tenderloin with Bacon and Veggies

(Prep + Cook Time: 48 minutes | Servings: 3)

Ingredients:
- 3 (6-oz.) pork tenderloins
- 3/4 lb. frozen green beans
- 3 potatoes
- 6 bacon slices
- 2 tbsp. olive oil

Directions:
1. Set the temperature of air fryer to 390°F. Grease an air fryer basket. With a fork, pierce the potatoes.
2. Place potatoes into the prepared air fryer basket and air fry for about 15 minutes. Wrap one bacon slice around 4 to 6 green beans.
3. Coat the pork tenderloins with oil After 15 minutes, add the pork tenderloins into air fryer basket with potatoes and air fry for about 5 to 6 minutes.
4. Remove the pork tenderloins from basket. Place bean rolls into the basket and top with the pork tenderloins.
5. Air fry for another 7 minutes. Remove from air fryer and transfer the pork tenderloins onto a platter.
6. Cut each tenderloin into desired size slices. Serve alongside the potatoes and green beans rolls.

Lamb Roast

(Prep + Cook Time: 1 hours 50 minutes | Servings: 6)

Ingredients:
- 2¾ lbs. half lamb leg roast
- 3 garlic cloves; cut into thin slices
- 2 tbsp. extra-virgin olive oil
- 1 tbsp. dried rosemary; crushed
- Salt and ground black pepper; as your liking

Directions:
1. In a small bowl, mix together the oil, rosemary, salt and black pepper.
2. With the tip of a sharp knife, make deep slits on the top of lamb roast fat.

3. Insert the garlic slices into the slits. Coat the lamb roast evenly with oil mixture.
4. Set the temperature of air fryer to 390°F. Grease an air fryer basket. Arrange lamb into the prepared air fryer basket in a single layer.
5. Air Fry for about 15 minutes and then another 1¼ hours at 320°F. Remove from air fryer and transfer the roast onto a platter.
6. With a piece of foil, cover the roast for about 10 minutes before slicing.
7. Cut the roast into desired size slices and serve.

Pork Tenderloin with Bell Peppers

(Prep + Cook Time: 35 minutes | Servings: 3)

Ingredients:
- 1 large red bell pepper, seeded and cut into thin strips
- 1 red onion, thinly sliced
- 10½-oz. pork tenderloin; cut into 4 pieces
- 1/2 tbsp. Dijon mustard
- 1 tbsp. olive oil
- 2 tsp. Herbs de Provence
- Salt and ground black pepper; as your liking

Directions:
1. In a bowl, add the bell pepper, onion, Herbs de Provence, salt, black pepper and 1/2 tbsp. of oil and toss to coat well.
2. Rub the pork pieces with mustard, salt and black pepper. Drizzle with the remaining oil.
3. Set the temperature of air fryer to 390°F. Grease an air fryer pan. Place bell pepper mixture into the prepared Air Fryer pan and top with the pork pieces.
4. Air fry for about 15 minutes, flipping once halfway through. Remove from air fryer and transfer the pork mixture onto serving plates. Serve hot.

Lamb Chops

(Prep + Cook Time: 16 minutes | Servings: 2)

Ingredients:
- 4 (4-oz.) lamb chops
- 1 tbsp. olive oil
- Salt and ground black pepper; as your liking

Directions:
1. In a large bowl, mix together the oil, salt and black pepper. Add the chops and coat evenly with the mixture.
2. Set the temperature of air fryer to 390°F. Grease an air fryer basket. Arrange chops into the prepared air fryer basket in a single layer.
3. Air fry for about 5 to 6 minutes. Remove from air fryer and transfer the chops onto plates. Serve hot.

Herbed Leg of Lamb

(Prep + Cook Time: 1 hour 25 minutes | Servings: 5)

Ingredients:
- 2 lbs. bone in leg of lamb
- 2 fresh rosemary sprigs
- 2 fresh thyme sprigs
- 2 tbsp. olive oil
- Salt and ground black pepper; as your liking

Directions:
1. Coat the leg of lamb with oil and sprinkle with salt and black pepper. Wrap the leg of lamb with herb sprigs.
2. Set the temperature of air fryer to 300°F. Grease an air fryer basket. Place leg of lamb into the prepared air fryer basket. Air fry for about 75 minutes.
3. Remove from air fryer and transfer the leg of lamb onto a platter.
4. With a piece of foil, cover the leg of lamb for about 10 minutes before slicing. Cut the leg of lamb into desired size pieces and serve.

Beef and Sauce

(**Prep + Cook Time:** 50 minutes | **Servings:** 6)

Ingredients:
- 3 lbs. beef roast
- 1¾ cups beef stock
- 2 tbsp. butter; melted
- 1 tbsp. mustard
- 3/4 cup red wine
- 3 garlic cloves; minced
- Salt and black pepper to taste

Directions:
1. In a bowl, mix the beef with the butter, mustard, garlic, salt and pepper; rub the meat thoroughly.
2. Put the beef roast in your air fryer's basket and cook at 400°F for 15 minutes
3. Heat up a pan over medium-high heat and add the stock and the wine
4. Then add the beef roast and place the pan in the fryer; cook at 380°F for 25 minutes more. Divide into bowls and serve.

Pork Sausage Casserole

(Prep + Cook Time: 45 minutes | Servings: 4)

Ingredients:
- 8 small sausages
- 8 fresh rosemary sprigs
- 6 oz. flour, sifted
- 3/4 cup milk
- 2/3 cup cold water
- 2 eggs
- 1 red onion, thinly sliced
- 1 garlic clove; minced
- Salt and ground black pepper; as your liking

Directions:
1. In a bowl, mix together the flour and eggs. Add the onion, garlic, salt and black pepper. Mix them well.
2. Gently, add in the milk and water and mix until well combined. In each sausage, pierce 1 rosemary sprig.
3. Set the temperature of air fryer to 320°F. Grease a baking dish.
4. Arrange sausages into the prepared baking dish and top evenly with the flour mixture.
5. Air fry for about 30 minutes. Remove from the air fryer and serve warm.

Beef and Mushroom

(**Prep + Cook Time:** 22 minutes | **Servings:** 2)

Ingredients:
- 8 oz. white mushrooms; sliced
- 1 yellow onion; chopped.
- 1 tsp. olive oil
- 2 tbsp. dark soy sauce
- 2 beef steaks; cut into strips
- Salt and black pepper to taste

Directions:
1. In a baking dish that fits your air fryer, combine all ingredients; toss well.
2. Place the pan in the fryer and cook at 390°F for 17 minutes. Divide everything between plates and serve

Tarragon Pork Loin

(**Prep + Cook Time:** 65 minutes | **Servings:** 6)

Ingredients:
- 3 lbs. pork loin roast; trimmed
- 1/4 cup olive oil
- 2 tbsp. tarragon; chopped.
- 2 tsp. sweet paprika
- 3 garlic cloves; minced
- Salt and black pepper to taste

Directions:

1. In a bowl, mix the roast with all the other ingredients and rub well
2. Transfer the roast to your air fryer and cook at 390°F for 55 minutes. Slice the roast, divide it between plates and serve

Lamb Chops with Veggies

(Prep + Cook Time: 28 minutes | Servings: 4)

Ingredients:

- 4 (6-oz.) lamb chops
- 1 purple carrot, peeled and cubed
- 1 parsnip, peeled and cubed
- 1 fennel bulb, cubed
- 1 yellow carrot, peeled and cubed
- 1 garlic clove; minced
- 2 tbsp. fresh rosemary; minced
- 2 tbsp. fresh mint leaves; minced
- 3 tbsp. olive oil
- Salt and ground black pepper, as required

Directions:

1. In a large bowl, mix together the herbs, garlic, oil, salt and black pepper.
2. Add the chops and generously coat with mixture. Refrigerate to marinate for about 3 hours.
3. In a large pan of water, soak the vegetables for about 15 minutes. Drain the vegetables completely.
4. Set the temperature of air fryer to 390°F. Grease an air fryer basket. Arrange chops into the prepared air fryer basket in a single layer. Air Fry for about 2 minutes. Remove chops from the air fryer.
5. Place vegetables into the air fryer basket and top with the chops in a single layer. Air Fry for about 6 minutes.
6. Remove from air fryer and transfer the chops and vegetables onto serving plates. Serve hot.

Smoked Pork Roast

(**Prep + Cook Time:** 60 minutes | **Servings:** 4)

Ingredients:

- 2 lbs. pork loin roast
- 2 tbsp. oregano; chopped.
- 3 tbsp. smoked paprika
- 1 tbsp. olive oil
- 1 tbsp. brown sugar
- 1 tsp. liquid smoke
- Salt and black pepper to taste

Directions:

1. Place all ingredients into a bowl, mix well and be sure the pork is thoroughly coated.
2. Transfer the roast to your air fryer and cook at 370°F for 55 minutes. Slice the roast, divide it between plates and serve

Beef Roast and Grapes

(**Prep + Cook Time:** 50 minutes | **Servings:** 4)

Ingredients:

- 1 lb. beef roast meat; cubed
- 1/2 lb. red grapes
- 1/2 red onion; chopped.
- 2 garlic cloves; minced
- 1 tsp. thyme; chopped
- 3 tbsp. olive oil
- 1½ cups chicken stock
- 1/2 cup dry white wine
- Salt and black pepper to taste

Directions:

1. Heat up the oil in a pan that fits your air fryer over medium-high heat.
2. Add the beef, salt and pepper; toss and brown for 5 minutes.
3. Add the stock, wine, garlic, thyme and onions; toss and cook for 5 minutes more
4. Transfer the pan to your air fryer and cook at 390°F for 25 minutes
5. Add the grapes, toss gently and cook everything for 5-6 minutes more. Divide between plates and serve right away.

Delicious Rack of Lamb

(**Prep + Cook Time:** 30 minutes | **Servings:** 4)

Ingredients:

- 28 oz. rack of lamb
- 1 egg; whisked
- 1 tbsp. vegetable oil
- 1 tbsp. oregano; chopped.
- 2 garlic cloves; minced
- 2 tbsp. macadamia nuts; toasted and crushed
- Salt and black pepper to taste

Directions:

1. In a bowl, mix the lamb with the salt, pepper, garlic and the oil; rub the lamb well.
2. In another bowl, mix the macadamia nuts with the oregano, salt and pepper; stir
3. Put the egg in a third bowl
4. Dredge the lamb in the egg, then in the macadamia nuts mix
5. Place the lamb in your air fryer's basket and cook at 380°F for 10 minutes on each side. Divide between plates and serve with a side salad.

Nut Crusted Rack of Lamb

(Prep + Cook Time: 50 minutes | Servings: 5)

Ingredients:

- 1¾ lbs. rack of lamb
- 3 oz. almonds; finely chopped
- 1 egg
- 1 tbsp. breadcrumbs
- 1 tbsp. olive oil
- 1 garlic clove; minced
- Salt and ground black pepper; as your liking

Directions:

1. In a bowl, mix together the oil, garlic, salt and black pepper. Coat the rack of lamb evenly with oil mixture.
2. Crack the egg in a shallow bowl and beat well. In another bowl, mix together the breadcrumbs and almonds.
3. Dip the rack of lamb in beaten egg and then, coat with almond mixture. Set the temperature of air fryer to 220°F. Grease an air fryer basket.
4. Place rack of lamb into the prepared air fryer basket. Air fry for about 30 minutes and then 5 more minutes at 390°F.
5. Remove from air fryer and place the rack of lamb onto a cutting board for about 5 minutes
6. With a sharp knife; cut the rack of lamb into individual chops and serve.

Pork and Bell Peppers

(**Prep + Cook Time:** 32 minutes | **Servings:** 2)

Ingredients:

- 7 oz. pork tenderloin; cut into strips
- 1 green bell pepper; cut into strips
- 1 yellow bell pepper; cut in strips
- 1 sweet onion; chopped.
- 1 red bell pepper; cut into strips
- 1 tbsp. olive oil
- Salt and black pepper to taste

Directions:

1. Place all of the ingredients into a pan that fits your air fryer and toss well.
2. Put the pan in the fryer and cook at 390°F for 22 minutes. Divide the mix between plates and serve

Spiced Lamb Steaks

(Prep + Cook Time: 30 minutes | Servings: 3)

Ingredients:

- 1½ lbs. boneless lamb sirloin steaks
- 1/2 onion, roughly chopped
- 5 garlic cloves, peeled
- 1 tbsp. fresh ginger, peeled
- 1/2 tsp. ground cinnamon
- 1/2 tsp. ground cumin
- 1/2 tsp. cayenne pepper
- 1 tsp. garam masala
- 1 tsp. ground fennel
- Salt and ground black pepper; as your liking

Directions:

1. In a blender, add the onion, garlic, ginger and spices and pulse until smooth.
2. Transfer the mixture into a large bowl. Add the lamb steaks and generously coat with the mixture.
3. Refrigerate to marinate for about 24 hours. Set the temperature of air fryer to 330°F. Grease an air fryer basket.
4. Arrange steaks into the prepared air fryer basket in a single layer. Air fry for about 15 minutes, flipping once halfway through. Once done, remove the steaks from air fryer and serve.

Leg of Lamb with Brussels Sprout

(Prep + Cook Time: 1 hour 50 minutes | Servings: 6)

Ingredients:

- 2¼ lbs. leg of lamb
- 1½ lbs. Brussels sprouts, trimmed
- 1 garlic clove; minced
- 1 tbsp. fresh rosemary; minced
- 1 tbsp. fresh lemon thyme
- 2 tbsp. honey
- 3 tbsp. olive oil; divided
- Salt and ground black pepper, as required

Directions:

1. With a sharp knife, score the leg of lamb at several places.
2. In a bowl, mix together 2 tbsp. of oil, herbs, garlic, salt and black pepper. Generously coat the leg of lamb with oil mixture.
3. Set the temperature of air fryer to 300°F. Grease an air fryer basket. Place leg of lamb into the prepared air fryer basket. Air fry for about 75 minutes.
4. Meanwhile, coat the Brussels sprout evenly with the remaining oil and honey. Now, set the temperature of air fryer to 392°F.
5. Arrange Brussels sprout into the air fryer basket with leg of lamb. Air Fry for about 15 minutes.
6. Remove from air Fryer and transfer the leg of lamb onto a platter. With a piece of foil, cover the leg of lamb for about 10 minutes before slicing. Cut the leg of lamb into desired size pieces and serve alongside the Brussels sprout.

Ground Beef

(**Prep + Cook Time:** 25 minutes | **Servings:** 4)

Ingredients:

- 1 lb. ground beef
- 1/4 cup tomato salsa
- 1 yellow onion; chopped.
- 1 tbsp. olive oil
- 1/2 tsp. cumin
- 2 garlic cloves; minced
- 1 green bell pepper; chopped.
- Salt and black pepper to taste

Directions:

1. Heat up the oil in a pan that fits your air fryer over medium heat.
2. Add the onion, garlic, bell peppers and the cumin; stir and sauté for 3 minutes
3. Add the meat, toss, cook for 3 minutes more and take off the heat.
4. Add the salsa, toss and place the pan in the fryer; cook at 380°F for 14 minutes more. Divide everything into bowls and serve

Rubbed Steaks

(Prep + Cook Time: 20 minutes | **Servings:** 4)

Ingredients:
- 1/4 cup ancho chili powder
- 4 flank steaks
- 2 tsp. ginger; grated
- 1 tbsp. dry mustard
- 2 tbsp. sweet paprika
- 1 tbsp. coriander; ground
- 1 tbsp. oregano; dried
- Cooking spray
- Salt and black pepper to taste

Directions:
1. In a bowl, mix all of the spices and then rub the steaks well with the mixture
2. Put the steaks in your air fryer's basket, grease with cooking spray and cook at 370°F for 7 minutes on each side. Serve the steaks with a side salad and enjoy!

Fennel Pork

(Prep + Cook Time: 20 minutes | **Servings:** 4)

Ingredients:
- 2 pork chops
- 1 tsp. fennel seeds; roasted
- 3 tbsp. olive oil
- 1 tbsp. rosemary; chopped.
- Salt and black pepper to taste

Directions:
1. In a bowl, mix the pork chops with the oil, salt, pepper, fennel and the rosemary; toss and make sure the pork chops are coated well
2. Transfer the chops to your air fryer and cook at 400°F for 15 minutes. Divide the chops between plates and serve

Mustard Pork Chops

(Prep + Cook Time: 25 minutes | **Servings:** 6)

Ingredients:
- 2 pork chops
- 2 garlic cloves; minced
- 1 tsp. sweet paprika
- 1 tbsp. mustard
- 1/4 cup olive oil
- Salt and black pepper to taste

Directions:
1. Place all of the ingredients in a bowl and coat the pork chops well
2. Transfer the pork chops to your air fryer's basket and cook at 400°F for 15 minutes. Divide the chops between plates and serve

Pork Steaks

(Prep + Cook Time: 20 minutes | **Servings:** 4)

Ingredients:
- 4 pork steaks
- 1 tbsp. butter; melted
- 1 tbsp. sweet paprika
- Salt and black pepper to taste

Directions:
1. Rub the pork steaks with the salt, pepper, butter and paprika until thoroughly coated
2. Transfer the steaks to your air fryer's basket and cook at 390°F for 7 minutes on each side. Divide the steaks between plates and serve

Pork and Broccoli

(Prep + Cook Time: 20 minutes | **Servings:** 4)

Ingredients:

- 1 lb. pork stew meat; cut into strips
- 1/3 cup oyster sauce
- 1 tsp. soy sauce
- 1 lb. broccoli florets
- 1 garlic clove; minced
- 2 tsp. olive oil

Directions:

1. In a bowl, mix the pork with all the other ingredients and toss well.
2. Put the mixture into your air fryer and cook at 390°F for 15 minutes. Divide into bowls and serve

Coconut Pork

(Prep + Cook Time: 20 minutes | **Servings:** 4)

Ingredients:

- 7 oz. coconut milk
- 14 oz. pork chops; cut into strips
- 2 garlic cloves; minced
- 2 tbsp. olive oil
- 3 tbsp. soy sauce
- 1 shallot; chopped.
- 1 tsp. ginger; grated
- 2 tsp. chili paste
- Salt and black pepper to taste

Directions:

1. In a baking dish that fits your air fryer, mix the pork with the ginger, chili paste, garlic, shallots, oil soy sauce, salt and pepper; toss well
2. Place the pan in the fryer and cook at 400°F for 12 minutes, shaking the fryer halfway
3. Add the coconut milk, toss and cook for 3-4 minutes more. Divide everything into bowls and serve.

Beef Roast

(Prep + Cook Time: 65 minutes | **Servings:** 4)

Ingredients:

- 2 lbs. beef roast
- 1 tbsp. smoked paprika
- 3 tbsp. garlic; minced
- 3 tbsp. olive oil
- Salt and black pepper to taste

Directions:

1. In a bowl, combine all the ingredients and coat the roast well.
2. Place the roast in your air fryer and cook at 390°F for 55 minutes. Slice the roast, divide it between plates and serve with a side salad

Jalapeno Beef

(Prep + Cook Time: 45 minutes | **Servings:** 6)

Ingredients:

- 1½ lbs. ground beef
- 16 oz. canned white beans; drained
- 20 oz. canned tomatoes; chopped.
- 1 cup beef stock
- 3 tbsp. chili powder
- 2 tbsp. olive oil
- 1 red onion; chopped.
- 6 garlic cloves; chopped.
- 7 jalapeno peppers; diced
- Salt and black pepper to taste

Directions:

1. Heat up the oil in a pan that fits your air fryer over medium heat.
2. Add the beef and the onions, stir and cook for 2 minutes
3. Add all remaining ingredients and stir; cook for 3 minutes more
4. Place the pan in the air fryer and cook at 380°F for 35 minutes. Divide everything into bowls and serve.

Oregano Pork Chops

(Prep + Cook Time: 20 minutes | **Servings:** 4)

Ingredients:
- 4 pork chops
- 4 garlic cloves; minced
- 2 tbsp. oregano; chopped.
- 2 tbsp. olive oil
- Salt and black pepper to taste

Directions:
1. Place all of the ingredients in a bowl and toss / mix well
2. Transfer the chops to your air fryer's basket and cook at 400°F for 15 minutes. Serve with a side salad and enjoy!

Lamb Chops and Dill

(Prep + Cook Time: 30 minutes | **Servings:** 6)

Ingredients:
- 1 lb. lamb chops
- 2 yellow onions; chopped.
- 1 tbsp. olive oil
- 2 tbsp. sweet paprika
- 2 tbsp. dill; chopped.
- 3 cups chicken stock
- 1½ cups heavy cream
- 1 garlic clove; minced
- Salt and black pepper to taste

Directions:
1. Put the lamb chops in your air fryer and season with the salt, pepper, garlic and paprika; rub the chops thoroughly
2. Cook at 380°F for 10 minutes
3. Transfer the lamb to a baking dish that fits your air fryer. Then add the onions, stock, cream and dill and toss.
4. Place the pan in the fryer and cook everything for 7-8 minutes more. Divide everything between plates and serve hot

Sage Pork

(Prep + Cook Time: 60 minutes | **Servings:** 6)

Ingredients:
- 2½ lbs. pork loin; boneless and cubed
- 3/4 cup beef stock
- 1 tsp. basil; dried
- 3 tsp. sage; dried
- 1 tsp. oregano; dried
- 1/2 tbsp. smoked paprika
- 1/2 tbsp. garlic powder
- 2 tbsp. olive oil
- Salt and black pepper to taste

Directions:
1. In a pan that fits your air fryer, heat up the oil over medium heat.
2. Add the pork, toss and brown for 5 minutes
3. Add the paprika, sage, garlic powder, basil, oregano, salt and pepper; toss and cook for 2 more minutes.
4. Next add the stock and toss
5. Place the pan in the fryer and cook at 360°F for 40 minutes. Divide everything between plates and serve.

Pork and Chives

(Prep + Cook Time: 32 minutes | **Servings:** 6)

Ingredients:

- 1 lb. pork tenderloin; cubed
- 1/4 cup tarragon; chopped.
- 2 tbsp. mustard
- 2 tbsp. chives; chopped.
- 1 cup mayonnaise
- 2 garlic cloves; minced
- Salt and black pepper to taste

Directions:

1. Place all ingredients except the mayo into a pan that fits your air fryer; mix well.
2. Put the pan in the fryer and cook at 400°F for 15 minutes
3. Add the mayo and toss
4. Put the pan in the fryer for 7 more minutes. Divide into bowls and serve.

Pork Chops and Spinach

(Prep + Cook Time: 20 minutes | **Servings:** 4)

Ingredients:

- 2 pork chops
- 1/4 cup beef stock
- 3 tbsp. spinach pesto
- 2 cups baby spinach
- Salt and black pepper to taste

Directions:

1. Place the pork chops, salt, pepper and spinach pesto in a bowl; toss well
2. Place the pork chops in the air fryer and cook at 400°F for 4 minutes on each side.
3. Transfer the chops to a pan that fits your air fryer and add the stock and the baby spinach
4. Put the pan in the fryer and cook at 400°F for 7 minutes more. Divide everything between plates and serve.

Pork and Sprouts

(Prep + Cook Time: 35 minutes | **Servings:** 4)

Ingredients:

- 1½ lbs. Brussels sprouts; trimmed
- 1 lb. pork tenderloin; cubed
- 1/2 cup sour cream
- 1 garlic clove; minced
- 2 tbsp. rosemary; chopped.
- 2 tbsp. olive oil
- Salt and black pepper to taste
- Salt and black pepper to taste

Directions:

1. In a pan that fits your air fryer, mix the pork with the oil, rosemary, salt, pepper, garlic, salt and pepper; toss well.
2. Place the pan in the fryer and cook at 400°F for 17 minutes
3. Next add the sprouts and the sour cream and toss
4. Place the pan in the fryer and cook for 8 more minutes. Divide everything into bowls and serve.

Cinnamon Beef

(Prep + Cook Time: 60 minutes | **Servings:** 6)

Ingredients:

- 2 lbs. beef roast
- 2 yellow onions; thinly sliced
- 2 garlic cloves; minced
- Juice of 1 lemon
- 1 tbsp. cilantro; chopped.
- 1½ tbsp. cinnamon powder
- 1 cup beef stock
- Salt and black pepper to taste

Directions:

1. In a baking dish that fits your air fryer, mix the roast with all other ingredients and toss well.
2. Place the dish in your fryer and cook at 390°F for 55 minutes, flipping the roast halfway

3. Carve the roast, divide between plates and serve with the cooking juices drizzled on top; enjoy!

Beef and Celery

(**Prep + Cook Time:** 65 minutes | **Servings:** 6)

Ingredients:
- 1 lb. yellow onion; chopped.
- 1 lb. celery; chopped.
- 3 lbs. beef roast
- 3 cups beef stock
- 2 tbsp. olive oil
- 16 oz. canned tomatoes; chopped.
- Salt and black pepper to taste

Directions:
1. Place all the ingredients into a baking dish that fits your air fryer and mix well
2. Put the pan in the fryer and cook at 390°F for 55 minutes
3. Slice the roast and then divide it and the celery mix between plates. Serve and enjoy!

Crispy Lamb Recipe

(**Prep + Cook Time:** 40 Minutes | **Servings:** 4)

Ingredients:
- 28-ounce rack of lamb
- 2 tbsp. macadamia nuts; toasted and crushed
- 1 tbsp. bread crumbs
- 1 tbsp. olive oil
- 1 egg;
- 1 tbsp. rosemary; chopped
- 1 garlic clove; minced
- Salt and black pepper to the taste

Directions:
1. In a bowl; mix oil with garlic and stir well
2. Season lamb with salt, pepper and brush with the oil.
3. In another bowl, mix nuts with breadcrumbs and rosemary
4. Put the egg in a separate bowl and whisk well.
5. Dip lamb in egg, then in macadamia mix, place them in your air fryer's basket, cook at 360°F and cook for 25 minutes; increase heat to 400°F and cook for 5 minutes more. Divide among plates and serve right away

Beef Kabobs Recipe

(**Prep + Cook Time:** 20 Minutes | **Servings:** 4)

Ingredients:
- 2 red bell peppers; chopped
- 2-pound sirloin steak; cut into medium pieces
- 2 tbsp. chili powder
- 2 tbsp. hot sauce
- 1 red onion; chopped
- 1 zucchini; sliced
- Juice form 1 lime
- 1/2 tbsp. cumin; ground
- 1/4 cup olive oil
- 1/4 cup salsa
- Salt and black pepper to the taste

Directions:
1. In a bowl; mix salsa with lime juice, oil, hot sauce, chili powder, cumin, salt and black pepper and whisk well.
2. Divide meat bell peppers, zucchini and onion on skewers, brush kabobs with the salsa mix you made earlier, put them in your preheated air fryer and cook them for 10 minutes at 370°F, flipping kabobs halfway. Divide among plates and serve with a side salad

Marinated Lamb and Veggies

(Prep + Cook Time: 40 Minutes **| Servings:** 4)

Ingredients:
- 1 carrot; chopped
- 1 onion; sliced
- 1/2 tbsp. olive oil

For the marinade:
- 1 garlic clove; minced
- 1/2 apple; grated
- 2 tbsp. orange juice
- 5 tbsp. soy sauce

- 8-ounce lamb loin; sliced
- 3-ounce bean sprouts

- 1 tbsp. sugar
- 1 tbsp. ginger; grated
- 1 small yellow onion; grated
- Salt and black pepper to the taste

Directions:
1. In a bowl; mix 1 grated onion with the apple, garlic, 1 tablespoon ginger, soy sauce, orange juice, sugar and black pepper, whisk well, add lamb and leave aside for 10 minutes
2. Heat up a pan that fits your air fryer with the olive oil over medium high heat, add 1 sliced onion, carrot and bean sprouts; stir and cook for 3 minutes.
3. Add lamb and the marinade, transfer pan to your preheated air fryer and cook at 360°F, for 25 minutes. Divide everything into bowls and serve

Garlicky Loin Roast

(Prep + Cook Time: 60 minutes **| Servings:** 4)

Ingredients:
- 1 lb. pork loin roast
- 3 garlic cloves; minced
- 2 tbsp. panko breadcrumbs

- 1 tbsp. olive oil
- 1 tbsp. rosemary; chopped.
- Salt and black pepper to taste

Directions:
1. Place all ingredients except the roast into a bowl; stir / mix well.
2. Spread the mixture over the roast. Place the roast in the air fryer and cook at 360°F for 55 minutes
3. Slice the roast, divide it between plates and serve with a side salad

Lamb Meatballs

(Prep + Cook Time: 22 minutes **| Servings:** 8)

Ingredients:
- 4 oz. lamb meat; minced
- 1 tbsp. oregano; chopped.
- 1/2 tbsp. lemon zest

- 1 egg; whisked
- Cooking spray
- Salt and black pepper to taste

Directions:
1. In a bowl, combine all of the ingredients except the cooking spray and stir well.
2. Shape medium-sized meatballs out of this mix
3. Place the meatballs in your air fryer's basket, grease them with cooking spray and cook at 400°F for 12 minutes. Divide between plates and serve

Hot Pork Delight

(Prep + Cook Time: 28 minutes **| Servings:** 4)

Ingredients:
- 1 lb. pork tenderloin; cubed
- 1 red onion; chopped.
- 2 tbsp. olive oil
- 3 tbsp. parsley; chopped.

- 1 garlic clove; minced
- 1/2 tsp. hot chili powder
- 1 tsp. cinnamon powder
- Salt and black pepper to taste

Directions:
1. In a bowl, combine the chili, cinnamon, garlic, salt, pepper and the oil. Then add the pork and rub it well with the mixture
2. Transfer the meat to your air fryer and cook at 280°F for 12 minutes. Add the onions and cook for 5 minutes more
3. Divide everything between plates and serve with the parsley sprinkled on top.

Paprika Beef

(Prep + Cook Time: 30 minutes | Servings: 4)

Ingredients:
- 1½ lbs. beef fillet
- 1 red onion; roughly chopped.
- 1 tbsp. tomato paste
- 1 tbsp. Worcestershire sauce
- 1/2 cup beef stock
- 3 tsp. sweet paprika
- 2 tbsp. olive oil
- Salt and black pepper to taste

Directions:
1. In a bowl, mix the beef with all remaining ingredients; toss well.
2. Transfer the mixture to a pan that fits your air fryer and cook at 400°F for 26 minutes, shaking the air fryer halfway. Divide everything between plates and serve

Lamb Ribs

(Prep + Cook Time: 20 minutes | Servings: 4)

Ingredients:
- 4 lamb ribs
- 1 cup veggie stock
- 1/4 tsp. smoked paprika
- 1/2 tsp. chili powder
- 2 tbsp. extra virgin olive oil
- 4 garlic cloves; minced
- Salt and black pepper to taste

Directions:
1. In a bowl; combine all of the ingredients except the ribs and mix well.
2. Then add the ribs and rub them thoroughly with the mixture
3. Transfer the ribs to your air fryer's basket and cook at 390°F for 7 minutes on each side. Serve with a side salad

Beef and Plums

(Prep + Cook Time: 50 minutes | Servings: 6)

Ingredients:
- 1½ lbs. beef stew meat; cubed
- 9 oz. plums; pitted and halved
- 8 oz. beef stock
- 1 tsp. ginger powder
- 1 tsp. cinnamon powder
- 1 tsp. turmeric powder
- 2 yellow onions; chopped.
- 2 garlic cloves; minced
- 3 tbsp. honey
- 2 tbsp. olive oil
- Salt and black pepper to tastes

Directions:
1. In a pan that fits your air fryer, heat up the oil over medium heat.
2. Add the beef, stir and brown for 2 minutes
3. Add the honey, onions, garlic, salt, pepper, turmeric, ginger and cinnamon; toss and cook for 2-3 minutes more
4. Add the plums and the stock; toss again.
5. Place the pan in the fryer and cook at 380°F for 30 minutes. Divide everything into bowls and serve

Chinese Style Beef

(**Prep + Cook Time:** 25 minutes | **Servings:** 4)

Ingredients:

- 1 lb. beef stew meat; cut into strips
- 1/4 cup sesame seeds; toasted
- 1 cup soy sauce
- 5 garlic cloves; minced
- 1 cup green onion; chopped
- Black pepper to taste

Directions:

1. In a pan that fits your air fryer, place all ingredients and mix well
2. Place the pan in the fryer and cook at 390°F for 20 minutes. Divide everything into bowls and serve

Beef and Peas

(**Prep + Cook Time:** 25 minutes | **Servings:** 2)

Ingredients:

- 2 beef steaks; cut into strips
- 2 tbsp. soy sauce
- 1 tbsp. olive oil
- 14 oz. snow peas
- Salt and black pepper to taste

Directions:

1. Put all of the ingredients into a pan that fits your air fryer; toss well.
2. Place the pan in the fryer and cook at 390°F for 25 minutes. Divide everything between plates and serve

Marinated Beef

(**Prep + Cook Time:** 30 minutes | **Servings:** 4)

Ingredients:

- 3 lbs. chuck roast; cut into thin strips
- 1/2 cup soy sauce
- 1/2 cup black soy sauce
- 3 red peppers; dried and crushed
- 1 tbsp. olive oil
- 5 garlic cloves; minced
- 2 tbsp. fish sauce

Directions:

1. In a bowl, combine the beef with all ingredients; toss well and place in the fridge for 10 minutes.
2. Transfer the beef to your air fryer's basket and cook at 380°F for 20 minutes. Serve with a side salad

Cumin Beef

(**Prep + Cook Time:** 40 minutes | **Servings:** 4)

Ingredients:

- 1 lb. ground beef
- 4 oz. canned kidney beans; drained
- 2 garlic cloves; minced
- 2 tbsp. olive oil
- 2 tsp. cumin; ground
- 8 oz. canned tomatoes; chopped.
- 1 yellow onion; chopped.
- Salt and black pepper to taste

Directions:

1. Heat up the oil in a pan that fits your air fryer over medium heat.
2. Add the onion and the beef, stir and cook for 2-3 minutes
3. Then add the garlic, salt, pepper, beans, tomatoes and the cumin; toss and cook for another 2 minutes
4. Transfer the pan to your air fryer and cook at 380°F for 30 minutes. Divide everything into bowls and serve.

Creamy Beef

(Prep + Cook Time: 55 minutes | **Servings:** 4)

Ingredients:

- 1½ lbs. cubed beef
- 4 oz. brown mushrooms; sliced
- 2 garlic cloves; minced
- 2½ tbsp. vegetable oil
- 1½ tbsp. white flour
- 1 tbsp. cilantro; chopped.
- 8 oz. sour cream
- 1 red onion; chopped.
- Salt and black pepper to taste

Directions:

1. In a bowl, mix the beef with the salt, pepper and flour; toss.
2. Heat up the oil in a pan that fits your air fryer over medium-high heat.
3. Add the beef, onions and garlic; stir and cook for 5 minutes
4. Add the mushrooms and toss
5. Place the pan in the fryer and cook at 380°F for 35 minutes
6. Add the sour cream and cilantro and toss; cook for 5 minutes more. Divide everything between plates and serve.

Lamb and Beans

(Prep + Cook Time: 35 minutes | **Servings:** 4)

Ingredients:

- 3 oz. canned kidney beans; drained
- 8 oz. lamb loin; cubed
- 1/2 tbsp. olive oil
- 1 tbsp. ginger; grated
- 3 tbsp. soy sauce
- 1 garlic clove; minced
- 1 yellow onion; sliced
- 1 carrot; chopped.
- Salt and black pepper to taste

Directions:

1. In baking dish that fits your air fryer, place all of the ingredients and mix well.
2. Place the dish in the fryer and cook at 390°F for 30 minutes. Divide everything into bowls and serve

Delicious Sausage

(Prep + Cook Time: 25 minutes | **Servings:** 4)

Ingredients:

- 6 pork sausage links; halved
- 1 red onion; sliced
- 1 tbsp. olive oil
- 1 tbsp. rosemary; chopped.
- 2 garlic cloves; minced
- 1 tbsp. sweet paprika
- Salt and black pepper to taste

Directions:

1. In a pan that fits your air fryer, mix all of the ingredients and toss.
2. Place the pan in the fryer and cook at 360°F for 20 minutes. Divide between plates and serve

Beef, Arugula and Leeks

(Prep + Cook Time: 22 minutes | **Servings:** 4)

Ingredients:

- 1 lb. ground beef
- 5 oz. baby arugula
- 1 tbsp. olive oil
- 2 tbsp. tomato paste
- 3 leeks; roughly chopped.
- Salt and black pepper to taste

Directions:

1. In a pan that fits your air fryer, mix the beef with the leeks, salt, pepper, oil and the tomato paste; toss well. Place the pan in the fryer and cook at 380°F for 12 minutes
2. Add the arugula and toss. Divide into bowls and serve.

Basil Beef Roast

(Prep + Cook Time: 60 minutes | **Servings:** 6)

Ingredients:

- 1½ lbs. beef roast
- 2 garlic cloves; minced
- 1 cup beef stock
- 2 carrots; sliced
- 1 tbsp. basil; dried
- Salt and black pepper to taste

Directions:

1. In a pan that fits your air fryer, combine all ingredients well.
2. Place the pan in the fryer and cook at 390°F for 55 minutes
3. Slice the roast, divide it and the carrots between plates and serve with cooking juices drizzled on top.

Snacks & Appetizers

Simple Roasted Peanuts

(Prep + Cook Time: 19 minutes | Servings: 10)

Ingredients:
- 2½ cups raw peanuts
- 1 tbsp. olive oil
- Salt; as your liking

Directions:
1. Set the temperature of Air Fryer to 320°F. Add the peanuts in an Air Fryer basket in a single layer.
2. Air Fry for about 9 minutes, tossing twice. Remove the peanuts from Air Fryer basket and transfer into a bowl.
3. Add the oil and salt and toss to coat well.
4. Return the nuts mixture into Air Fryer basket.
5. Air Fry for about 5 minutes. Once done, transfer the hot nuts in a glass or steel bowl and serve.

Broccoli Poppers

(Prep + Cook Time: 25 minutes | Servings: 4)

Ingredients:
- 1 lb. broccoli; cut into small florets
- 2 tbsp. chickpea flour
- 2 tbsp. plain yogurt
- 1/4 tsp. ground cumin
- 1/4 tsp. ground turmeric
- 1/2 tsp. red chili powder
- Salt, to taste

Directions:
1. In a bowl, mix together the yogurt and spices. Add the broccoli and generously coat with marinade.
2. Refrigerate for about 20 minutes. Set the temperature of Air Fryer to 400°F.
3. Sprinkle the broccoli florets with chickpea flour. Add the broccoli florets in an Air Fryer basket in a single layer. Air Fry for about 10 minutes, tossing once halfway through. Serve hot.

Onion Rings

(Prep + Cook Time: 30 minutes | Servings: 4)

Ingredients:
- 1 large onion; cut into ¼ inch slices
- 3/4 cup dry breadcrumbs
- 1 cup milk
- 1 egg
- 1¼ cups all-purpose flour
- 1 tsp. baking powder
- Salt; as your liking

Directions:
1. Separate the onion slices into rings. In a shallow dish, mix together the flour, baking powder and salt.
2. In a second dish, mix well milk and egg. In a third dish, put the breadcrumbs.
3. Coat each onion ring with flour mixture, then dip into egg mixture and finally, coat evenly with the breadcrumbs.
4. Set the temperature of Air Fryer to 360°F. Place the onion rings in an Air Fryer basket in a single layer.
5. Air Fry for about 7 to 10 minutes. Serve hot.

Easy Spicy Chickpeas

(Prep + Cook Time: 25 minutes | Servings: 4)

Ingredients:

- 1 (15-oz.) can chickpeas, rinsed and drained
- 1 tbsp. olive oil
- 1/2 tsp. smoked paprika
- 1/2 tsp. cayenne pepper
- 1/2 tsp. ground cumin
- Salt, to taste

Directions:

1. Set the temperature of Air Fryer to 390°F. In a bowl, add all the Ingredients and toss to coat well.
2. Add the chickpeas in an Air Fryer basket in 2 batches. (you can lay a piece of grease-proof baking paper)
3. Air Fry for about 8 to 10 minutes. Once done, transfer the hot nuts in a glass or steel bowl and serve.

Salmon Croquettes

(Prep + Cook Time: 29 minutes | Servings: 16)

Ingredients:

- 1 large can red salmon, drained
- 1 cup breadcrumbs
- 1/3 cup vegetable oil
- 2 eggs, lightly beaten
- 2 tbsp. fresh parsley; chopped
- Salt and freshly ground black pepper, as needed

Directions:

1. Set the temperature of Air Fryer to 390°F. In a bowl, add the salmon and mash it completely using a fork.
2. Add the eggs, parsley, salt and black pepper. Mix until well combined.
3. Make 16 equal-sized croquettes from the mixture. In a shallow dish, mix together the oil and breadcrumbs. Coat the croquettes evenly with the breadcrumb mixture.
4. Place the croquettes in an Air Fryer basket in a single layer in 2 batches. Air Fry for about 7 minutes. Serve.

Broccoli Bites

(Prep + Cook Time: 27 minutes | Servings: 10)

Ingredients:

- 1/4 cup Parmesan cheese; grated
- 1¼ cups panko breadcrumbs
- 1¼ cups cheddar cheese; grated
- 2 cups broccoli florets
- 2 eggs, beaten
- Salt and freshly ground black pepper, as needed

Directions:

1. In a food processor, add the broccoli and pulse until finely crumbled.
2. Take a large bowl, mix together the broccoli and remaining ingredients.
3. Make small equal-sized balls from the mixture. Arrange the balls in a baking sheet and refrigerate for at least 30 minutes.
4. Set the temperature of Air Fryer to 350°F. Put the balls in an Air fryer basket Air Fry for about 12 minutes. Serve.

Pepper Rolls

(Prep + Cook Time: 20 minutes | **Servings:** 8)

Ingredients:
- 4 oz. feta cheese; crumbled
- 2 tbsp. oregano; chopped.
- 1 green onion; chopped.
- 1 yellow bell pepper; deseeded and halved
- 1 orange bell pepper; deseeded and halved
- Salt and black pepper to taste

Directions:
1. Place the bell pepper halves in your air fryer's basket and cook at 400°F for 10 minutes.
2. Transfer the bell peppers to a cutting board, cool down, peel and arrange them on a working surface.
3. In a bowl, mix the cheese, salt, pepper, cilantro and green onions; stir well
4. Spread the cheese mixture on each pepper half, roll the peppers and secure them with toothpicks. Serve as an appetizer, or even as a great side

Mozzarella Sticks

(Prep + Cook Time: 39 minutes | Servings: 4)

Ingredients:
- 1 lb. Mozzarella cheese block cut into 3x½-inch sticks
- 1 cup plain breadcrumbs
- 1/4 cup white flour
- 2 eggs
- 3 tbsp. nonfat milk

Directions:
1. Add the flour in a shallow dish. In a second dish, mix together the eggs and milk. In a third dish, put the breadcrumbs.
2. Coat the Mozzarella sticks with flour, then dip into egg mixture and finally, coat evenly with the breadcrumbs.
3. Arrange the Mozzarella sticks onto a baking sheet and freeze for about 1 to 2 hours.
4. Set the temperature of Air Fryer to 440°F.
5. Arrange the Mozzarella sticks in an Air Fryer basket in a single layer in 2 batches. Air Fry for about 12 minutes.

Chocolate Cookie Dough Balls

(Prep + Cook Time: 35 minutes | Servings: 6)

Ingredients:
- 16½ oz. store-bought chilled chocolate chip cookie dough
- 1/2 cup chocolate cookie crumbs
- 1/4 cup butter, melted
- 2 tbsp. sugar

Directions:
1. Cut the cookie dough into 12 equal-sized pieces and then, shape each into a ball.
2. Add the melted butter in a shallow dish. In another dish, mix together the cookie crumbs and sugar.
3. Dip each cookie ball in the melted butter and then evenly coat with the cookie crumbs.
4. In the bottom of a baking sheet, place the coated cookie balls and freeze for at least 2 hours.
5. Preheat the air fryer to 350°F. Line the air fryer basket with a piece of foil. Place the cookies balls in an Air Fryer basket in a single layer in 2 batches. Air Fry for about 10 minutes.

Bacon Wrapped Shrimp

(Prep + Cook Time: 22 minutes | Servings: 6)

Ingredients:
- 1 lb. shrimp, peeled and deveined
- 1 lb. bacon, thinly sliced

Directions:
1. Wrap each shrimp with one bacon slice. Add the shrimp in a baking dish and refrigerate for about 20 minutes.
2. Set the temperature of Air Fryer to 390°F.
3. Add the shrimp in an Air Fryer basket in a single layer. Air Fry for about 5 to 7 minutes.

Cauliflower Poppers

(Prep + Cook Time: 26 minutes | Servings: 6)

Ingredients:
- 1 large head cauliflower; cut into bite-sized florets
- 2 tbsp. olive oil
- Salt and freshly ground black pepper, as needed

Directions:
1. Drizzle the cauliflower florets with oil. Sprinkle with salt and black pepper.
2. Set the temperature of Air Fryer to 390°F. Place the cauliflower florets in a greased Air Fryer basket in a single layer in 2 batches.
3. Air Fry for about 8 minutes, shaking once halfway through. Serve hot.

Simple Roasted Mixed Nuts

(Prep + Cook Time: 25 minutes | Servings: 6)

Ingredients:
- 1 packet stevia
- 1/2 cup pecans
- 1/2 cup almonds
- 1/2 cup walnuts
- 2 tbsp. egg white
- 1/2 tbsp. ground cinnamon
- A pinch of cayenne pepper

Directions:
1. Set the temperature of Air Fryer to 320°F. Take a bowl and mix together all the listed ingredients.
2. Place the nuts in an Air Fryer basket in a single layer. (you can lay a piece of grease-proof baking paper)
3. Air Fry for about 20 minutes, stirring once halfway through.
4. Once done, transfer the hot nuts in a glass or steel bowl and serve.

Fried Corn

(**Prep + Cook Time:** 15 minutes | **Servings:** 4)

Ingredients:
- 2½ tbsp. butter
- 2 tbsp. corn kernels

Directions:
1. In a pan that fits your air fryer, mix the corn with the butter.
2. Place the pan in the fryer and cook at 400°F for 10 minutes. Serve as a snack and enjoy!

Simple Roasted Cashews

(Prep + Cook Time: 24 minutes | Servings: 8)

Ingredients:
- 2 cups raw cashew nuts
- 1 tsp. butter, melted
- Salt and freshly ground black pepper, as needed

Directions:
1. Set the temperature of Air Fryer to 355°F. In a bowl, mix together all the ingredients.
2. Place the cashews nuts in an Air Fryer basket in a single layer. (you can lay a piece of grease-proof baking paper)
3. Air Fry for about 4 minutes, shaking once halfway through. Once done, transfer the hot nuts in a glass bowl and serve.

Potato Chips

(Prep + Cook Time: 45 minutes | Servings: 6)

Ingredients:
- 4 small russet potatoes, thinly sliced
- 2 tbsp. fresh rosemary; finely chopped
- 1 tbsp. olive oil
- 1/4 tsp. salt

Directions:
1. In a large bowl, add the water and potato slices. Set aside for about 30 minutes, changing the water once halfway through.
2. Drain the potato slices well and pat them dry with the paper towels. Set the temperature of Air Fryer to 350°F.
3. In a bowl, mix together the potato slices, olive oil, rosemary and salt. Add the potato chips in an Air Fryer basket in a single layer. Air Fry for about 30 minutes. Serve.

Squash Fries

(Prep + Cook Time: 45 minutes | Servings: 2)

Ingredients:
- 14 oz. butternut squash, peeled, seeded and cut into strips
- 1/2 tsp. red chili powder
- 1/4 tsp. garlic salt
- 2 tsp. olive oil
- 1/2 tsp. ground cinnamon
- Salt and freshly ground black pepper, as needed

Directions:
1. Set the temperature of Air Fryer to 440°F. Line a baking sheet with parchment paper. Take a bowl, add all the listed Ingredients and toss to coat well.
2. Place the butternut squash strips onto the prepared baking sheet in a single layer. Arrange the baking sheet in an Air Fryer basket. Air Fry for about 35 minutes. Serve.

Zucchini Fries

(Prep + Cook Time: 30 minutes | Servings: 4)

Ingredients:
- 1 lb. zucchini, sliced into 2½-inch sticks
- 2 tbsp. olive oil
- 3/4 cup panko breadcrumbs
- Salt; as your liking

Directions:
1. In a colander, add the zucchini and sprinkle with salt. Set aside for about 10 minutes. Set the temperature of Air Fryer to 390°F.
2. Gently pat dry the zucchini sticks with the paper towels and coat with oil. In a shallow dish, add the breadcrumbs. Coat the zucchini sticks evenly with breadcrumbs.
3. Place the zucchini sticks in an Air Fryer basket in a single layer in 2 batches. Set the temperature of Air Fryer to 425°F and Air Fry for about 10 minutes. Serve.

Carrot Sticks

(Prep + Cook Time: 22 minutes | Servings: 2)

Ingredients:
- 1 large carrot, peeled and cut into sticks
- 1 tbsp. olive oil
- 1 tbsp. fresh rosemary; finely chopped
- 1/4 tsp. cayenne pepper
- 2 tsp. sugar
- Salt and freshly ground black pepper, as needed

Directions:
1. Set the temperature of Air Fryer to 390°F. In a bowl, add all the Ingredients and toss to coat well.
2. Place the carrot sticks in an Air Fryer basket in a single layer.
3. Air Fry for about 12 minutes. Serve.

Beet Chips

(Prep + Cook Time: 25 minutes | Servings: 6)

Ingredients:
- 4 medium beetroots, peeled and thinly sliced
- 1/4 tsp. smoked paprika
- 2 tbsp. olive oil
- 1/2 tsp. salt

Directions:
1. Set the temperature of Air Fryer to 325°F. In a bowl, add all the Ingredients and toss to coat well.
2. Arrange the beet slices in an Air Fryer basket in a single layer. Air Fry for about 12 to 15 minutes. Serve.

Spinach Rolls

(Prep + Cook Time: 24 minutes | Servings: 6)

Ingredients:
- 1 (16-oz.) package frozen spinach, thawed
- 1 package frozen filo dough, thawed
- 1 cup feta cheese, crumbled
- 1/2 cup Romano cheese; grated
- 1 red onion; chopped
- 1 cup fresh parsley; chopped
- 1 cup fresh mint leaves; chopped
- 1 egg
- 1/4 tsp. ground cardamom
- 2 tbsp. olive oil
- Salt and freshly ground black pepper, as needed

Directions:
1. Put all the listed Ingredients except filo dough and oil in a food processor and pulse until smooth.
2. Place one filo sheet on the cutting board and cut into three rectangular strips. Brush each strip with the oil.
3. Add about one tsp. of spinach mixture along with the short side of a strip.
4. Roll the dough to secure the filling. Repeat with the remaining filo sheets and spinach mixture.
5. Set the temperature of Air Fryer to 355°F. Grease an Air Fryer basket. Place rolls into the prepared basket in a single layer. Air Fry for about 4 minutes.

Banana Chips

(Prep + Cook Time: 20 minutes | Servings: 8)

Ingredients:
- 2 tbsp. olive oil
- 2 raw bananas, peeled and sliced
- Salt and freshly ground black pepper, as needed

Directions:
1. Set the temperature of Air Fryer to 355°F. Drizzle the banana slices evenly with oil.
2. Arrange the banana slices in an Air Fryer basket in a single layer. Air Fry for about 10 minutes. Sprinkle with salt and black pepper. Serve.

Crispy Prawns

(Prep + Cook Time: 23 minutes | Servings: 4)

Ingredients:
- 1/2 lb. nacho chips; crushed
- 1 egg
- 18 prawns, peeled and deveined

Directions:
1. In a shallow dish, crack the egg and beat well. Put the crushed nacho chips in another dish.
2. dip the prawn into beaten egg and then, coat with the nacho chips.
3. Set the temperature of Air Fryer to 355°F. Place the prawns in an Air Fryer basket in a single layer.
4. Air Fry for about 8 minutes. Serve hot.

Tomatoes and Dates Salsa

(**Prep + Cook Time:** 20 minutes | **Servings:** 12)

Ingredients:
- 1½ lbs. tomatoes; peeled and cubed
- 6 oz. sultanas; chopped.
- 3 oz. dates; roughly chopped.
- 1 yellow onion; chopped.
- 1 tbsp. balsamic vinegar
- 1 tsp. whole spice
- 1 apple; cored and cubed
- 1/2 tbsp. brown sugar
- Salt and black pepper to taste

Directions:
1. In a pan that fits your air fryer, add and toss all the ingredients. Place the pan in the fryer and cook at 370°F for 15 minutes
2. Remove the salsa, place in a bowl and chill. Serve the salsa cold as a snack or appetizer

Eggplant Slices

(Prep + Cook Time: 31 minutes | Servings: 4)

Ingredients:
- 1 medium eggplant, peeled and cut into 1/2-inch round slices
- 1 cup Italian-style breadcrumbs
- 1/2 cup all-purpose flour
- 2 eggs, beaten
- 1/4 cup olive oil
- Salt; as your liking

Directions:
1. In a colander, add the eggplant slices and sprinkle with salt. Set aside for about 45 minutes and pat dry the eggplant slices.
2. Add the flour in a shallow dish. Crack the eggs in a second dish and beat well. In a third dish, mix together the oil and breadcrumbs.
3. Coat each eggplant slice with flour, then dip into beaten eggs and finally, evenly coat with the breadcrumbs mixture. Set the temperature of Air Fryer to 390°F. Arrange the eggplant slices in an Air Fryer basket in a single layer in 2 batches. Air Fry for about 8 minutes. Serve.

Spring Rolls

(Prep + Cook Time: 35 minutes | Servings: 6)

Ingredients:
- 3½ oz. cooked shrimps
- 12 spring roll wrappers
- 1 egg, beaten
- 1¾ oz. fresh mushrooms, sliced
- 1 oz. canned water chestnuts, sliced
- 1 oz. bean sprouts
- 1 small carrot, peeled and cut into matchsticks
- 2 scallions (green part); chopped
- 2 tbsp. vegetable oil; divided
- 1 tbsp. soy sauce
- 1 tsp. fresh ginger; finely grated
- 1 tsp. Chinese five-spice powder

Directions:
1. Take a skillet, heat one tbsp. of oil over medium heat and sauté the mushrooms, water chestnuts and ginger for about 2 to 3 minutes.
2. Add in the beans sprouts, carrot, scallion, soy sauce and five-spice powder. Sauté for about 1 minute.
3. Stir in the shrimps and remove from heat. Set aside to cool.
4. Divide the veggie mixture evenly between spring rolls. Roll the wrappers around the filling and seal with beaten egg. Coat each roll with the remaining oil.
5. Set the temperature of Air Fryer to 390°F. Grease an Air Fryer basket.
6. Place rolls into the prepared Air Fryer basket in a single layer in 2 batches. Air Fry for about 5 minutes. Serve.

Potato Croquettes

(Prep + Cook Time: 38 minutes | Servings: 4)

Ingredients:
- 2 medium Russet potatoes, peeled and cubed
- 2 eggs
- 1/2 cup breadcrumbs
- 1/2 cup Parmesan cheese; grated
- 1 egg yolk
- 2 tbsp. all-purpose flour
- 2 tbsp. chives; minced
- 2 tbsp. vegetable oil
- Salt and freshly ground black pepper, as needed
- A pinch of ground nutmeg

Directions:
1. Add potatoes in the pan of a boiling water and cook for about 15 minutes. Drain the potatoes well and transfer into a large bowl.
2. With a potato masher, mash the potatoes and set aside to cool completely.
3. In the same bowl of mashed potatoes, add in the flour, Parmesan cheese, egg yolk, chives, nutmeg, salt and black pepper. Whisk until well combined. Make small equal-sized balls from the mixture. Now, roll each ball into a cylinder shape.
4. In a shallow dish, crack the eggs and beat well. In another dish, mix together the breadcrumbs and oil.
5. Dip the croquettes in egg mixture and then evenly coat with the breadcrumbs mixture.
6. Set the temperature of Air Fryer to 390°F. Place the croquettes in an Air Fryer basket in a single layer. Air Fry for about 7 to 8 minutes.

Pork Bites

(**Prep + Cook Time:** 25 minutes | **Servings:** 4)

Ingredients:
- 1 lb. ground pork
- 3/4 cup panko breadcrumbs
- 3/4 cup coconut; shredded
- 2 tsp. garlic powder
- 2 eggs
- A drizzle of olive oil
- Salt and black pepper to taste

Directions:
1. In a bowl, mix coconut with panko and stir well. In another bowl, mix the pork, salt, pepper, eggs and garlic powder and then shape medium meatballs out of this mix
2. Dredge the meatballs in the coconut mix, place them in your air fryer's basket, introduce in the air fryer and cook at 350°F for 15 minutes. Serve and enjoy!

Basil and Cilantro Crackers

(**Prep + Cook Time:** 26 minutes | **Servings:** 6)

Ingredients:
- 1¼ cups flour
- 1 garlic clove; minced
- 4 tbsp. butter; melted
- 2 tbsp. basil; minced
- 2 tbsp. cilantro; minced
- 1/2 tsp. baking powder
- Salt and black pepper to taste

Directions:
1. Add all of the ingredients to a bowl and stir until you obtain a dough.
2. Spread this on a lined baking sheet that fits your air fryer. Place the baking sheet in the fryer at 325°F and cook for 16 minutes. Cool down, cut and serve

French Fries

(Prep + Cook Time: 45 minutes | Servings: 8)

Ingredients:
- 1¾ lbs. potatoes, peeled and cut into strips
- 1/4 cup olive oil
- 1 tsp. garlic powder
- 2 tsp. paprika
- 1 tsp. onion powder

Directions:
1. In a large bowl, add the water and potato strips. Set aside for about 1 hour.
2. Drain the potato strips well and pat them dry with the paper towels.
3. Take a large bowl, add the potato strips and the remaining ingredients. Toss to coat well.
4. Set the temperature of Air Fryer to 375°F.
5. Add the potato strips in an Air Fryer basket in a single layer. Air Fry for about 30 minutes. Serve.

Avocado Fries

(Prep + Cook Time: 27 minutes | Servings: 2)

Ingredients:
- 1 avocado, peeled, pitted and sliced into 8 pieces
- 1/4 cup all-purpose flour
- 1/2 cup panko breadcrumbs
- 1 egg
- 1 tsp. water
- Non stick cooking spray
- Salt and freshly ground black pepper, as needed

Directions:
1. In a shallow bowl, mix together the flour, salt and black pepper. In a second bowl, mix well egg and water. In a third bowl, put the breadcrumbs.
2. Coat the avocado slices with flour mixture, then dip into egg mixture and finally, coat evenly with the breadcrumbs.
3. spray the avocado slices evenly with cooking spray. Set the temperature of Air Fryer to 400°F.
4. Place the avocado slices in an Air Fryer basket in a single layer. Air Fry for about 7 minutes, flipping once halfway through. Enjoy!

Cauliflower Poppers

(Prep + Cook Time: 30 minutes | Servings: 4)

Ingredients:
- 1 large egg white
- 3/4 cup panko breadcrumbs
- 4 cups cauliflower florets
- 2 tbsp. hot sauce
- 3 tbsp. ketchup

Directions:
1. In a bowl, mix together the egg white, ketchup and hot sauce. Add the breadcrumbs in another bowl. Dip the cauliflower florets in ketchup mixture and then evenly coat with the breadcrumbs.
2. Set the temperature of Air Fryer to 320°F. Arrange the cauliflower florets in an Air Fryer basket in a single layer. Air Fry for about 20 minutes. Serve.

Cheesey Sandwich

(Prep + Cook Time: 15 minutes | Servings: 2)

Ingredients:
- 1/2 cup sharp cheddar cheese; grated
- 1/2 cup butter; softened
- 4 white bread slices

Directions:
1. Set the temperature of Air Fryer to 355°F. Spread the butter evenly over one side of each bread slice.
2. Sprinkle the cheese over buttered side of 2 slices.
3. Top with the remaining slices of bread. Place the sandwiches in an Air Fryer basket in a single layer. Air Fry for about 4 to 5 minutes. Serve.

Squash Dip

(**Prep + Cook Time:** 35 minutes | **Servings:** 6)

Ingredients:
- 1 yellow onion; chopped.
- 1 cup veggie stock
- 1/4 cup lemon juice
- 8 garlic cloves; minced
- 1 bunch basil; chopped.
- 8 carrots; chopped.
- 2 butternut squash; chopped.
- 2 tbsp. olive oil
- Salt and black pepper to taste

Directions:
1. In a pan that fits your air fryer, mix all the ingredients except the lemon juice.
2. Place the pan in the fryer and cook at 380°F for 25 minutes
3. Transfer the entire mixture to a blender, add the lemon juice and pulse well. Divide into bowls and serve as a party dip or an appetizer

Buttered Corn

(Prep + Cook Time: 25 minutes | Servings: 2)

Ingredients:
- 2 corn on the cob
- 2 tbsp. butter; softened and divided
- Salt and freshly ground black pepper, as needed

Directions:
1. Set the temperature of Air Fryer to 320°F. Sprinkle the cobs evenly with salt and black pepper.
2. After that, rub with 1 tbsp. of butter.
3. With 1 piece of foil, wrap each cob and place in an Air Fryer basket. Air Fry for about 20 minutes.
4. Top with the remaining butter and serve.

Apple Chips

(Prep + Cook Time: 26 minutes | Servings: 2)

Ingredients:
- 1 apple, peeled, cored and thinly sliced
- 1 tbsp. sugar
- 1/2 tsp. ground cinnamon
- A pinch of ground ginger
- A pinch of ground cardamom
- A pinch of salt

Directions:
1. Set the temperature of Air Fryer to 390°F. In a bowl, add all the Ingredients and toss to coat well.
2. Arrange the apple slices in an Air Fryer basket in a single layer in 2 batches. Air Fry for about 7 to 8 minutes, flipping once halfway through. Serve.

Polenta Sticks

(Prep + Cook Time: 16 minutes | Servings: 4)

Ingredients:
- 1/4 cup Parmesan cheese; shredded
- 2½ cups cooked polenta
- Salt; as your liking

Directions:
1. Add the polenta evenly into a greased baking dish and with the back of a spoon, smooth the top surface.
2. Cover the baking dish and refrigerate for about 1 hour or until set.
3. Remove from the refrigerator and cut down the polenta into the desired size slices. Set the temperature of Air Fryer to 350°F. Grease a baking dish.
4. Arrange the polenta sticks into the prepared baking dish in a single layer and sprinkle with salt.
5. Place the baking dish into an Air Fryer basket. Air Fry for about 5 to 6 minutes. Top with the cheese and serve.

Dill Pickle Fries

(Prep + Cook Time: 43 minutes | Servings: 12)

Ingredients:
- 1½ (16-oz.) jars spicy dill pickle spears, drained and pat dried
- 1 egg, beaten
- 1/4 cup milk
- 1 cup panko breadcrumbs
- 1 cup all-purpose flour
- 1/2 tsp. paprika
- Nonstick cooking spray

Directions:
1. In a shallow dish, mix together the flour and paprika. In a second dish, mix well milk and egg.
2. In a third dish, put the breadcrumbs. Coat the pickle spears with flour mixture, then dip into egg mixture and finally, coat evenly with the breadcrumbs.
3. Spray the pickle spears evenly with cooking spray. Set the temperature of Air Fryer to 440°F. Arrange the pickle spears in an Air Fryer basket in a single layer in 2 batches. Air Fry for about 14 minutes, flipping once halfway through. Serve.

Kale Chips

(Prep + Cook Time: 23 minutes | Servings: 4)

Ingredients:
- 1 head fresh kale; stems and ribs removed and cut into 1½ inch pieces
- 1/8 tsp. cayenne pepper
- 1 tbsp. olive oil
- 1 tsp. soy sauce
- A pinch of freshly ground black pepper

Directions:
1. Set the temperature of Air Fryer to 390°F. Take a large bowl and mix together all the ingredients.
2. Place the kale leaves in an Air Fryer basket in a single layer.
3. Air Fry for about 2 to 3 minutes, tossing once halfway through. Serve.

Coconut Shrimp Snack

(**Prep + Cook Time:** 22 minutes | **Servings:** 4)

Ingredients:
- 12 large shrimp; deveined and peeled
- 2 cups coconut; shredded
- 2 eggs; whisked
- 1 cup white flour
- Salt and black pepper to taste

Directions:
1. Put the coconut in one bowl, the flour in a second one and the eggs in a third.
2. Season the shrimp with the salt and pepper, then dredge them in the flour, then the eggs and then the coconut
3. Place the shrimp in your air fryer's basket and cook at 360°F for 12 minutes, flipping them halfway
4. Divide the shrimp into bowls and serve as a snack (or an appetizer, or even an entrée!)

Lemon Biscuits

(Prep + Cook Time: 20 minutes | Servings: 10)

Ingredients:
- 3½ oz. caster sugar
- 8½ oz. Self rising flour
- 3½ oz. cold butter
- 1 small egg
- 2 tbsp. fresh lemon juice
- 1 tsp. fresh lemon zest; finely grated
- 1 tsp. vanilla extract

Directions:
1. In a bowl, mix together the flour and sugar. Using two forks; cut in the butter until coarse crumb forms.
2. Add in the egg, vanilla extract, lemon juice and zest. Mix until a soft dough forms.
3. After that, take out the dough from bowl and put onto a floured surface. Now, roll it into an even thickness. (1/2 inch)
4. Cut the dough into medium-sized biscuits using a cookie cutter. Set the temperature of Air Fryer to 355°F. Place the biscuits in a baking sheet in a single layer.
5. Put the baking sheet in an Air Fryer basket. Air Fry for about 5 minutes or until golden brown.

Turmeric Carrot Chips

(**Prep + Cook Time:** 30 minutes | **Servings:** 4)

Ingredients:
- 4 carrots; thinly sliced
- 1/2 tsp. chaat masala
- 1/2 tsp. turmeric powder
- 1 tsp. olive oil
- Salt and black pepper to taste

Directions:
1. Place all ingredients in a bowl and toss well. Put the mixture in your air fryer's basket and cook at 370°F for 25 minutes, shaking the fryer from time to time. Serve as a snack

Rice Bites

(Prep + Cook Time: 35 minutes | Servings: 4)

Ingredients:
- 3 oz. mozzarella cheese, cubed
- 1/3 cup Parmesan cheese; grated
- 3/4 cup breadcrumbs
- 3 cups cooked risotto
- 1 egg, beaten

Directions:
1. In a bowl, mix together the risotto, Parmesan cheese and egg. Make 20 equal-sized balls from the mixture.
2. Insert a mozzarella cube in the center of each ball and using your fingers, smooth the risotto mixture to cover the mozzarella.

3. In a shallow dish, add the breadcrumbs. Coat the balls evenly with breadcrumbs.
4. Set the temperature of Air Fryer to 390°F.
5. Arrange the balls in an Air Fryer basket in a single layer in 2 batches. Air Fry for about 10 minutes or until they turn golden brown. Serve.

Coconut Cookies

(Prep + Cook Time: 27 minutes | Servings: 8)

Ingredients:
- 2¼ oz. caster sugar
- 1¼ oz. white chocolate; chopped
- 5 oz. Self rising flour
- 3½ oz. butter
- 1 small egg
- 3 tbsp. desiccated coconut
- 1 tsp. vanilla extract

Directions:
1. In a large bowl, add the sugar and butter and beat until fluffy and light.
2. Add the egg and vanilla extract and whisk until well combined. Now, add the flour and chocolate and mix well.
3. In a shallow bowl, place the coconut. With your hands, make small balls from the mixture and roll evenly into the coconut.
4. Place the balls onto an ungreased baking sheet about 1- inch apart and gently, press each ball.
5. Set the temperature of air fryer to 355°F. Place baking sheet into the air fryer basket. Air fry for about 8 minutes and then, another 4 minutes at 320°F.
6. Remove from air fryer and place the baking sheet onto a wire rack to cool for about 5 minutes.
7. Invert the cookies onto wire rack to cool completely before serving. Serve.

Balsamic Zucchini Slices

(**Prep + Cook Time:** 55 minutes | **Servings:** 6)

Ingredients:
- 3 zucchinis; thinly sliced
- 2 tbsp. avocado oil
- 2 tbsp. balsamic vinegar
- Salt and black pepper to taste

Directions:
1. Add all of the ingredients to a bowl and mix. Put the zucchini mixture in your air fryer's basket and cook at 220°F for 50 minutes. Serve as a snack and enjoy!

Cheesey Pastries

(Prep + Cook Time: 20 minutes | Servings: 6)

Ingredients:
- 4 oz. feta cheese, crumbled
- 2 frozen filo pastry sheets, thawed
- 2 tbsp. olive oil
- 1 scallion; finely chopped
- 1 egg yolk
- 2 tbsp. fresh parsley; finely chopped
- Salt and ground black pepper, as needed

Directions:
1. In a large bowl, add the egg yolk and beat well. Add in the feta cheese, scallion, parsley, salt and black pepper. Mix well.
2. Cut each filo pastry sheet in three strips. Add about 1 tsp. of feta mixture on the underside of a strip.
3. Fold the tip of sheet over the filling in a zigzag manner to form a triangle.
4. Repeat with the remaining strips and fillings. Set the temperature of Air Fryer to 390°F. Coat each pastry evenly with oil.
5. Place the pastries in an Air Fryer basket in a single layer.
6. Air Fry for about 3 minutes, then air fryer for about 2 minutes on 360°F. Serve.

Bacon Croquettes

(Prep + Cook Time: 23 minutes | Servings: 6)

Ingredients:
- 1 lb. thin bacon slices
- 1 lb. sharp cheddar cheese block; cut into 1-inch rectangular pieces
- 1/4 cup olive oil
- 1 cup breadcrumbs
- 1 cup all-purpose flour
- 3 eggs
- Salt; as your liking

Directions:
1. Wrap 2 bacon slices around 1 piece of cheddar cheese, covering completely. Repeat with the remaining bacon and cheese pieces.
2. Arrange the croquettes in a baking dish and freeze for about 5 minutes. Add the flour in a shallow dish.
3. In a second dish, crack the eggs and beat well. In a third dish, mix together the breadcrumbs, salt and oil.
4. Coat the croquettes with flour, then dip into beaten eggs and finally, evenly coat with the breadcrumbs mixture.
5. Set the temperature of Air Fryer to 390°F. Arrange the croquettes in an Air Fryer basket in a single layer. Air Fry for about 7 to 8 minutes. Serve hot.

Buttermilk Biscuits

(Prep + Cook Time: 23 minutes | Servings: 4)

Ingredients:
- 1/2 cup cake flour
- 1/4 cup cold unsalted butter; cut into cubes
- 3/4 cup buttermilk
- 1¼ cups all-purpose flour
- 2 tbsp. butter, melted
- 1 tsp. granulated sugar
- 1/4 tsp. baking soda
- 1/2 tsp. baking powder
- Salt; as your liking

Directions:
1. In a large bowl, sift together the flours, baking soda, baking powder, sugar and salt. Using two forks; cut in the butter until coarse crumb forms. Slowly, add in the buttermilk and mix until a smooth dough forms.
2. After that, take out the dough from bowl and put onto a floured surface. Using your hands, press it into 1/2 inch thickness.
3. With a 1 ¾-inch round cookie cutter; cut the biscuits.
4. Cut out the remaining biscuits from dough. Set the temperature of Air Fryer to 400°F. Place the biscuits in a pie pan in a single layer and coat with butter.
5. Put the pie pan in an Air Fryer basket. Air Fry for about 8 minutes. Serve.

Tortilla Chips

(Prep + Cook Time: 16 minutes | Servings: 6)

Ingredients:
- 8 corn tortillas; cut into triangles
- 1 tbsp. olive oil
- Salt, to taste

Directions:
1. Set the temperature of Air Fryer to 390°F. Coat the tortilla chips with oil.
2. Sprinkle each side of the tortillas with salt Place them in an Air Fryer basket in a single layer in 2 batches. Air Fry for about 3 minutes. Enjoy with your favorite salsa.

Cod Nuggets

(Prep + Cook Time: 25 minutes | Servings: 4)

Ingredients:

- 1 lb. cod; cut into 1x2½-inch strips
- 3/4 cup breadcrumbs
- 1 cup all-purpose flour
- 2 eggs
- 2 tbsp. olive oil
- A pinch of salt

Directions:

1. Add the flour in a shallow dish. Crack the eggs in a second dish and beat well. In a third dish, mix together the breadcrumbs, salt and oil.
2. Coat the nuggets with flour, then dip into beaten eggs and finally, evenly coat with the breadcrumbs.
3. Set the temperature of Air Fryer to 390°F. Add the croquettes in an Air Fryer basket in a single layer.
4. Air Fry for about 8 to 10 minutes.

Cream Cheese Balls

(**Prep + Cook Time:** 10 minutes | **Servings:** 6)

Ingredients:

- 4 oz. cream cheese
- 14 pepperoni slices; chopped.
- 1 tbsp. basil; chopped.
- 8 black olives; pitted and minced
- 2 tbsp. basil pesto
- Salt and black pepper to taste

Directions:

1. In a bowl, place all of the ingredients and stir.
2. Shape the mixture into medium balls and then place them in your lined air fryer's basket. Cook at 360°F for 5 minutes. Serve as a snack

Beef Dip

(**Prep + Cook Time:** 40 minutes | **Servings:** 6)

Ingredients:

- 2 lbs. ground beef; browned
- 28 oz. canned tomatoes; crushed
- 1/4 cup beef stock
- 2 carrots; chopped.
- 4 garlic cloves; minced
- 2 celery ribs; chopped.
- 1 yellow onion; chopped.
- 1 tbsp. olive oil
- A splash of red wine
- A pinch of basil; dried
- A pinch of oregano; dried
- Salt and black pepper to taste

Directions:

1. Place all the ingredients in a pan that fits your air fryer and whisk.
2. Put the pan in the fryer and cook at 380°F for 30 minutes. Divide into bowls and serve as a snack or appetizer

Veggie Bread Rolls

(Prep + Cook Time: 53 minutes | Servings: 8)

Ingredients:

- 5 large potatoes, peeled
- 8 bread slices, trimmed
- 2 small onions; finely chopped
- 2 green chilies, seeded and chopped
- 2 curry leaves
- 2 tbsp. vegetable oil; divided
- 1/2 tsp. ground turmeric
- Salt; as your liking

Directions:

1. In the pan of a boiling water, add the potatoes and cook for about 15 to 20 minutes.
2. Drain the potatoes well and with a potato masher, mash the potatoes.
3. In a skillet, heat 1 tsp. of oil over a medium heat and sauté the onion for about 4 to 5 minutes.
4. Add the green chilies, curry leaves and turmeric. Sauté for about 1 minute.

5. Add in the mashed potatoes and salt and mix them well. Once done, remove from the heat and set aside to cool completely.
6. Make 8 equal-sized oval-shaped patties from the mixture. Wet the bread slices completely with water.
7. Using your hands, press each bread slice between your hands to remove the excess water.
8. Place 1 bread slice in your palm and place 1 patty in the center.
9. Roll the bread slice in a spindle shape and seal the edges to secure the filling.
10. Coat the roll with some oil. Repeat with the remaining slices, filling and oil.
11. Set the temperature of Air Fryer to 390°F. Grease the Air Fryer basket with cooking spray.
12. Add rolls into the prepared basket in a single layer. Air Fry for about 12 to 13 minutes. Serve.

Lemony Apple Bites

(**Prep + Cook Time:** 10 minutes | **Servings:** 4)

Ingredients:
- 3 big apples; cored, peeled and cubed
- 1/2 cup caramel sauce
- 2 tsp. lemon juice

Directions:
1. In your air fryer, mix all the ingredients; toss well.
2. Cook at 340°F for 5 minutes. Divide into cups and serve as a snack

Veggie Pastries

(Prep + Cook Time: 57 minutes | Servings: 8)

Ingredients:
- 2 large potatoes, peeled
- 1/2 cup carrot, peeled and chopped
- 1/2 cup green peas, shelled
- 3 puff pastry sheets
- 1/2 cup onion; chopped
- 2 garlic cloves; minced
- 1 tbsp. olive oil
- 2 tbsp. fresh ginger; minced
- Salt and ground black pepper, as needed

Directions:
1. In the pan of a boiling water, put the potatoes and cook for about 15 to 20 minutes. Drain the potatoes well and with a potato masher, mash the potatoes.
2. In a skillet, heat the oil over medium heat and sauté the carrot, onion, ginger and garlic for about 4 to 5 minutes. Drain all the fat from the skillet.
3. Stir in the mashed potatoes, peas, salt and black pepper. Cook for about 1 to 2 minutes.
4. Once done, remove the potato mixture from heat and set aside to cool completely.
5. Put the puff pastry onto a smooth surface. Cut each puff pastry sheet into four pieces and then cut each piece in a round shape. Add about two tablespoons of veggie filling over each pastry round.
6. Moisten the edges using your wet fingers. Fold each pastry round in half to seal the filling.
7. Using a fork, firmly press the edges. Set the temperature of Air Fryer to 390°F. Add the pastries in an Air Fryer basket in a single layer in 2 batches. Air Fry for about 5 minutes. Serve.

Lentils Snack

(**Prep + Cook Time:** 17 minutes | **Servings:** 4)

Ingredients:
- 15 oz. canned lentils; drained
- 1 tsp. sweet paprika
- 1/2 tsp. cumin; ground
- 1 tbsp. olive oil
- Salt and black pepper to taste

Directions:
1. Place all ingredients in a bowl and mix well. Transfer the mixture to your air fryer and cook at 400°F for 12 minutes
2. Divide into bowls and serve as a snack (or a side, or appetizer!)

Carrot Dip

(**Prep + Cook Time:** 25 minutes | **Servings:** 6)

Ingredients:
- 2 cups carrots; grated
- 4 tbsp. butter; melted
- A pinch of cayenne pepper
- 1 tbsp. chives
- Salt and black pepper to taste

Directions:
1. Add all ingredients to a pan that fits your air fryer and mix. Place the pan in the fryer and cook at 380°F for 15 minutes
2. Blend a bit using an immersion blender and then divide into bowls. Serve as a dip.

Minty Cauliflower Spread

(**Prep + Cook Time:** 20 minutes | **Servings:** 6)

Ingredients:
- 3 cups veggie stock
- 8 garlic cloves; minced
- 2 tbsp. butter; melted
- 6 cups cauliflower florets
- Salt and black pepper to taste
- A handful of mint; chopped.

Directions:
1. Place all the ingredients into a pan that fits your air fryer; mix well.
2. Put the pan into the air fryer and cook at 370°F for 15 minutes. Blend using an immersion blender, divide into bowls and serve

Broccoli Bites

(**Prep + Cook Time:** 20 minutes | **Servings:** 6)

Ingredients:
- 1 broccoli head; florets separated
- 1 tsp. butter; melted
- 2 tsp. garlic powder
- 1 tsp. olive oil
- Salt and black pepper to taste

Directions:
1. Spread the broccoli florets on a lined baking sheet that fits your air fryer; then add all other ingredients and toss.
2. Cook at 450°F for 15 minutes. Divide into bowls and serve as a snack (or as a side)

Banana Chips

(**Prep + Cook Time:** 10 minutes | **Servings:** 8)

Ingredients:
- 1 banana; peeled and sliced into 16 pieces
- 1/4 cup peanut butter; soft
- 1 tbsp. vegetable oil

Directions:
1. Put the banana slices in your air fryer's basket and drizzle the oil over them
2. Cook at 360°F for 5 minutes. Transfer to bowls and serve them dipped in peanut butter.

Kale Crackers

(**Prep + Cook Time:** 30 minutes | **Servings:** 6)

Ingredients:
- 4 cups flax seed; soaked overnight, drained and ground
- 4 bunches kale; chopped.
- 1/3 cup avocado oil
- 4 garlic cloves; minced
- 1 bunch basil; chopped.

Directions:
1. Place all ingredients in your food processor and pulse well. Spread the mixture in your air fryer's pan and cut into medium crackers.
2. Cook in the air fryer cook at 380°F for 20 minutes. Cool and serve as a snack

Chili Dip

(Prep + Cook Time: 22 minutes | **Servings:** 4)

Ingredients:
- 6 ancho chilies; dried, seedless and chopped.
- 2 garlic cloves; minced
- 2 tbsp. apple cider vinegar
- 1 cup water
- 1/2 tsp. oregano; dried
- 1½ tsp. sugar
- Salt and black pepper to taste

Directions:
1. Mix all the ingredients together in a pan that fits your air fryer; stir well.
2. Place the pan in the air fryer and cook at 380°F for 12 minutes. Transfer the mixture to a blender and pulse. Divide into bowls and serve as a dip

Coriander Bites

(Prep + Cook Time: 30 minutes | **Servings:** 4)

Ingredients:
- 12 oz. tofu; cubed
- 2 tsp. olive oil
- 1 tsp. sweet paprika
- 2 tbsp. fish sauce
- 2 tbsp. soy sauce
- 1 tbsp. coriander paste

Directions:
1. In a bowl, mix the tofu, paprika, 1 tsp. of the oil, coriander paste, soy sauce and fish sauce; toss and set aside for 10 minutes
2. Transfer the coriander tofu bites to your air fryer's basket, drizzle the remaining tsp. of the oil over them and cook at 350°F for 20 minutes, shaking halfway. Serve as a snack

Tomato Dip

(Prep + Cook Time: 15 minutes | **Servings:** 4)

Ingredients:
- 1 cup tomato puree
- 2 garlic cloves; minced
- 1 yellow onion; chopped.
- 1/8 tsp. cumin powder
- 4 tbsp. white vinegar
- 4 tbsp. honey
- 1 tsp. liquid smoke
- 1 tsp. Tabasco sauce
- 1 tbsp. olive oil
- Salt and black pepper to taste

Directions:
1. Place all the ingredients in a pan that fits your air fryer and mix well
2. Put the pan into the fryer and cook at 370°F for 10 minutes. Whisk well, divide into bowls and serve as a dip.

Crab Bites

(Prep + Cook Time: 17 minutes | **Servings:** 6)

Ingredients:
- 10 crabsticks; cut into medium bites
- 2 tsp. olive oil
- Salt and black pepper to taste

Directions:
1. Mix all the ingredients in your air fryer.
2. Cook at 350°F for 12 minutes. Divide into bowls and serve

Corn Dip

(Prep + Cook Time: 23 minutes | **Servings:** 4)

Ingredients:
- 2 cups corn kernels
- 1 cup chicken stock
- 2 tbsp. white wine
- 2 tsp. butter; melted
- 1 yellow onion; chopped.
- 1 tbsp. olive oil
- 1 tsp. thyme; chopped.
- Salt and black pepper to taste

Directions:
1. Put a pan that fits your air fryer over medium heat and add the oil and the butter; heat up.
2. Add the onion; stir and sauté for 3 minutes. Add the corn, stock, wine, salt, pepper and thyme; stir
3. Place the pan in the fryer and cook at 390°F for 15 minutes
4. Blend a bit using an immersion blender, divide into bowls and serve as a party dip or appetizer.

Sausage Bites

(Prep + Cook Time: 25 minutes | **Servings:** 9)

Ingredients:
- 5 oz. ground sausage meat
- 1 yellow onion; chopped.
- 3 tbsp. breadcrumbs
- 1/2 tsp. garlic; minced
- Salt and black pepper to taste

Directions:
1. Mix all of the ingredients in a bowl; stir well. Shape medium balls out of this mix, place them in your air fryer and cook at 360°F for 15 minutes
2. Serve as an appetizer, or, would be a great breakfast food!

Zucchini and Mint Spread

(Prep + Cook Time: 22 minutes | **Servings:** 4)

Ingredients:
- 1½ lbs. zucchini; chopped.
- 1/2 cup veggie stock
- 1 yellow onion; chopped.
- 1 tbsp. olive oil
- 1 bunch mint; chopped.
- 2 garlic cloves; minced
- Salt and white pepper to taste

Directions:
1. Over medium heat, heat up the oil in a pan that fits your air fryer
2. Add the onions and garlic, stir and cook for 1-2 minutes. Add the remaining ingredients; stir well.
3. Place the pan in the air fryer and cook at 380°F for 10 minutes
4. Blend using an immersion blender and serve as an appetizer or party spread.

Italian Mozzarella Sticks

(Prep + Cook Time: 18 minutes | **Servings:** 12)

Ingredients:
- 2 eggs; whisked
- 8 mozzarella cheese strings; halved
- 1 tbsp. Italian seasoning
- 1 cup parmesan cheese; grated
- A drizzle of olive oil
- Salt and black pepper to taste

Directions:
1. In a bowl, mix the parmesan, salt, pepper and Italian seasoning; stir. Put the whisked eggs in another bowl.
2. Dip the mozzarella sticks in the egg mixture, then in the parmesan mix
3. Dip the sticks one more time in egg and parmesan and place them in your air fryer's basket. Drizzle the oil over them and cook at 390°F for 8 minutes, flipping them halfway. Serve as an appetizer

Chives Radish Snack

(**Prep + Cook Time:** 15 minutes | **Servings:** 4)

Ingredients:
- 16 radishes; sliced
- 1 tbsp. chives; chopped.
- A drizzle of olive oil
- Salt and black pepper to taste

Directions:
1. In a bowl, mix the radishes, salt, pepper and oil; toss well
2. Place the radishes in your air fryer's basket and cook at 350°F for 10 minutes. Divide into bowls and serve with chives sprinkled on top

Zucchini Balls

(**Prep + Cook Time:** 22 minutes | **Servings:** 8)

Ingredients:
- 3 zucchinis; grated
- 1/2 cup dill; chopped.
- 1 egg
- 1/2 cup white flour
- 2 garlic cloves; minced
- Cooking spray
- Salt and black pepper to taste

Directions:
1. In a bowl, mix all the ingredients and stir. Shape the mix into medium balls and place them into your air fryer's basket
2. Cook at 375°F for 12 minutes, flipping them halfway. Serve them as a snack right away.

Potato Chips

(**Prep + Cook Time:** 17 minutes | **Servings:** 4)

Ingredients:
- 4 potatoes; thinly sliced
- 1 tbsp. olive oil
- Sour cream for serving
- Salt and black pepper to taste

Directions:
1. Brush the potato slices with the oil and place them in your air fryer's basket. Cook at 400°F for 12 minutes, flipping them halfway. Serve as a snack along with the sour cream

Buttery Onion Dip

(**Prep + Cook Time:** 40 minutes | **Servings:** 8)

Ingredients:
- 2½ lbs. red onions; chopped.
- 6 tbsp. butter; softened
- 1/2 tsp. baking soda
- Salt and black pepper to taste

Directions:
1. Place the butter into a pan that fits your air fryer and heat over medium heat.
2. Add the onions and the baking soda, stir and sauté for 5 minutes. Transfer the pan to your air fryer and cook at 370°F for 25 minutes. Serve warm as a party dip

Cheesy Tomatoes and Sausage Dip

(**Prep + Cook Time:** 15 minutes | **Servings:** 4)

Ingredients:
- 5 oz. canned tomatoes; chopped.
- 2 cups processed cheese; cut into chunks
- 1 cup Italian sausage; cooked and chopped.
- 4 tbsp. chicken stock

Directions:
1. Place all the ingredients into a pan that fits your air fryer and mix well.
2. Put the pan into the fryer and cook at 378°F for 10 minutes. Stir well and serve as a party dip or appetizer; enjoy!

Lentils Spread

(Prep + Cook Time: 25 minutes | **Servings:** 4)

Ingredients:

- 30 oz. canned tomatoes; crushed
- 1 cup chicken stock
- 3 garlic cloves; minced
- 2 cups canned red lentils; drained
- Salt and black pepper to taste

Directions:

1. Add all of the ingredients to a pan that fits your air fryer and stir
2. Place the pan into the fryer and cook at 370°F for 20 minutes. Blend the mix with an immersion blender. Divide into bowls and serve as a snack or an appetizer

Cheesy Beef Meatballs

(Prep + Cook Time: 18 minutes | **Servings:** 8)

Ingredients:

- 4 oz. beef meat; minced
- 1/2 tbsp. lemon peel; grated
- 1 tbsp. breadcrumbs
- 2 tbsp. feta cheese; crumbled
- 1 tbsp. oregano; chopped.
- Salt and black pepper to taste

Directions:

1. Place all of the ingredients in a bowl and stir well. Shape medium meatballs out of this mix.
2. Place the meatballs in your air fryer's basket and cook at 400°F for 8 minutes. Serve as an appetizer, or even as an entrée

Minty Shrimp Mix

(Prep + Cook Time: 13 minutes | **Servings:** 12)

Ingredients:

- 10 oz. shrimp; peeled and deveined
- 2 tbsp. olive oil
- 1/3 cup red wine
- 1 tbsp. mint; chopped.

Directions:

1. In your air fryer, mix / toss all the ingredients.
2. Cook at 390°F for 8 minutes. Divide into bowls and serve as an appetizer

Lemony Endives Appetizer

(Prep + Cook Time: 20 minutes | **Servings:** 4)

Ingredients:

- 6 endives; halved lengthwise
- 1/2 cup yogurt
- 1 tsp. garlic powder
- 3 tbsp. lemon juice
- Salt and black pepper to taste

Directions:

1. In a bowl, mix all ingredients except the endives; whisk. Now add the endives, toss and set them aside for 10 minutes.
2. Place the endives in your air fryer's basket and cook at 360°F for 10 minutes. Serve as an appetizer

Chicken Sticks

(Prep + Cook Time: 26 minutes | **Servings:** 4)

Ingredients:

- 1 lb. chicken breast; skinless, boneless and cut in medium sticks
- 3/4 cup white flour
- 1 cup breadcrumbs
- 1 egg; whisked
- 1/2 tbsp. olive oil
- Salt and black pepper to taste

Directions:

1. Combine the flour, salt and pepper in a bowl. Put the egg in another bowl and the breadcrumbs in a third one.
2. Dredge the chicken pieces in the flour, then the egg and then the breadcrumbs
3. Place the chicken pieces in your air fryer's basket, drizzle the oil over them and cook at 400°F for 16 minutes, flipping them halfway. Serve right away and enjoy

Mushroom Salad

(Prep + Cook Time: 35 minutes | **Servings:** 6)

Ingredients:

- 10 oz. shiitake mushrooms; chopped.
- 1 oz. parmesan cheese; grated
- 10 oz. cremini mushrooms; chopped.
- 10 oz. Portobello mushrooms; chopped.
- 1/4 cup olive oil
- 1/4 cup coconut cream
- 1 yellow onion; chopped.
- 1 tbsp. thyme; chopped.
- 1 cup chicken stock
- 3 garlic cloves; minced
- 1 tbsp. parsley; minced
- Salt and black pepper to taste

Directions:

1. In a pan that fits your air fryer, heat up the oil over medium heat. Add the onions, garlic, thyme, salt and pepper; stir and cook for 3-4 minutes
2. Add the stock and the mushrooms; stir and cook for 1-2 minutes more
3. Place the pan in the air fryer and cook at 350°F for 20 minutes
4. Add the cream, parmesan and parsley and stir well. Divide into bowls and serve as an appetizer.

Leek Spread

(Prep + Cook Time: 20 minutes | **Servings:** 6)

Ingredients:

- 3 leeks; roughly chopped.
- 1/2 cup whipping cream
- 2 tbsp. butter; melted
- 3 tbsp. lemon juice
- Salt and pepper to taste

Directions:

1. In a pan that fits your air fryer, mix the leeks, butter, lemon juice, salt and pepper; stir well.
2. Put the pan into the fryer and cook at 380°F for 15 minutes
3. Transfer the mixture to a blender, add the cream and pulse. Divide into bowls and serve cold

Fish & Seafood

Coconut Cod Fillets

(Prep + Cook Time: 15 minutes | **Servings:** 4)

Ingredients:
- 4 medium cod fillets; boneless
- 1/2 cup parsley; chopped.
- 2 garlic cloves; chopped.
- 1/2 jalapeno; chopped.
- 1/2 cup coconut milk
- 1 tsp. ginger; grated
- A drizzle of olive oil
- Salt and black pepper to taste

Directions:
1. Place all ingredients except the fish in your blender; pulse well
2. In a baking dish that fits your air fryer, place the fish along with the coconut milk mixture and toss gently.
3. Place the dish in your air fryer and cook at 380°F for 10 minutes. Divide between plates and serve hot.

Cod Cakes

(Prep + Cook Time: 34 minutes | Servings: 6)

Ingredients:
- 1 lb. cod fillet
- 1/3 cup coconut; grated and divided
- 1 scallion, finely chopped
- 1 egg
- 1 tbsp. fresh lime juice
- 2 tbsp. fresh parsley; chopped
- 1 tsp. fresh lime zest, finely grated
- 1 tsp. red chili paste
- Salt; as your liking

Directions:
1. **For cod cakes:** in a food processor, add the cod fillet, lime zest, egg, chili paste, salt and lime juice and pulse until smooth.
2. Transfer the cod mixture into a bowl. Add 2 tbsp. of coconut, scallion and parsley. Mix until well combined.
3. Make 12 equal-sized round cakes from the mixture. In a shallow bowl; place the remaining coconut. Coat the cod cakes evenly with coconut.
4. Set the temperature of air fryer to 375°F. Grease an air fryer basket.
5. Arrange cod cakes into the prepared air fryer basket in 2 batches in a single layer.
6. Air fry for about 7 minutes.
7. Remove from air fryer and place 2 cod cakes onto each serving plate. Serve warm.

Cajun Spiced Salmon

(Prep + Cook Time: 17 minutes | Servings: 2)

Ingredients:
- 2 (7-oz) salmon fillets
- 1 tbsp. fresh lemon juice
- 1 tbsp. Cajun seasoning
- 1/2 tsp. sugar

Directions:
1. Set the temperature of air fryer to 356°F. Grease an air fryer grill pan.
2. Sprinkle the salmon evenly with Cajun seasoning and sugar.
3. Arrange fish into the prepared air fryer grill pan, skin-side up. Air fry for about 7 minutes.
4. Remove from air fryer and place the salmon fillets onto the serving plates. Drizzle with the lemon juice and serve hot.

Asian Style Cod

(Prep + Cook Time: 35 minutes | Servings: 2)

Ingredients:

- 2 (7-oz) cod fillets
- 2 scallions (green part), sliced
- 1/4 cup fresh cilantro; chopped
- 1 cup water
- 5 little squares rock sugar
- 5 ginger slices
- 5 tbsp. light soy sauce
- 3 tbsp. olive oil
- 1/4 tsp. sesame oil
- 1 tsp. dark soy sauce
- Salt and ground black pepper; as your liking

Directions:

1. Season each cod fillet evenly with salt and black pepper and drizzle with sesame oil. Set aside at room temperature for about 15 to 20 minutes.
2. Set the temperature of air fryer to 355°F. Grease an air fryer basket.
3. Arrange cod fillets into the prepared air fryer basket in a single layer. Air fry for about 12 minutes.
4. Meanwhile; in a small pan, add the water and bring it to a boil.
5. Add the rock sugar and both soy sauces and cook until sugar is dissolved, stirring continuously. Remove from the heat and set aside.
6. Remove cod fillets from air fryer and transfer them onto serving plates. Top each fillet with scallion and cilantro.
7. Heat the olive oil in a small frying pan over medium heat and sauté ginger slices for about 2 to 3 minutes.
8. Remove the frying pan from heat and discard the ginger slices. Carefully; pour the hot oil evenly over cod fillets. Top with the sauce mixture and serve.

Sweet and Sour Glazed Salmon

(Prep + Cook Time: 32 minutes | Servings: 2)

Ingredients:

- 4 (3 ½ -oz) salmon fillets
- 1/3 cup honey
- 1/3 cup soy sauce
- 1 tsp. water
- 3 tsp. rice wine vinegar

Directions:

1. In a small bowl; mix together the soy sauce, honey, vinegar and water.
2. In another bowl; reserve about half of the mixture. Add salmon fillets in the remaining mixture and coat well.
3. Cover the bowl and refrigerate to marinate for about 2 hours.
4. Set the temperature of air fryer to 355°F. Grease an air fryer basket. Arrange salmon fillets into the prepared air fryer basket in a single layer.
5. Air fry for about 12 minutes, flipping once halfway through and coating with the reserved marinade after every 3 minutes.
6. Remove from air fryer and place the salmon fillets onto serving plates. Serve hot.

Salmon with Broccoli

(Prep + Cook Time: 27 minutes | Servings: 2)

Ingredients:

- 2 (6-oz) skin-on salmon fillets
- 1 scallion, thinly sliced
- 1 ½ cups small broccoli florets
- 1 (½-inch) piece fresh ginger; grated
- 2 tbsp. vegetable oil, divided
- 1 tbsp. soy sauce
- 1 tsp. light brown sugar
- 1/4 tsp. cornstarch
- 1 tsp. rice vinegar
- Salt and ground black pepper; as your liking

Directions:

1. In a bowl; mix together the broccoli, 1 tbsp. of oil, salt and black pepper.
2. In another bowl; mix well the ginger, soy sauce, vinegar, sugar and cornstarch.
3. Coat the salmon fillets evenly with remaining oil and then with the ginger mixture.
4. Set the temperature of air fryer to 375°F. Grease an air fryer basket. Arrange broccoli florets into the prepared air fryer basket.
5. Place the salmon fillets on top of broccoli, flesh-side down. Air fry for about 12 minutes.
6. Remove from air fryer and place the salmon fillets onto serving plates. Serve hot alongside the broccoli.

Coconut Crusted Shrimp

(Prep + Cook Time: 55 minutes | Servings: 3)

Ingredients:

- 1/2 cup panko breadcrumbs
- 1 lb. large shrimp; peeled and deveined
- 8-oz coconut milk
- 1/2 cup sweetened coconut, shredded
- Salt and ground black pepper; as your liking

Directions:

1. In a shallow bowl; add the coconut milk. In another bowl; mix well coconut, breadcrumbs, salt and black pepper.
2. Dip the shrimp into coconut milk and then, coat with the coconut mixture.
3. Set the temperature of air fryer to 350°F. Grease an air fryer basket.
4. Arrange shrimp into the prepared air fryer basket in 2 batches in a single layer.
5. Air fry for about 17 to 20 minutes.
6. Remove from air fryer and transfer the shrimp onto serving plates. Serve hot.

Salmon with Shrimp and Pasta

(Prep + Cook Time: 38 minutes | Servings: 4)

Ingredients:

- 1/2 lb. cherry tomatoes; chopped
- 8 large prawns; peeled and deveined
- 4 (4-oz) salmon steaks
- 14-oz pasta (of your choice)
- 2 tbsp. olive oil
- 2 tbsp. fresh lemon juice
- 2 tbsp. fresh thyme; chopped
- 4 tbsp. pesto, divided

Directions:

1. In a large pan of salted boiling water, add the pasta and cook for about 8 to 10 minutes or until desired doneness.
2. Meanwhile; in the bottom of a baking dish, spread 1 tbsp. of pesto. Place salmon steaks and tomatoes over pesto in a single layer and drizzle evenly with the oil.
3. Add the prawns on top in a single layer. Drizzle with lemon juice and sprinkle with thyme.
4. Set the temperature of air fryer to 390°F. Arrange the baking dish in air fryer and air fry for about 8 minutes. Once done, remove the salmon mixture from air fryer. Drain the pasta and transfer into a large bowl.
5. Add the remaining pesto and toss to coat well. Add the pasta evenly onto each serving plate and top with salmon mixture. Serve immediately.

Eastern Style Catfish

(Prep + Cook Time: 30 minutes | Servings: 5)

Ingredients:

- 5 (6-oz) catfish fillets
- 1/2 cup yellow mustard
- 1/2 cup cornmeal
- 1/4 cup all-purpose flour
- 1 cup milk
- 2 tbsp. dried parsley flakes
- 1/4 tsp. onion powder
- 1/4 tsp. garlic powder
- 1/4 tsp. red chili powder
- 2 tsp. fresh lemon juice
- 1/4 tsp. cayenne pepper
- Olive oil cooking spray
- Salt and ground black pepper; as your liking

Directions:

1. In a large bowl; place the catfish, milk and lemon juice and refrigerate for about 15 minutes. In a shallow bowl; add the mustard.
2. In another bowl; mix together the cornmeal, flour, parsley flakes and spices.
3. Remove the catfish fillets from milk mixture and with paper towels, pat them dry.
4. Coat each fish fillet with mustard and then, roll evenly into cornmeal mixture.
5. Set the temperature of air fryer to 400°F. Grease an air fryer basket.
6. Arrange catfish fillets into the prepared air fryer basket in a single layer and spray with the cooking spray.
7. Air fry for about 10 minutes. Flip the side and spray with the cooking spray. Air fry for about 3-5 minutes.
8. Remove from air fryer and transfer the catfish fillets onto serving plates. Serve hot.

Spicy Salmon

(Prep + Cook Time: 21 minutes | Servings: 2)

Ingredients:

- 2 (6-oz) 1½-inch thick salmon fillets
- 1 tsp. onion powder
- 1 tsp. garlic powder
- 2 tsp. olive oil
- 1 tsp. smoked paprika
- 1 tsp. cayenne pepper
- Salt and ground black pepper; as your liking

Directions:

1. Add the spices in a bowl and mix well. Drizzle the salmon fillets with oil and then, rub with the spice mixture.
2. Set the temperature of air fryer to 390°F. Grease an air fryer basket.
3. Arrange salmon fillets into the prepared air fryer basket in a single layer. Air fry for about 9-11 minutes.
4. Remove from air fryer and place the salmon fillets onto the serving plates. Serve hot.

Prawn Burgers

(Prep + Cook Time: 26 minutes | Servings: 2)

Ingredients:

- 3 cups fresh baby greens
- 1/2 cup breadcrumbs
- 1/2 cup prawns, peeled, deveined and finely chopped
- 2 to 3 tbsp. onion, finely chopped
- 1/2 tsp. red chili powder
- 1/2 tsp. ground cumin
- 1/4 tsp. ground turmeric
- 1/2 tsp. ginger, minced
- 1/2 tsp. garlic, minced
- Salt and ground black pepper; as your liking

Directions:

1. In a large bowl; mix together the prawns, breadcrumbs, onion, ginger, garlic and spices. Make small-sized patties from the mixture.

2. Set the temperature of air fryer to 390°F. Grease an air fryer basket.
3. Arrange patties into the prepared air fryer basket in a single layer.
4. Air fry for about 5 to 6 minutes. Remove from air fryer and transfer the prawn burgers onto serving plates. Serve warm alongside the baby greens.

Maple Glazed Salmon

(Prep + Cook Time: 18 minutes | Servings: 2)

Ingredients:
- 2 (6-oz) salmon fillets
- 2 tbsp. maple syrup
- Salt; as your liking

Directions:
1. Sprinkle the salmon fillets evenly with salt and then, coat with maple syrup.
2. Set the temperature of air fryer to 355°F. Grease an air fryer basket.
3. Arrange salmon fillets into the prepared air fryer basket in a single layer. Air Fry for about 8 minutes.
4. Remove from air fryer and place the salmon fillets onto serving plates. Serve hot.

Breaded Flounder

(Prep + Cook Time: 27 minutes | Servings: 3)

Ingredients:
- 3 (6-oz) flounder fillets
- 1 lemon, sliced
- 1 cup dry breadcrumbs
- 1/4 cup vegetable oil
- 1 egg

Directions:
1. In a shallow bowl; beat the egg in another bowl; add the breadcrumbs and oil. Mix until crumbly mixture is formed.
2. Dip flounder fillets into the beaten egg and then, coat with the breadcrumb mixture.
3. Set the temperature of air fryer to 356°F. Grease an air fryer basket.
4. Arrange flounder fillets into the prepared air fryer basket in a single layer. Air fry for about 12 minutes.
5. Remove from air fryer and transfer the flounder fillets onto serving plates. Garnish with the lemon slices and serve hot.

Easy Salmon

(Prep + Cook Time: 15 minutes | Servings: 2)

Ingredients:
- 2 (6-oz) salmon fillets
- 1 tbsp. olive oil
- Salt and ground black pepper; as your liking

Directions:
1. Set the temperature of air fryer to 360°F. Grease an air fryer basket. Season each salmon fillet with salt and black pepper and then, coat with the oil.
2. Arrange salmon fillets into the prepared air fryer basket in a single layer.
3. Air fry for about 8 to 10 minutes. Remove from air fryer and place the salmon fillets onto the serving plates. Serve hot.

Salmon with Asparagus

(Prep + Cook Time: 26 minutes | Servings: 2)

Ingredients:
- 2 (6-oz) boneless salmon fillets
- 1 bunch asparagus
- 2 tbsp. fresh parsley; roughly chopped
- 2 tbsp. fresh dill; roughly chopped
- 1 ½ tbsp. fresh lemon juice
- 1 tbsp. olive oil
- Salt and ground black pepper; as your liking

Directions:
1. In a small bowl; mix well the lemon juice, oil, herbs, salt and black pepper.
2. In another large bowl; mix together the salmon and 3/4 of oil mixture.
3. In a second large bowl; add the asparagus and remaining oil mixture. Mix them well.
4. Set the temperature of air fryer to 400°F. Grease an air fryer basket. Arrange asparagus into the prepared air fryer basket. Air fry for about 2 to 3 minutes.
5. Place the salmon fillets on top of asparagus and air fry for about 8 minutes.
6. Remove from air fryer and place the salmon fillets onto serving plates. Serve hot alongside the asparagus.

Salmon with Green Beans

(Prep + Cook Time: 27 minutes | Servings: 4)

Ingredients:

For Green Beans:
- 5 cups frozen green beans
- 1 tbsp. avocado oil
- Salt; as your liking

For Salmon:
- 4 (6-oz) salmon fillets
- 2 garlic cloves, minced
- 2 tbsp. fresh lemon juice
- 1 tbsp. olive oil
- 2 tbsp. fresh dill; chopped
- Salt; as your liking

Directions:
1. Set the temperature of air fryer to 375°F. Grease an air fryer basket. In a large bowl; mix well the green beans, oil and salt.
2. Arrange green beans into the prepared air fryer basket. Air fry for about 6 minutes.
3. Meanwhile; for salmon: in a bowl; mix together the garlic, dill, lemon juice and olive oil.
4. Remove the basket from air fryer. Flip the green beans and top with salmon fillets.
5. Place the garlic mixture evenly on top of each salmon fillet and then, sprinkle with the salt. Air fry for about 6 minutes.
6. Remove from air fryer and place the salmon fillets onto serving plates. Serve hot alongside the green beans.

Zesty Salmon

(Prep + Cook Time: 18 minutes | Servings: 3)

Ingredients:
- 1 ½ lbs. salmon
- 1 lemon; cut into slices
- 1 tbsp. fresh dill; chopped
- 1/2 tsp. red chili powder
- Salt and ground black pepper; as your liking

Directions:
1. Set the temperature of air fryer to 375°F. Grease an air fryer basket.
2. Season the salmon evenly with chili powder, salt and black pepper. Arrange salmon into the prepared air fryer basket.
3. Place the lemon slices over the salmon. Air fry for about 8 minutes.
4. Remove from air fryer and place the salmon fillets onto serving plates.
5. Garnish with fresh dill and serve.

Parmesan Clams

(**Prep + Cook Time:** 22 minutes | **Servings:** 4)

Ingredients:
- 24 clams; shucked
- 3 garlic cloves; minced
- 4 tbsp. butter; softened
- 1/4 cup parsley; chopped.
- 1 cup breadcrumbs
- 1/4 cup parmesan cheese; grated
- 1 tsp. oregano; dried

Directions:
1. In a bowl, combine the breadcrumbs, parmesan, oregano, parsley, butter and garlic; mix well.
2. Divide the breadcrumb mixture into the exposed clams
3. Put the clams in your air fryer and cook at 380°F for 12 minutes. Serve and enjoy!

Crispy Cod Sticks

(Prep + Cook Time: 27 minutes | Servings: 2)

Ingredients:
- 3 (4-oz) skinless cod fillets; cut into rectangular pieces
- 1 green chili, finely chopped
- 2 garlic cloves, minced
- 3/4 cup flour
- 4 eggs
- 2 tsp. light soy sauce
- Salt and ground black pepper; as your liking

Directions:
1. In a shallow bowl; add the flour. In another bowl; mix well eggs, garlic, green chili, soy sauce, salt and black pepper.
2. Coat each piece with flour and then, dip into the egg mixture.
3. Set the temperature of air fryer to 375°F. Grease an air fryer basket.
4. Arrange cod pieces into the prepared air fryer basket in a single layer. Air fry for about 7 minutes.
5. Remove from air fryer and place the cod sticks onto serving plates. Serve warm.

Buttered Scallops

(Prep + Cook Time: 19 minutes | Servings: 2)

Ingredients:
- 3/4 lb. sea scallops, cleaned and patted very dry
- 1/2 tbsp. fresh thyme, minced
- 1 tbsp. butter; melted
- Salt and ground black pepper; as your liking

Directions:
1. In a large bowl; add the scallops, butter, thyme, salt and black pepper. Toss to coat well.
2. Set the temperature of air fryer to 390°F. Grease an air fryer basket.
3. Arrange scallops into the prepared air fryer basket in a single layer. Air fry for about 4 minutes.
4. Remove from air fryer and transfer the scallops onto serving plates. Serve hot.

Salmon and Orange Marmalade Recipe

(**Prep + Cook Time:** 25 Minutes | **Servings:** 4)

Ingredients:
- 1-pound wild salmon; skinless, boneless and cubed
- 2 lemons; sliced
- 1/4 cup balsamic vinegar
- 1/3 cup orange marmalade
- 1/4 cup orange juice
- A pinch of salt and black pepper

Directions:
1. Heat up a pot with the vinegar over medium heat; add marmalade and orange juice; stir, bring to a simmer, cook for 1 minute and take off heat

2. Thread salmon cubes and lemon slices on skewers, season with salt and black pepper, brush them with half of the orange marmalade mix, arrange in your air fryer's basket and cook at 360°F, for 3 minutes on each side. Brush skewers with the rest of the vinegar mix; divide among plates and serve right away with a side salad

Creamy Tuna Cakes

(Prep + Cook Time: 30 minutes | Servings: 4)

Ingredients:
- 2 (6-oz) cans tuna; drained
- 1 ½ tbsp. mayonnaise
- 1 ½ tbsp. almond flour
- 1 tbsp. fresh lemon juice
- 1 tsp. dried dill
- 1 tsp. garlic powder
- 1/2 tsp. onion powder
- Pinch of salt and ground black pepper

Directions:
1. In a large bowl; mix together the tuna, mayonnaise, flour, lemon juice, dill and spices. Make 4 equal-sized patties from the mixture.
2. Set the temperature of air fryer to 400°F. Grease an air fryer basket.
3. Arrange tuna cakes into the prepared air fryer basket in a single layer.
4. Air fry for about 10 minutes. Flip the side and air fry for another 4 to 5 minutes.
5. Remove from air fryer and transfer the tuna cakes onto serving plates. Serve warm.

Nacho Chips Crusted Prawns

(Prep + Cook Time: 23 minutes | Servings: 2)

Ingredients:
- 5-oz Nacho flavored chips, finely crushed
- 3/4 lb. prawns; peeled and deveined
- 1 large egg

Directions:
1. In a shallow bowl; beat the egg. In another bowl; place the nacho chips Dip each prawn into the beaten egg and then, coat with the crushed nacho chips.
2. Set the temperature of air fryer to 350°F. Grease an air fryer basket.
3. Arrange prawns into the prepared air fryer basket.
4. Air fry for about 8 minutes. Remove from air fryer and transfer the prawns onto serving plates. Serve hot.

Baby Shrimp

(**Prep + Cook Time:** 22 minutes | **Servings:** 4)

Ingredients:
- 1 lb. baby shrimp; peeled and deveined
- 1 cup mayonnaise
- 1 cup red bell pepper; chopped.
- 1 tbsp. olive oil
- 1 tsp. sweet paprika
- 1/2 cup yellow onion; chopped.
- 1 cup green bell pepper; chopped.
- Salt and black pepper to taste

Directions:
1. In a pan that fits your air fryer, add all the ingredients except the mayo; toss well
2. Place the pan in the fryer and cook at 380°F for 12 minutes
3. Cool the mixture down and then add the mayo. Toss and serve.

Cod and Veggie Parcel

(Prep + Cook Time: 35 minutes | Servings: 4)

Ingredients:

- 2 (5-oz) frozen cod fillets, thawed
- 1/2 cup carrots; peeled and julienned
- 1/2 cup fennel bulbs, julienned
- 1/2 cup red bell peppers, seeded and thinly sliced
- 2 tbsp. butter; melted
- 1 tbsp. fresh lemon juice
- 1 tbsp. olive oil
- 1/2 tsp. dried tarragon
- Salt and ground black pepper; as your liking

Directions:

1. In a large bowl; mix well butter, lemon juice, tarragon, salt and black pepper.
2. Add the bell pepper, carrot and fennel bulb and generously coat with the mixture. Arrange 2 large parchment squares onto a smooth surface.
3. Coat the cod fillets with oil and then, sprinkle evenly with salt and black pepper.
4. Arrange 1 cod fillet onto each parchment square and top each evenly with the vegetables. Top with any remaining sauce from the bowl.
5. Fold the parchment paper and crimp the sides to secure fish and vegetables. Set the temperature of air fryer to 350°F.
6. Arrange fish parcels into the air fryer basket. Air fry for about 15 minutes.
7. Remove from air fryer and place the parcels onto serving plates. Carefully; open each parcel and serve warm.

Salmon Patties

(Prep + Cook Time: 47 minutes | Servings: 6)

Ingredients:

- 3 large russet potatoes; peeled and cubed
- 3/4 cup frozen vegetables (of your choice), parboiled and drained
- 1 (6-oz) salmon fillet
- 1 cup breadcrumbs
- 1/4 cup olive oil
- 1 egg
- 2 tbsp. fresh parsley; chopped
- 1 tsp. fresh dill; chopped
- Salt and ground black pepper; as your liking

Directions:

1. In a pan of boiling water, cook the potatoes for about 10 minutes. Drain the potatoes well.
2. Transfer the potatoes into a bowl and mash them using a potato masher. Set aside to cool completely.
3. Set the temperature of air fryer to 355°F. Grease an air fryer basket. Arrange salmon fillet into the prepared air fryer basket. Air fry for about 5 minutes.
4. Remove from air fryer and transfer the salmon fillet into a large bowl. With a fork, flake the salmon.
5. Add the mashed potatoes, egg, vegetables, herbs, salt and black pepper into the bowl of salmon and mix until well combined.
6. Make 6 equal-sized patties from the mixture. Coat patties evenly with breadcrumbs and then, drizzle with the oil. Transfer the patties into air fryer basket
7. Once again, set the temperature of air fryer to 355°F. Line an air fryer basket with a lightly greased piece of foil.
8. Arrange patties into the prepared air fryer basket in a single layer.
9. Air fry for about 10 to 12 minutes, flipping once halfway through. Remove from air fryer and place the patties onto serving platesServe warm.

Sesame Seeds Coated Tuna

(Prep + Cook Time: 21 minutes | Servings: 2)

Ingredients:

- 2 (6-oz) tuna steaks
- 1/4 cup white sesame seeds
- 1 egg white
- 1 tbsp. black sesame seeds
- Salt and ground black pepper; as your liking

Directions:

1. In a shallow bowl; whisk the egg white. In another bowl; mix together the sesame seeds, salt and black pepper.
2. Dip the tuna steaks into egg white and then, coat with the sesame seeds mixture.
3. Set the temperature of air fryer to 400°F. Grease an air fryer basket.
4. Arrange tuna steaks into the prepared air fryer basket in a single layer. Air fry for about 3 minutes per side.
5. Remove from air fryer and transfer the tuna steaks onto serving plates. Serve hot.

Cheesy Shrimp

(Prep + Cook Time: 40 minutes | Servings: 4)

Ingredients:

- 2 lbs. shrimp; peeled and deveined
- 2/3 cup Parmesan cheese; grated
- 4 garlic cloves, minced
- 2 tbsp. olive oil
- 1 to 2 tbsp. fresh lemon juice
- 1/2 tsp. dried oregano
- 1 tsp. onion powder
- 1/2 tsp. red pepper flakes; crushed
- 1 tsp. dried basil
- Ground black pepper; as your liking

Directions:

1. In a large bowl; mix well Parmesan cheese, garlic, oil, herbs and spices. Add the shrimp and toss to combine.
2. Set the temperature of air fryer to 350°F. Grease an air fryer basket.
3. Arrange shrimp into the prepared air fryer basket in 2 batches in a single layer. Air fry for about 8 to 10 minutes.
4. Remove from air fryer and transfer the shrimp onto serving plates.
5. Drizzle with lemon juice and serve immediately.

Creamy Breaded Shrimp

(Prep + Cook Time: 35 minutes | Servings: 3)

Ingredients:

- 1 lb. shrimp; peeled and deveined
- 1/2 cup mayonnaise
- 1/4 cup sweet chili sauce
- 1 cup panko breadcrumbs
- 1/4 cup all-purpose flour
- 1 tbsp. Sriracha sauce

Directions:

1. In a shallow bowl; place the flour. In a second bowl; mix together the mayonnaise, chili sauce and Sriracha sauce.
2. In a third bowl; add the breadcrumbs. Coat each shrimp with the flour, then dip into mayonnaise mixture and finally, coat with the breadcrumbs.
3. Set the temperature of air fryer to 400°F. Grease an air fryer basket.
4. Arrange shrimp into the prepared air fryer basket in 2 batches in a single layer.
5. Air fry for about 10 minutes. Remove from air fryer and transfer the shrimp onto serving plates. Serve hot.

Glazed Calamari

(Prep + Cook Time: 33 minutes | Servings: 3)

Ingredients:
For Calamari:
- 1/2 lb. calamari tubes
- 1 cup flour
- 1 cup club soda

For Sauce:
- 2 tbsp. Sriracha sauce
- 1/2 cup honey

- 1/2 tbsp. red pepper flakes; crushed
- Salt and ground black pepper; as your liking

- 1/4 tsp. red pepper flakes; crushed

Directions:
1. Wash calamari and cut into ¼ inch rings. Transfer the calamari into a bowl and cover with club soda. Set aside for about 10 minutes.
2. In another bowl; mix well flour, red pepper flakes, salt and black pepper. Drain the club soda from calamari.
3. With the paper towels, pat dry the calamari rings. Coat the calamari rings evenly with flour mixture.
4. Set the temperature of air fryer to 375°F. Grease an air fryer basket.
5. Arrange calamari rings into the prepared air fryer basket. Air fry for about 11 minutes, shaking occasionally. Meanwhile; in a bowl; mix together the honey, Sriracha sauce and red pepper flakes.
6. Remove from air fryer and coat calamari rings with the sauce. Air fry for about 2 minutes.
7. Remove from air Fryer and transfer the calamari rings onto serving plates. Serve hot.

Spicy Shrimp

(Prep + Cook Time: 18 minutes | Servings: 2)

Ingredients:
- 3/4 lb. tiger shrimp; peeled and deveined
- 1 ½ tbsp. olive oil
- 1/4 tsp. smoked paprika

- 1/4 tsp. cayenne pepper
- 1/2 tsp. old bay seasoning
- Salt; as your liking

Directions:
1. Set the temperature of air fryer to 390°F. Grease an air fryer basket.
2. In a large bowl; mix well shrimp, oil and spices.
3. Arrange shrimp into the prepared air fryer basket in a single layer. Air fry for about 5 minutes.
4. Remove from air fryer and transfer the shrimp onto serving plates. Serve hot.

Breaded Hake

(Prep + Cook Time: 27 minutes | Servings: 2)

Ingredients:
- 4-oz breadcrumbs
- 4 (6-oz) hake fillets
- 1 lemon; cut into wedges

- 1 egg
- 2 tbsp. vegetable oil

Directions:
1. In a shallow bowl; whisk the egg. In another bowl; add the breadcrumbs and oil and mix until a crumbly mixture forms.
2. Dip fish fillets into the egg and then, coat with the breadcrumbs mixture.
3. Set the temperature of air fryer to 350°F. Grease an air fryer basket.
4. Arrange haddock fillets into the prepared air fryer basket in a single layer. Air fry for about 12 minutes.
5. Remove from air fryer and transfer the hake fillets onto serving plates.
6. Garnish with lemon wedges and serve hot.

Tuna and Potato Cakes

(Prep + Cook Time: 32 minutes | Servings: 4)

Ingredients:

- 2 (6-oz) cans tuna; drained
- 1 cup breadcrumbs
- 1 green chili, seeded and finely chopped
- 1 onion; chopped
- 1 medium boiled potato; mashed
- 1 egg
- 1 tbsp. fresh ginger; grated
- 2 tbsp. celery, finely chopped
- 1/2 tbsp. olive oil
- Salt; as your liking

Directions:

1. Heat the olive oil in a frying pan and sauté onions, ginger and green chili for about 30 seconds.
2. Add the tuna and stir fry for about 2 to 3 minutes or until all the liquid is absorbed.
3. Remove from heat and transfer the tuna mixture onto a large bowl. Set aside to cool.
4. In the bowl of tuna mixture, mix well mashed potato, celery and salt. Make 4 equal-sized patties from the mixture.
5. In a shallow bowl; place the breadcrumbs. In another bowl; beat the egg. Coat each patty with breadcrumbs, then dip into egg and finally, again coat with the breadcrumbs.
6. Set the temperature of air fryer to 390°F. Grease an air fryer basket.
7. Arrange tuna cakes into the prepared air fryer basket in a single layer. Air fry for about 2 to 3 minutes.
8. Flip the side and air fry for about 4 to 5 minutes.
9. Remove from air fryer and transfer the tuna cakes onto serving plates. Serve warm.

Pesto Haddock

(Prep + Cook Time: 23 minutes | Servings: 2)

Ingredients:

- 2 (6-oz) haddock fillets
- 1/3 cup extra-virgin olive oil
- 1 tbsp. Parmesan cheese; grated
- 1 tbsp. olive oil
- 2 tbsp. pine nuts
- 3 tbsp. fresh basil; chopped
- Salt and ground black pepper; as your liking

Directions:

1. Set the temperature of air fryer to 355°F. Grease an air fryer basket. Coat the fish fillets evenly with oil and then, sprinkle with salt and black pepper.
2. Arrange fish fillets into the prepared air fryer basket in a single layer. Air fry for about 8 minutes.
3. Meanwhile; for the pesto: add the remaining Ingredients in a food processor and pulse until smooth.
4. Remove from air fryer and transfer the flounder fillets onto serving plates. Top with the pesto and serve.

Lemon Garlic Shrimp

(Prep + Cook Time: 23 minutes | Servings: 2)

Ingredients:

- 3/4 lb. medium shrimp; peeled and deveined
- 1 tbsp. olive oil
- 1 ½ tbsp. fresh lemon juice
- 1/4 tsp. paprika
- 1/4 tsp. garlic powder
- 1 tsp. lemon pepper

Directions:

1. In a large bowl; mix well lemon juice, oil and spices. Add the shrimp and toss to combine.
2. Set the temperature of air fryer to 400°F. Grease an air fryer basket.
3. Arrange shrimp into the prepared air fryer basket in a single layer.
4. Air fry for about 6 to 8 minutes.
5. Remove from air fryer and transfer the shrimp onto serving plates. Serve hot.

Glazed Halibut

(Prep + Cook Time: 35 minutes | Servings: 3)

Ingredients:

- 1 lb. halibut steak
- 1/2 cup low-sodium soy sauce
- 1/4 cup fresh orange juice
- 1/4 cup sugar
- 1/2 cup cooking wine
- 1 garlic clove, minced
- 2 tbsp. lime juice
- 1/4 tsp. red pepper flakes; crushed
- 1/4 tsp. fresh ginger, finely grated

Directions:

1. In a medium pan, add the garlic, ginger, wine, soy sauce, juices, sugar and red pepper flakes and bring to a boil.
2. Cook for about 3 to 4 minutes, stirring continuously. Remove the pan of marinade from heat and let it cool.
3. In a small bowl; add half of the marinade and reserve in a refrigerator.
4. In a resealable bag, add the remaining marinade and halibut steak.
5. Seal the bag and shake to coat well. Refrigerate for about 30 minutes. Set the temperature of air fryer to 390°F. Grease an air fryer basket.
6. Place halibut steak into the prepared air fryer basket. Air fry for about 9-11 minutes.
7. Remove from air fryer and place the halibut steak onto a platter. Cut the steak into 3 equal-sized pieces and coat with the remaining glaze. Serve immediately.

Bacon Wrapped Scallops

(Prep + Cook Time: 27 minutes | Servings: 4)

Ingredients:

- 20 sea scallops, cleaned and patted very dry
- 5 center-cut bacon slices, cut each in 4 pieces
- Olive oil cooking spray
- 1 tsp. lemon pepper seasoning
- 1/2 tsp. paprika
- Salt and ground black pepper; as your liking

Directions:

1. With a piece of bacon, wrap each scallop and secure each with a toothpick. Sprinkle each scallop evenly with lemon pepper seasoning and paprika.
2. Set the temperature of air fryer to 400°F. Grease an air fryer basket.
3. Arrange scallops into the prepared air fryer basket in 2 batches in a single layer.
4. Spray the scallops evenly with cooking spray and sprinkle with salt and black pepper.
5. Air fry for about 5 to 6 minutes, flipping once halfway through.
6. Remove from air fryer and transfer the scallops onto a paper towel-lined plate. Serve hot.

Rice Flour Coated Shrimp

(Prep + Cook Time: 40 minutes | Servings: 3)

Ingredients:

- 1 lb. shrimp; peeled and deveined
- 2 tbsp. olive oil
- 3 tbsp. rice flour
- 1 tsp. powdered sugar
- Salt and ground black pepper, as required

Directions:

1. In a bowl; mix well flour, oil, sugar, salt and black pepper. Add the shrimp and toss to coat well.
2. Set the temperature of air fryer to 325°F. Grease an air fryer basket.
3. Arrange shrimp into the prepared air fryer basket in 2 batches in a single layer.
4. Air fry for about 8 to 10 minutes, tossing once halfway through.
5. Remove from air fryer and transfer the shrimp onto serving plates. Serve hot.

Shrimp Scampi

(Prep + Cook Time: 27 minutes | Servings: 4)

Ingredients:
- 1 lb. shrimp; peeled and deveined
- 2 tbsp. fresh basil; chopped
- 1 tbsp. fresh lemon juice
- 1 tbsp. garlic, minced
- 1 tbsp. fresh chives; chopped
- 2 tbsp. dry white wine
- 4 tbsp. salted butter
- 2 tsp. red pepper flakes; crushed

Directions:
1. Arrange a 7-inch round baking pan in the air fryer basket. Set the temperature of air fryer to 325°F for about 8 minutes.
2. Carefully remove the pan from air fryer basket. In the heated pan, place butter, lemon juice, garlic and red pepper flakes and return the pan to air fryer basket.
3. Air fry for about 2 minutes, stirring once halfway through. Carefully remove the pan from air fryer basket and stir in shrimp, basil, chives and wine.
4. Return the pan to air fryer basket and air fry for about 5 minutes, stirring once halfway through.
5. Remove from air fryer and place the pan onto a wire rack for about 1 minute.
6. Stir the mixture and transfer onto serving plates. Serve hot.

Shrimp Kebabs

(Prep + Cook Time: 23 minutes | Servings: 2)

Ingredients:
- 3/4 lb. shrimp; peeled and deveined
- 1 tbsp. fresh cilantro; chopped
- 2 tbsp. fresh lemon juice
- 1/2 tsp. paprika
- 1/2 tsp. ground cumin
- 1 tsp. garlic, minced
- Salt and ground black pepper; as your liking

Directions:
1. Set the temperature of air fryer to 350°F. Grease an air fryer basket.
2. In a bowl; mix together the lemon juice, garlic and spices. Add the shrimp and mix well.
3. Thread the shrimp onto presoaked wooden skewers. Arrange shrimp skewers into the prepared air fryer basket.
4. Air fry for about 5 to 8 minutes, flipping once halfway through. Remove from air fryer and transfer the shrimp kebabs onto serving plates.
5. Garnish with fresh cilantro and serve immediately.

Chili Salmon Fillets

(**Prep + Cook Time:** 14 minutes | **Servings:** 2)

Ingredients:
- 2 salmon fillets; boneless
- 3 red chili peppers; chopped.
- 2 tbsp. garlic; minced
- 2 tbsp. olive oil
- 2 tbsp. lemon juice
- Salt and black pepper to taste

Directions:
1. In a bowl, combine the ingredients, toss and coat fish well.
2. Transfer everything to your air fryer and cook at 365°F for 8 minutes, flipping the fish halfway. Divide between plates and serve right away

Breaded Shrimp with Lemon

(Prep + Cook Time: 29 minutes | Servings: 3)

Ingredients:

- 1 lb. large shrimp; peeled and deveined
- 2 egg whites
- 1 cup breadcrumbs
- 1/2 cup plain flour
- 2 tbsp. vegetable oil
- 1/4 tsp. lemon zest
- 1/4 tsp. cayenne pepper
- 1/4 tsp. red pepper flakes; crushed
- Salt and ground black pepper; as your liking

Directions:

1. In a shallow bowl; mix together the flour, salt and black pepper. In a second bowl; whisk the egg whites.
2. In a third bowl; mix well breadcrumbs, lime zest and spices.
3. Coat each shrimp with flour, then dip into egg whites and finally, coat with the breadcrumbs mixture.
4. Drizzle the shrimp evenly with oil. Set the temperature of air fryer to 400°F. Grease an air fryer basket.
5. Arrange shrimp into the prepared air fryer basket in 2 batches in a single layer.
6. Air fry for about 6 to 7 minutes. Remove from air fryer and transfer the shrimp onto serving plates. Serve hot.

Scallops with Capers Sauce

(Prep + Cook Time: 21 minutes | Servings: 2)

Ingredients:

- 10 (1-oz) sea scallops, cleaned and patted very dry
- 1/4 cup extra-virgin olive oil
- 2 tbsp. fresh parsley, finely chopped
- 1 tsp. fresh lemon zest, finely grated
- 1/2 tsp. garlic, finely chopped
- 2 tsp. capers, finely chopped
- Salt and ground black pepper; as your liking

Directions:

1. Season each scallop evenly with salt and black pepper. Set the temperature of air fryer to 400°F. Grease an air fryer basket.
2. Arrange scallops into the prepared air fryer basket in a single layer. Air fry for about 6 minutes.
3. Meanwhile; for the sauce: in a bowl; mix the remaining ingredients.
4. Remove from air fryer and transfer the scallops onto serving plates.
5. Top with the sauce and serve immediately.

Bacon Wrapped Shrimp

(Prep + Cook Time: 34 minutes | Servings: 4)

Ingredients:

- 1 ½ lbs. tiger shrimp; peeled and deveined
- 1 lb. bacon

Directions:

1. With a slice of bacon, wrap each shrimp. Refrigerate for about 20 minutes.
2. Set the temperature of air fryer to 390°F. Grease an air fryer basket.
3. Arrange shrimp into the prepared air fryer basket in 2 batches in a single layer.
4. Air fry for about 5 to 7 minutes.
5. Remove from air fryer and transfer the shrimp onto serving plates. Serve hot.

Roasted Cod and Parsley

(**Prep + Cook Time:** 20 minutes | **Servings:** 4)

Ingredients:
- 4 medium cod filets; boneless
- 1 shallot; chopped.
- 3 tbsp. parsley; chopped.
- 2 tbsp. lemon juice
- 1/4 cup butter; melted
- 2 garlic cloves; minced
- Salt and black pepper to taste

Directions:
1. In a bowl, mix all ingredients except the fish; whisk well.
2. Spread this mixture over the cod fillets
3. Put them in your air fryer and cook at 390°F for 10 minutes. Divide the fish between plates and serve

Salmon Fillets

(**Prep + Cook Time:** 18 minutes | **Servings:** 4)

Ingredients:
- 4 salmon fillets; boneless
- 1 tsp. cumin; ground
- 1 tsp. garlic powder
- 1 tsp. sweet paprika
- 1/2 tsp. chili powder
- 1 tbsp. olive oil
- Juice of 1 lime
- Salt and black pepper to taste

Directions:
1. In a bowl, mix the salmon with the other ingredients, rub / coat well and transfer to your air fryer.
2. Cook at 350°F for 6 minutes on each side
3. Divide the fish between plates and serve right away with a side salad

Shrimp and Veggies

(**Prep + Cook Time:** 30 minutes | **Servings:** 4)

Ingredients:
- 1 lb. shrimp; peeled and deveined
- 1/2 cup red onion; chopped.
- 1 tbsp. butter; melted
- 1 tsp. sweet paprika
- 1 cup red bell pepper; chopped.
- 1 cup celery; chopped.
- 1 tsp. Worcestershire sauce
- Salt and black pepper to taste

Directions:
1. Add all the ingredients to a bowl and mix well
2. Transfer everything to your air fryer and cook 320°F for 20 minutes, shaking halfway. Divide between plates and serve

Crispy Scallops

(**Prep + Cook Time:** 21 minutes | **Servings:** 4)

Ingredients:
- 18 sea scallops, cleaned and patted very dry
- 1/2 egg
- 1/4 cup cornflakes; crushed
- 1/8 cup all-purpose flour
- 1/2 tsp. paprika
- 1 tbsp. 2% milk
- Olive oil cooking spray
- Salt and ground black pepper; as your liking

Directions:
1. In a shallow bowl; mix together the flour, paprika, salt and black pepper. In another bowl; add the milk and egg. Beat until well combined.
2. In a third bowl; place the cornflakes. Coat each scallop with the flour mixture, then dip into the egg mixture and finally, coat with the cornflakes.

3. Spray the scallops evenly with cooking spray. Set the temperature of air fryer to 400°F. Grease an air fryer basket.
4. Arrange scallops into the prepared air fryer basket in a single layer.
5. Air fry for about 5 to 6 minutes, flipping once halfway through.
6. Remove from air fryer and transfer the scallops onto serving plates. Serve hot.

Scallops with Spinach

(Prep + Cook Time: 30 minutes | Servings: 2)

Ingredients:
- 8 jumbo sea scallops
- 1 (12-oz) package frozen spinach, thawed and drained
- 3/4 cup heavy whipping cream
- Olive oil cooking spray
- 1 tbsp. fresh basil; chopped
- 1 tbsp. tomato paste
- 1 tsp. garlic, minced
- Salt and ground black pepper, as required

Directions:
1. In the bottom of a 7-inch heatproof pan, place the spinach. Spray each scallop evenly with cooking spray and then, sprinkle with a little salt and black pepper.
2. Arrange scallops on top of the spinach in a single layer.
3. In a bowl; mix well cream, tomato paste, garlic, basil, salt and black pepper.
4. Add cream mixture evenly over the spinach and scallops. Set the temperature of air fryer to 350°F.
5. Air fry for about 10 minutes. Remove from air fryer and transfer the scallops mixture onto serving plates. Serve hot.

Salmon Fillets and Bell Peppers

(**Prep + Cook Time:** 20 minutes | **Servings:** 6)

Ingredients:
- 6 medium salmon fillets; skinless and boneless
- 3 red bell peppers; cut into medium pieces
- 3 tbsp. olive oil
- 2 tbsp. cilantro; chopped.
- 1 cup green olives; pitted
- 1/2 tsp. smoked paprika
- Salt and black pepper to taste

Directions:
1. In a baking dish that fits your air fryer, mix all the ingredients and toss gently
2. Place the baking dish in your air fryer and cook at 360°F for 15 minutes. Divide the fillets between plates and serve.

Maple Salmon

(**Prep + Cook Time:** 15 minutes | **Servings:** 2)

Ingredients:
- 2 salmon fillets; boneless
- 1 tbsp. olive oil
- 2 tbsp. mustard
- 1 tbsp. maple syrup
- Salt and black pepper to taste

Directions:
1. In a bowl, mix the mustard with the oil and the maple syrup; whisk well and brush the salmon with this mix.
2. Place the salmon in your air fryer and cook it at 370°F for 5 minutes on each side. Serve immediately with a side salad

Crab Cakes

(Prep + Cook Time: 40 minutes | Servings: 4)

Ingredients:

- 1 lb. lump crab meat
- 1 tsp. Dijon mustard
- 1 tsp. Worcestershire sauce
- 1/3 cup panko breadcrumbs
- 1/4 cup scallion, finely chopped
- 2 large eggs
- 2 tbsp. mayonnaise
- 1 ½ tsp. Old Bay seasoning
- Ground black pepper; as your liking

Directions:

1. In a large bowl; add all the Ingredients and gently, stir to combine. Cover the bowl and refrigerate for about 1 hour.
2. Make 8 equal-sized patties from the mixture. Set the temperature of air fryer to 375°F. Grease an air fryer basket.
3. Arrange crab cakes into the prepared air fryer basket in 2 batches in a single layer.
4. Air fry for about 5 minutes per side.
5. Remove from air fryer and transfer the crab cakes onto serving plates. Serve warm.

Balsamic Cod Fillets

(**Prep + Cook Time:** 18 minutes | **Servings:** 2)

Ingredients:

- 2 cod fillets; boneless
- 3 shallots; chopped
- 2 tbsp. olive oil
- 2 tbsp. lemon juice
- 1/3 cup water
- 1/3 cup balsamic vinegar
- 1/2 tsp. garlic powder
- Salt and black pepper to taste

Directions:

1. In a bowl, toss the cod with the salt, pepper, lemon juice, garlic powder, water, vinegar and oil; coat well.
2. Transfer the fish to your fryer's basket and cook at 360°F for 12 minutes, flipping them halfway
3. Divide the fish between plates, sprinkle the shallots on top and serve

Saffron Shrimp Mix

(**Prep + Cook Time:** 18 minutes | **Servings:** 4)

Ingredients:

- 20 shrimp; peeled and deveined
- 1/4 cup parsley; chopped.
- 2 tbsp. butter; melted
- 4 garlic cloves; minced
- 1/2 tsp. saffron powder
- Juice of 1 lemon
- Salt and black pepper to taste

Directions:

1. In a pan that fits your air fryer, mix the shrimp with all the other ingredients; toss well
2. Place the pan in the fryer and cook at 380°F for 8 minutes. Divide between plates and serve hot.

Salmon and Orange Vinaigrette

(Prep + Cook Time: 15 minutes | Servings: 2)

Ingredients:

- 2 salmon fillets; boneless
- 2 tsp. honey
- 2 tbsp. parsley; chopped.
- 1 tbsp. dill; chopped.
- 2 tbsp. mustard
- 2 tbsp. olive oil
- A pinch of salt and black pepper
- Zest of 1/2 orange
- Juice of 1/2 orange

Directions:

1. In a bowl, mix the orange zest with the orange juice, salt, pepper, mustard, honey, oil, dill and parsley and whisk well
2. Add the salmon to this mix, toss and transfer the fish to your air fryer
3. Cook at 350°F for 10 minutes, flipping halfway. Divide the fish between plates, drizzle the orange vinaigrette all over and serve.

Tiger Shrimp

(Prep + Cook Time: 15 minutes | Servings: 2)

Ingredients:

- 20 tiger shrimp; peeled and deveined
- 1/4 tsp. smoked paprika
- 1/2 tsp. Italian seasoning
- 1 tbsp. extra virgin olive oil
- Salt and black pepper to taste

Directions:

1. Add all the ingredients to a bowl and toss
2. Put the shrimp in the air fryer's basket and cook at 380°F for 10 minutes. Divide into bowls and serve.

Coconut Shrimp

(Prep + Cook Time: 15 minutes | Servings: 4)

Ingredients:

- 12 large shrimp; deveined and peeled
- 1 tbsp. parsley; chopped.
- 1 tbsp. cornstarch
- 1 cup coconut cream
- Salt and black pepper to taste

Directions:

1. Add all ingredients to a pan that fits your air fryer and toss.
2. Place the pan in the fryer and cook at 360°F for 10 minutes. Serve hot and enjoy!

White Fish and Peas

(Prep + Cook Time: 22 minutes | Servings: 4)

Ingredients:

- 4 white fish fillets; boneless
- 2 cups peas; cooked and drained
- 2 tbsp. cilantro; chopped.
- 4 tbsp. veggie stock
- 2 garlic cloves; minced
- 1/2 tsp. basil; dried
- 1/2 tsp. sweet paprika
- Salt and pepper to taste

Directions:

1. In a bowl, mix the fish with all ingredients except the peas; toss to coat the fish well.
2. Transfer everything to your air fryer and cook at 360°F for 12 minutes
3. Add the peas, toss and divide everything between plates, Serve

Salmon and Balsamic Orange Sauce

(Prep + Cook Time: 20 minutes | **Servings:** 4)

Ingredients:
- 4 salmon fillets; boneless and cubed
- 1/4 cup balsamic vinegar
- 2 lemons; sliced
- 1/4 cup orange juice
- A pinch of salt and black pepper

Directions:
1. In a pan that fits your air fryer, mix all ingredients except the fish; whisk.
2. Heat the mixture up over medium-high heat for 5 minutes and add the salmon
3. Toss gently and place the pan in the air fryer and cook at 360°F for 10 minutes. Divide between plates and serve right away with a side salad

Cod Fillets

(Prep + Cook Time: 25 minutes | **Servings:** 4)

Ingredients:
- 4 cod fillets; boneless
- 4 ginger slices
- 3 tbsp. olive oil + a drizzle
- 2 tbsp. coriander; chopped.
- 4 tbsp. light soy sauce
- 3 spring onions; chopped.
- 1 cup water
- 1 tbsp. sugar
- Salt and black pepper to taste

Directions:
1. Season the fish with salt and pepper, then drizzle some oil over it and rub well.
2. Put the fish in your air fryer and cook at 360°F for 12 minutes.
3. Put the water in a pot and heat up over medium heat; add the soy sauce and sugar, stir, bring to a simmer and remove from the heat
4. Heat up a pan with the olive oil over medium heat; add the ginger and green onions, stir, cook for 2-3 minutes and remove from the heat
5. Divide the fish between plates and top with ginger, coriander and green onions. Drizzle the soy sauce mixture all over, serve and enjoy!

Salmon and Fennel

(Prep + Cook Time: 30 minutes | **Servings:** 4)

Ingredients:
- 2 red onions; chopped.
- 2 small fennel bulbs; trimmed and sliced
- 2 tbsp. olive oil
- 5 tsp. fennel seeds; toasted
- 1/4 cup almonds; toasted and sliced
- 4 salmon fillets; boneless
- Salt and black pepper to taste

Directions:
1. Season the fish with salt and pepper, grease it with 1 tbsp. of the oil and place in your air fryer's basket.
2. Cook at 350°F for 5-6 minutes on each side and divide between plates
3. Heat up a pan with the remaining tbsp. of oil over medium-high heat; add the onions, stir and sauté for 2 minutes
4. Add the fennel bulbs and seeds, almonds, salt and pepper and cook for 2-3 minutes more. Spread the mixture over the fish and serve right away; enjoy!

Salmon and Capers

(**Prep + Cook Time:** 18 minutes | **Servings:** 4)

Ingredients:
- 4 salmon fillets; boneless
- 1 tbsp. capers; drained
- 1 tbsp. dill; chopped.
- 2 tsp. olive oil
- Juice of 1 lemon
- Salt and black pepper to taste

Directions:
1. In your air fryer, mix the capers, dill, salt, pepper and the oil and then rub the fish gently with this mixture.
2. Cook at 360°F for 6 minutes on each side. Divide the fish between plates, drizzle the lemon juice all over and serve

Shrimp and Mushrooms

(**Prep + Cook Time:** 15 minutes | **Servings:** 2)

Ingredients:
- 1 lb. shrimp; peeled and deveined
- 8 oz. mushrooms; roughly sliced
- 1/2 cup beef stock
- 1/4 cup heavy cream
- 2 garlic cloves; minced
- 1 tbsp. butter; melted
- 1 tbsp. chives; chopped.
- 1 tbsp. parsley; chopped.
- A drizzle of olive oil
- A pinch of red pepper flakes
- Salt and black pepper to taste

Directions:
1. Season the shrimp with salt and pepper and grease with the oil.
2. Place the shrimp in your air fryer, cook at 360°F for 7 minutes and divide between plates
3. Heat up a pan with the butter over medium heat, add the mushrooms, stir and cook for 3-4 minutes.
4. Add all remaining ingredients; stir and then cook for a few minutes more
5. Drizzle the butter / garlic mixture over the shrimp and serve.

Chili Tomato Shrimp

(**Prep + Cook Time:** 20 minutes | **Servings:** 4)

Ingredients:
- 1 lb. shrimp; peeled and deveined
- 1 cup tomato juice
- 1 tsp. chili powder
- 2 tbsp. olive oil
- 1 yellow onion; chopped.
- 1/2 tsp. sugar
- 2 tsp. vinegar
- Salt and black pepper to taste

Directions:
1. Place all of the ingredients into a pan that fits your air fryer and mix well.
2. Put the pan in the fryer and cook at 370°F for 10 minutes. Divide into bowls and serve

Butter Shrimp

(**Prep + Cook Time:** 15 minutes | **Servings:** 2)

Ingredients:
- 8 large shrimp
- 2 tbsp. butter; melted
- 4 garlic cloves; minced
- 1 tbsp. rosemary; chopped.
- Salt and black pepper to taste

Directions:
1. Add all the ingredients to a bowl and toss
2. Transfer the shrimp to your air fryer and cook at 360°F for 10 minutes. Divide into bowls, serve and enjoy!

Salmon and Carrots

(Prep + Cook Time: 25 minutes | **Servings:** 2)

Ingredients:
- 2 salmon fillets; boneless
- 3 garlic cloves; minced
- 1/4 cup veggie stock
- 1 cup baby carrots
- 1 tbsp. olive oil
- Salt and black pepper to taste

Directions:
1. In your air fryer, mix all the ingredients.
2. Cook at 370°F for 20 minutes. Divide everything between plates and serve

Trout and Almond Butter Sauce

(Prep + Cook Time: 25 minutes | **Servings:** 5)

Ingredients:
- 4 trout fillets; boneless
- Cooking spray
- Salt and black pepper to taste

For the sauce:
- 1 cup almond butter
- 1/4 cup lemon juice
- 4 tsp. soy sauce
- 1/4 cup water
- 1 tsp. almond oil

Directions:
1. Put the fish fillets in your air fryer, season with salt and pepper and grease with the cooking spray.
2. Cook at 380°F for 5 minutes on each side and divide between plates
3. Heat up a pan with the almond butter over medium heat; then add the soy sauce, lemon juice, almond oil and the water
4. Whisk the sauce well and cook for 2-3 minutes. Drizzle the almond butter sauce over the fish and serve.

Rosemary Shrimp Kabobs

(Prep + Cook Time: 13 minutes | **Servings:** 2)

Ingredients:
- 8 shrimps; peeled and deveined
- 8 red bell pepper slices
- 4 garlic cloves; minced
- 1 tbsp. olive oil
- 1 tbsp. rosemary; chopped.
- Salt and black pepper to taste

Directions:
1. Place all ingredients in a bowl and toss them well.
2. Thread 2 shrimp and 2 bell pepper slices on a skewer and then repeat with 2 more shrimp and bell pepper slices.
3. Thread another 2 shrimp and 2 bell pepper slices on the other skewer and then repeat with the last 2 shrimp and 2 bell pepper slices
4. Put the kabobs in your air fryer's basket., cook at 360°F for 7 minutes and serve immediately with a side salad

Tarragon Shrimp

(Prep + Cook Time: 22 minutes | **Servings:** 4)

Ingredients:

- 1 lb. shrimp; peeled and deveined
- 2 garlic cloves; minced
- 1 yellow onion; chopped.
- 3/4 cup parmesan cheese; grated
- 1/4 cup tarragon; chopped.
- 1/2 cup chicken stock
- 2 tbsp. olive oil
- 2 tbsp. dry white wine
- Salt and black pepper to taste

Directions:

1. In a pan that fits your air fryer, add all ingredients except the parmesan cheese and stir well
2. Place the pan in the air fryer and cook at 380°F for 12 minutes
3. Add the parmesan and toss. Divide everything between plates and serve.

Cod and Lime Sauce

(Prep + Cook Time: 18 minutes | **Servings:** 4)

Ingredients:

- 4 cod fillets; boneless
- 2 tsp. lime juice
- 2 tbsp. olive oil
- 3 tbsp. chives; chopped.
- 3 tsp. lime zest
- 6 tbsp. butter; melted
- Salt and black pepper to taste

Directions:

1. Season the fish with the salt and pepper, rub it with the oil and then put it in your air fryer.
2. Cook at 360°F for 10 minutes, flipping once
3. Heat up a pan with the butter over medium heat and then add the chives, salt, pepper, lime juice and zest, whisk; cook for 1-2 minutes. Divide the fish between plates, drizzle the lime sauce all over and serve immediately

Salmon and Blackberry Sauce

(Prep + Cook Time: 18 minutes | **Servings:** 2)

Ingredients:

- 2 salmon fillets; boneless
- 1/2 cup blackberries
- 1 tbsp. honey
- Juice of 1/2 lemon
- 1 tbsp. olive oil
- Salt and black pepper to taste

Directions:

1. In a blender, mix the blackberries with the honey, oil, lemon juice, salt and pepper; pulse well
2. Spread the blackberry mixture over the salmon and then place the fish in your air fryer's basket
3. Cook at 380°F for 12 minutes, flipping the fish halfway. Serve hot and enjoy!

Pistachio Crusted Cod

(Prep + Cook Time: 20 minutes | **Servings:** 4)

Ingredients:

- 4 cod fillets; boneless
- 1/4 cup lime juice
- 1 tbsp. mustard
- 1 tsp. parsley; chopped.
- 1 cup pistachios; chopped.
- 2 tbsp. honey
- Salt and black pepper to taste

Directions:

1. Place all the ingredients except the fish into a bowl; whisk.
2. Spread the mixture over the fish fillets, put them in your air fryer and cook at 350°F for 10 minutes
3. Divide the fish between plates and serve immediately with a side salad

Salmon Steaks

(Prep + Cook Time: 20 minutes | **Servings:** 6)

Ingredients:
- 6 salmon steaks
- 2 garlic cloves; minced
- 2 tbsp. olive oil
- 2 tbsp. parsley; chopped.
- 2 tbsp. lemon juice
- 1 tsp. sherry
- 1 cup clam juice
- 1/3 cup dill; chopped.
- Salt and white pepper to taste

Directions:
1. In a pan that fits your air fryer, mix the salmon with all the other ingredients
2. Place the pan in the fryer and cook at 370°F for 15 minutes. Divide everything between plates and serve.

Cod Fillets with Leeks

(Prep + Cook Time: 25 minutes | **Servings:** 2)

Ingredients:
- 2 black cod fillets; boneless
- 1/2 cup pecans; chopped.
- 2 leeks; sliced
- 1 tbsp. olive oil
- Salt and black pepper to taste

Directions:
1. In a bowl, mix the cod with the oil, salt, pepper and the leeks; toss / coat well.
2. Transfer the cod to your air fryer and cook at 360°F for 15 minutes. Divide the fish and leeks between plates, sprinkle the pecans on top and serve immediately

Salmon Fillets and Pineapple Mix

(Prep + Cook Time: 15 minutes | **Servings:** 2)

Ingredients:
- 20 oz. canned pineapple pieces
- 2 tsp. garlic powder
- 1 tbsp. balsamic vinegar
- 2 medium salmon fillets; boneless
- 1/2 tsp. ginger; grated
- A drizzle of olive oil
- Salt and black pepper to taste

Directions:
1. Grease a pan that fits your air fryer with the oil and add the fish inside.
2. Add the remaining ingredients and place the pan in the air fryer.
3. Cook at 350°F for 10 minutes. Divide between plates and serve

Herbed Tuna

(Prep + Cook Time: 18 minutes | **Servings:** 4)

Ingredients:
- 1/2 cup cilantro; chopped.
- 1/3 cup olive oil
- 1 jalapeno pepper; chopped.
- 2 tbsp. parsley; chopped.
- 2 tbsp. basil; chopped.
- 1 tsp. red pepper flakes
- 1 tsp. thyme; chopped.
- 4 sushi tuna steaks
- 3 garlic cloves; minced
- 1 small red onion; chopped.
- 3 tbsp. balsamic vinegar
- Salt and black pepper to taste

Directions:
1. Place all ingredients except the fish into a bowl and stir well.
2. Add the fish and toss, coating it well
3. Transfer everything to your air fryer and cook at 360°F for 4 minutes on each side. Divide the fish between plates and serve

Shrimp and Tomatoes

(Prep + Cook Time: 25 minutes | **Servings:** 4)

Ingredients:

- 2 lbs. shrimp; peeled and deveined
- 1 lb. tomatoes; peeled and chopped
- 4 onions; chopped.
- 1 tsp. coriander; ground
- Juice of 1 lemon
- 1/4 cup veggie stock
- 4 tbsp. olive oil
- Salt and black pepper to taste

Directions:

1. In a pan that fits your air fryer, mix all the ingredients well
2. Place the pan in the fryer and cook at 360°F for 15 minutes. Divide into bowls and serve; enjoy!

Peas and Cod Fillets

(Prep + Cook Time: 20 Minutes | **Servings:** 4)

Ingredients:

- 4 cod fillets; boneless
- 2 cups peas
- 1/2 tsp. oregano; dried
- 1/2 tsp. sweet paprika
- 2 tbsp. parsley; chopped
- 4 tbsp. wine
- 2 garlic cloves; minced
- Salt and pepper to the taste

Directions:

1. In your food processor mix garlic with parsley, salt, pepper, oregano, paprika and wine and blend well.
2. Rub fish with half of this mix, place in your air fryer and cook at 360°F, for 10 minutes
3. Meanwhile; put peas in a pot, add water to cover, add salt, bring to a boil over medium high heat, cook for 10 minutes; drain and divide among plates. Also divide fish on plates, spread the rest of the herb dressing all over and serve

Awesome Shrimp Mix

(Prep + Cook Time: 20 minutes | **Servings:** 4)

Ingredients:

- 18 oz. shrimp; peeled and deveined
- 2 green chilies; minced
- 1 tbsp. olive oil
- 1 tsp. turmeric powder
- 2 onions; chopped.
- 4 oz. curd; beaten
- 1-inch ginger; chopped.
- 1/2 tbsp. mustard seeds
- Salt and black pepper to taste

Directions:

1. In a pan that fits your air fryer, place and mix all the ingredients.
2. Place the pan in the fryer and cook at 380°F for 10 minutes. Divide into bowls and serve

Pea Pods and Shrimp Mix

(Prep + Cook Time: 18 minutes | **Servings:** 4)

Ingredients:

- 1 lb. shrimp; peeled and deveined
- 3/4 cup pineapple juice
- 2 tbsp. soy sauce
- 1/2 lb. pea pods
- 3 tbsp. sugar
- 3 tbsp. balsamic vinegar

Directions:

1. In a pan that fits your air fryer, mix all the ingredients.
2. Place the pan in the fryer and cook at 380°F for 8 minutes. Divide into bowls and serve

Halibut and Sun Dried Tomatoes

(Prep + Cook Time: 20 Minutes | **Servings:** 2)

Ingredients:
- 2 medium halibut fillets
- 2 garlic cloves; minced
- 9 black olives; pitted and sliced
- 6 sun dried tomatoes; chopped
- 2 small red onions; sliced
- 1 fennel bulb; sliced
- 4 rosemary springs; chopped
- 1/2 tsp. red pepper flakes; crushed
- 2 tsp. olive oil
- Salt and black pepper to the taste

Directions:
1. Season fish with salt, pepper, rub with garlic and oil and put in a heat proof dish that fits your air fryer.
2. Add onion slices, sun dried tomatoes, fennel, olives, rosemary and sprinkle pepper flakes, transfer to your air fryer and cook at 380°F, for 10 minutes. Divide fish and veggies on plates and serve

Baked Cod

(Prep + Cook Time: 18 minutes | **Servings:** 4)

Ingredients:
- 4 cod fillets; boneless
- 3/4 tsp. sweet paprika
- 1/2 tsp. oregano; dried
- 1/2 tsp. thyme; dried
- 1/2 tsp. basil; dried
- 2 tbsp. parsley; chopped.
- 2 tbsp. butter; melted
- A drizzle of olive oil
- Juice of 1 lemon
- Salt and black pepper to taste

Directions:
1. Add all ingredients to a bowl and toss gently.
2. Transfer the fish to your air fryer and cook at 380°F for 6 minutes on each side. Serve right away

Simple Lime Salmon

(Prep + Cook Time: 17 minutes | **Servings:** 5)

Ingredients:
- 1/2 cup butter; melted
- 1/2 cup olive oil
- 2 salmon fillets; boneless
- 1 lime; sliced
- 6 green onions; chopped.
- 3 garlic cloves; minced
- 2 shallots; chopped.
- Juice of 1 lime
- Salt and black pepper to taste

Directions:
1. In a bowl, mix the salmon with the lime juice, butter, oil, garlic, shallots, salt, pepper and the green onions; rub well
2. Transfer the fish to your air fryer, top with the lime slices and cook at 380°F for 6 minutes on each side. Serve with a side salad.

Sea Bass Paella

(Prep + Cook Time: 35 minutes | **Servings:** 4)

Ingredients:
- 1 lb. sea bass fillets; cubed
- 1 red bell pepper; deseeded and chopped.
- 6 scallops
- 8 shrimp; peeled and deveined
- 5 oz. wild rice
- 2 oz. peas
- 14 oz. dry white wine
- 3½ oz. chicken stock
- A drizzle of olive oil
- Salt and black pepper to taste

Directions:
1. In a heatproof dish that fits your air fryer, place all the ingredients and toss

2. Place the dish in your air fryer and cook at 380°F and cook for 25 minutes, stirring halfway. Divide between plates and serve.

Spicy Cod

(Prep + Cook Time: 15 minutes | Servings: 4)

Ingredients:
- 4 cod fillets; boneless
- 2 tbsp. assorted chili peppers
- 1 lemon; sliced
- Juice of 1 lemon
- Salt and black pepper to taste

Directions:
1. In your air fryer, mix the cod with the chili pepper, lemon juice, salt and pepper
2. Arrange the lemon slices on top and cook at 360°F for 10 minutes. Divide the fillets between plates and serve.

Cilantro Trout Fillets

(Prep + Cook Time: 18 minutes | Servings: 4)

Ingredients:
- 4 trout fillets; boneless
- 4 garlic cloves; minced
- 1 cup black olives; pitted and chopped.
- 1 tbsp. olive oil
- 3 tbsp. cilantro; chopped.

Directions:
1. Add all of the ingredients to your air fryer and mix well
2. Cook at 360°F for 6 minutes on each side. Divide everything between plates and serve.

Snapper Fillets

(Prep + Cook Time: 20 minutes | Servings: 4)

Ingredients:
- 4 medium snapper fillets; boneless
- 8 garlic cloves; minced
- 1/3 cup olive oil
- 1 tbsp. lemon zest
- 1½ tbsp. green olives; pitted and sliced
- Juice of 2 limes
- Salt and black pepper to taste

Directions:
1. Add all the ingredients except the fish to a baking dish that fits your air fryer; mix well.
2. Add the fish and toss gently, then place in the fryer
3. Cook at 360°F for 15 minutes. Divide everything between plates and serve

Salmon and Jasmine Rice

(Prep + Cook Time: 35 minutes | Servings: 2)

Ingredients:
- 2 wild salmon fillets; boneless
- 1/2 cup jasmine rice
- 1 tbsp. butter; melted
- 1/4 tsp. saffron
- 1 cup chicken stock
- Salt and black pepper to taste

Directions:
1. Add all ingredients except the fish to a pan that fits your air fryer; toss well
2. Place the pain in the air fryer and cook at 360°F for 15 minutes
3. Add the fish, cover and cook at 360°F for 12 minutes more. Divide everything between plates and serve right away.

Mussels and Shrimp

(Prep + Cook Time: 25 minutes | **Servings:** 4)

Ingredients:
- 1½ lbs. large shrimp; peeled and deveined
- 20 oz. canned tomatoes; chopped.
- 1/2 cup parsley; chopped.
- 1/2 tsp. marjoram; dried
- 1 tbsp. basil; dried
- 8 oz. clam juice
- 12 mussels
- 2 tbsp. butter; melted
- 2 yellow onions; chopped.
- 3 garlic cloves; minced
- Salt and black pepper to taste

Directions:
1. Place all the ingredients in a pan that fits your air fryer; toss well
2. Put the pan into the fryer and cook at 380°F for 15 minutes. Divide into bowls and serve right away.

Fried Salmon

(Prep + Cook Time: 22 minutes | **Servings:** 4)

Ingredients:
- 4 salmon fillets; boneless
- 1 white onion; chopped.
- 3 tbsp. olive oil
- 3 tomatoes; sliced
- 4 thyme sprigs; chopped.
- 4 cilantro sprigs; chopped.
- 1 lemon; sliced
- Salt and black pepper to taste

Directions:
1. In your air fryer, mix the salmon with the oil, onions, tomatoes, thyme, cilantro, salt and pepper
2. Top with the lemon slices and cook at 360°F for 12 minutes. Divide everything between plates and serve.

Trout Bites

(Prep + Cook Time: 18 minutes | **Servings:** 4)

Ingredients:
- 1 lb. trout fillets; boneless and cut into cubes
- 1 sweet onion; chopped.
- 2 celery stalks; sliced
- 1 garlic clove; crushed
- 1 shallot; sliced
- 1/3 cup sake
- 1/3 cup mirin
- 1/4 cup miso
- 1-inch ginger piece; chopped
- 1 tsp. mustard
- 1 tsp. sugar
- 1 tbsp. rice vinegar

Directions:
1. Add all ingredients to a pan that fits your air fryer and toss
2. Place the pan in the fryer and cook at 370°F for 12 minutes. Divide into bowls and serve.

Shrimp and Spaghetti

(Prep + Cook Time: 20 minutes | **Servings:** 4)

Ingredients:
- 1 lb. shrimp; cooked, peeled and deveined
- 10 oz. canned tomatoes; chopped.
- 1 cup parmesan cheese; grated
- 2 tbsp. olive oil
- 1/4 tsp. oregano; dried
- 12 oz. spaghetti; cooked
- 1 garlic clove; minced
- 1 tbsp. parsley; finely chopped.

Directions:
1. In a pan that fits your air fryer, add the shrimp with the oil, garlic, tomatoes, oregano and parsley; toss well.
2. Place the pan in the fryer and cook at 380°F for 10 minutes

3. Add the spaghetti and the parmesan; toss well. Divide between plates, serve and enjoy!

Hawaiian Salmon Recipe

(**Prep + Cook Time:** 20 Minutes | **Servings:** 2)

Ingredients:
- 20-ounce canned pineapple pieces and juice
- 2 medium salmon fillets; boneless
- 1/2 tsp. ginger; grated
- 2 tsp. garlic powder
- 1 tsp. onion powder
- 1 tbsp. balsamic vinegar
- Salt and black pepper to the taste

Directions:
1. Season salmon with garlic powder, onion powder, salt and black pepper, rub well, transfer to a heat proof dish that fits your air fryer, add ginger and pineapple chunks and toss them really gently
2. Drizzle the vinegar all over, put in your air fryer and cook at 350°F, for 10 minutes. Divide everything on plates and serve

Easy Trout

(**Prep + Cook Time:** 25 minutes | **Servings:** 4)

Ingredients:
- 4 whole trout
- 3 oz. breadcrumbs
- 1 tbsp. chives; chopped.
- 1 tbsp. olive oil
- 1 egg; whisked
- 1 tbsp. butter
- Juice of 1 lemon
- Salt and black pepper to taste

Directions:
1. In a bowl, combine the breadcrumbs, lemon juice, salt, pepper, egg and chives; stir very well.
2. Coat the trout with the breadcrumb mix
3. Heat up your air fryer with the oil and the butter at 370°F; add the trout and cook for 10 minutes on each side. Divide between plates and serve with a side salad

Clams and Potatoes

(**Prep + Cook Time:** 20 minutes | **Servings:** 4)

Ingredients:
- 1 lb. baby red potatoes; scrubbed
- 10 oz. beer
- 15 small clams; shucked
- 2 tbsp. cilantro; chopped.
- 2 chorizo links; sliced
- 1 yellow onion; chopped.
- 1 tsp. olive oil

Directions:
1. In a pan that fits your air fryer, add all of the ingredients and toss
2. Place the pan in the fryer and cook at 390°F for 15 minutes. Divide into bowls and serve.

Mussels Bowls

(**Prep + Cook Time:** 18 minutes | **Servings:** 4)

Ingredients:
- 2 lbs. mussels; scrubbed
- 8 oz. spicy sausage; chopped.
- 1 yellow onion; chopped.
- 1 tbsp. olive oil
- 12 oz. black beer
- 1 tbsp. paprika

Directions:
1. Combine all the ingredients in a pan that fits your air fryer
2. Place the pan in the air fryer and cook at 400°F for 12 minutes. Divide the mussels into bowls, serve and enjoy!

Shrimp and Corn

Ingredients:

- 1½ lbs. shrimp; peeled and deveined
- 2 cups corn
- 1/4 cup chicken stock
- 2 sweet onions; cut into wedges
- 1 tbsp. old bay seasoning
- 1 tsp. red pepper flakes; crushed
- 8 garlic cloves; crushed
- A drizzle of olive oil
- Salt and black pepper to taste

Directions:

1. Grease a pan that fits your air fryer with the oil.
2. Add all other ingredients to the oiled pan and toss well
3. Place the pan in the fryer and cook at 390°F for 10 minutes. Divide everything into bowls and serve

Salmon Thyme and Parsley

(**Prep + Cook Time:** 25 Minutes | **Servings:** 4)

Ingredients:

- 4 salmon fillets; boneless
- 4 thyme springs
- 4 parsley springs
- 3 tbsp. extra virgin olive oil
- 1 yellow onion; chopped
- 3 tomatoes; sliced
- Juice from 1 lemon
- Salt and black pepper to the taste

Directions:

1. Drizzle 1 tablespoon oil in a pan that fits your air fryer; add a layer of tomatoes, salt and pepper, drizzle 1 more tablespoon oil, add fish, season them with salt and pepper, drizzle the rest of the oil, add thyme and parsley springs, onions, lemon juice, salt and pepper, place in your air fryer's basket
2. Cook at 360°F, for 12 minutes shaking once. Divide everything on plates and serve right away

Vegan & Vegetarian

Parmesan Broccoli

(Prep + Cook Time: 50 minutes | Servings: 2)

Ingredients:
- 10-oz frozen broccoli
- 2 tbsp. Parmesan cheese; grated
- 1 tbsp. olive oil
- 3 tbsp. balsamic vinegar
- 1/8 tsp. cayenne pepper
- Salt and ground black pepper; as your liking

Directions:
1. In a bowl; add the broccoli, vinegar, oil, cayenne, salt and black pepper and toss to coat well.
2. Set the temperature of air fryer to 400°F. Grease an air fryer basket.
3. Arrange broccoli into the prepared air fryer basket. Air fry for about 20 minutes, tossing several times while frying.
4. Remove from air fryer and transfer the broccoli onto serving plates. Immediately, sprinkle with cheese and serve hot.

Radish Salad

(Prep + Cook Time: 45 minutes | Servings: 4)

Ingredients:
For Radishes:
- 1 ½ lbs. radishes, trimmed and halved
- 2 tbsp. olive oil
- Salt and ground black pepper, as required

For Salad:
- 6 cups fresh salad greens
- 1/2 lb. fresh mozzarella, sliced
- 1 tbsp. balsamic vinegar
- 1 tsp. olive oil
- 1 tsp. honey
- Salt and ground black pepper, as required

Directions:
1. In a bowl; add the radishes, salt, black pepper and oil and toss to coat well.
2. Set the temperature of air fryer to 350°F. Grease an air fryer basket.
3. Arrange radishes into the prepared air fryer basket in a single layer. Air fry for about 30 minutes, tossing 2 to 3 times.
4. Remove from air fryer and place the radishes into a bowl to cool. For salad: in a large serving bowl; mix together the cooked radishes, mozzarella and greens.
5. Place the dressing over salad and toss to coat well. Serve immediately.

For dressing: in a small bowl; mix together the honey, oil, vinegar, salt and black pepper.

Caramelized Carrots

(Prep + Cook Time: 25 minutes | Servings: 3)

Ingredients:
- 1 small bag baby carrots
- 1/2 cup brown sugar
- 1/2 cup butter; melted

Directions:
1. Set the temperature of air fryer to 400°F. Grease an air fryer basket.
2. In a bowl; mix together the butter and brown sugar. Add the carrots and coat well.
3. Arrange carrots into the prepared air fryer basket in a single layer.
4. Air fry for about 15 minutes. Remove from air fryer and transfer the carrots onto serving plates. Serve hot.

Cauliflower Salad

(Prep + Cook Time: 30 minutes | Servings: 4)

Ingredients:

For Salad:

- 1 head cauliflower; cut into small florets
- 1/4 cup pecans; toasted and chopped
- 1/4 cup golden raisins
- 1 cup boiling water

- 1/4 cup olive oil
- 2 tbsp. fresh mint leaves; chopped
- 1 tbsp. curry powder
- Salt, to taste

For Dressing:

- 1 cup mayonnaise
- 1 tbsp. fresh lemon juice

- 2 tbsp. sugar

Directions:

1. **For the salad:** in a bowl; add the cauliflower, curry powder, salt and oil and toss to coat well.
2. Set the temperature of air fryer to 390°F. Grease an air fryer basket.
3. Arrange cauliflower florets into the prepared air fryer basket in a single layer. Air fry for about 8 to 10 minutes.
4. Meanwhile; in a bowl; add the raisins and boiling water and set aside until using.
5. Remove from air fryer and transfer the cauliflower florets onto a plate. Set aside to cool. Drain the raisins well.
6. **For Salad dressing:** in a bowl; add all the Ingredients and mix until well combined.
7. In another bowl; mix together the cauliflower, raisins and pecans. Add the dressing and gently, stir to combine.
8. Refrigerate to chill before serving. Garnish with mint and serve

Eggplant Salad

(Prep + Cook Time: 30 minutes | Servings: 2)

Ingredients:

For Salad:

- 1 avocado, peeled, pitted and chopped
- 1 eggplant; cut into ½-inch-thick slices crosswise
- 2 tbsp. canola oil

- 1 tsp. fresh lemon juice
- Salt and ground black pepper; as your liking

For Dressing:

- 1 tbsp. honey
- 1 tbsp. fresh oregano leaves; chopped
- 1 tbsp. extra-virgin olive oil
- 1 tbsp. red wine vinegar

- 1 tsp. Dijon mustard
- 1 tsp. fresh lemon zest; grated
- Salt and ground black pepper; as your liking

Directions:

1. Set the temperature of air fryer to 400°F. Grease an air fryer basket.
2. **For the salad:** in a bowl; add the eggplant, oil, salt and black pepper and toss to coat well.
3. Arrange eggplants pieces into the prepared air fryer basket in a single layer.
4. Air fry for about 15 minutes, shaking after every 5 minutes.
5. Remove from air fryer and transfer the eggplant pieces onto a plate. Set aside to cool slightly.
6. In a bowl; mix together the avocado and lemon juice.
7. In a serving bowl; mix together the eggplants pieces and avocado mixture.
8. **For the dressing:** in a bowl; add all the Ingredients and beat until well combined. Add the dressing and gently, stir to combine. Serve immediately.

Lemony Green Beans

(Prep + Cook Time: 27 minutes | Servings: 3)

Ingredients:

- 1 lb. green beans, trimmed and halved
- 1 tbsp. fresh lemon juice
- 1/4 tsp. garlic powder
- 1 tsp. butter; melted
- Salt and ground black pepper; as your liking

Directions:

1. In a large bowl; add all the Ingredients and toss to coat well. Set the temperature of air fryer to 400°F. Grease an air fryer basket.
2. Arrange green beans into the prepared air fryer basket. Air fry for about 10 to 12 minutes.
3. Remove from air fryer and transfer the green beans onto serving plates. Serve hot.

Potato Salad

(Prep + Cook Time: 50 minutes | Servings: 6)

Ingredients:

- 4 Russet potatoes
- 3 hard-boiled eggs; peeled and chopped
- 1/4 cup mayonnaise
- 1 cup celery; chopped
- 1/2 cup red onion; chopped
- 1 tbsp. olive oil
- 1 tbsp. prepared mustard
- 1/4 tsp. celery salt
- 1/4 tsp. garlic salt
- Salt; as your liking

Directions:

1. Set the temperature of air fryer to 390°F. Grease an air fryer basket. With a fork, prick the potatoes. Drizzle with oil and rub with the salt.
2. Arrange potatoes into the prepared air fryer basket. Air fry for about 35 to 40 minutes.
3. Remove from air fryer and transfer the potatoes into a bowl. Set aside to cool.
4. After cooling, chop the potatoes. In a serving bowl; add the potatoes and remaining Ingredients and gently, mix them well. Refrigerate to chill before serving. Serve.

Stuffed Pumpkin

(Prep + Cook Time: 50 minutes | Servings: 5)

Ingredients:

- 1/2 of butternut pumpkin, seeded
- 1/2 cup fresh peas, shelled
- 1 onion; chopped
- 2 garlic cloves, minced
- 1 sweet potato; peeled and chopped
- 1 egg, beaten
- 1 parsnip; peeled and chopped
- 1 carrot; peeled and chopped
- 2 tsp. mixed dried herbs
- Salt and ground black pepper; as your liking

Directions:

1. In a large bowl; mix well vegetables, garlic, egg, herbs, salt and black pepper. Stuff the pumpkin half with vegetable mixture.
2. Set the temperature of air fryer to 355°F. Grease an air fryer basket. Arrange pumpkin half into the prepared air fryer basket.
3. Air fry for about 30 minutes. Remove from air fryer and transfer the pumpkin onto a serving platter.
4. Set aside to cool slightly. Serve warm.

Hassel-back Potatoes

(Prep + Cook Time: 50 minutes | Servings: 4)

Ingredients:
- 4 potatoes
- 2 tbsp. Parmesan cheese, shredded
- 1 tbsp. fresh chives; chopped
- 2 tbsp. olive oil

Directions:
1. With a sharp knife, cut slits along each potato the short way about ¼-inch apart, making sure slices should stay connected at the bottom.
2. Set the temperature of air fryer to 355°F. Grease an air fryer basket. Gently brush each potato evenly with oil.
3. Arrange potatoes into the prepared air fryer basket.
4. Air fry for about 30 minutes, coating with the oil once halfway through.
5. Remove from air fryer and transfer the potatoes onto a platter. Garnish with the cheeses and chives. Serve immediately.

Cheesy Mushroom Pizza

(Prep + Cook Time: 21 minutes | Servings: 2)

Ingredients:
- 2 Kalamata olives, pitted and sliced
- 2 Portobello mushroom caps, stemmed
- 2 tbsp. mozzarella cheese, shredded
- 2 tbsp. Parmesan cheese; grated freshly
- 2 tbsp. olive oil
- 2 tbsp. canned tomatoes; chopped
- 1/8 tsp. dried Italian seasonings
- 1 tsp. red pepper flakes; crushed
- Salt, to taste

Directions:
1. Set the temperature of air fryer to 320°F. Grease an air fryer basket. With a spoon, scoop out the center of each mushroom cap.
2. Coat each mushroom cap with oil from both sides. Sprinkle the inside of caps with Italian seasoning and salt.
3. Place the canned tomato evenly over both caps, followed by the olives and mozzarella cheese.
4. Arrange mushroom caps into the prepared air fryer basket. Air fry for about 5 to 6 minutes.
5. Remove from air fryer and immediately sprinkle with the Parmesan cheese and red pepper flakes. Serve.

Curried Eggplant

(Prep + Cook Time: 25 minutes | Servings: 2)

Ingredients:
- 1 large eggplant; cut into 1/2-inch thick slices
- 1/2 fresh red chili; chopped
- 1 garlic clove, minced
- 1 tbsp. vegetable oil
- 1/4 tsp. curry powder
- Salt; as your liking

Directions:
1. Set the temperature of air fryer to 300°F. Grease an air fryer basket. In a bowl; add all the Ingredients and toss to coat well.
2. Arrange eggplant slices into the prepared air fryer basket in a single layer.
3. Air fry for about 10 minutes, shaking once halfway through.
4. Remove from air fryer and transfer the eggplant slices onto serving plates. Serve hot.

Buttered Dinner Rolls

(Prep + Cook Time: 45 minutes | Servings: 12)

Ingredients:
- 1 cup milk
- 1 tbsp. coconut oil
- 1 tbsp. olive oil
- 3 cups plain flour
- 7½ tbsp. unsalted butter
- 1 tsp. yeast
- Salt and ground black pepper; as your liking

Directions:
1. In a pan, add the milk, coconut oil and olive oil and cook until lukewarm. Remove from the heat and stir well.
2. In a large bowl; add the flour, butter, yeast, salt, black pepper and milk mixture and mix until a dough forms. With your hands, knead for about 4 to 5 minutes
3. With a damp cloth, cover the dough and set aside in a warm place for about 5 minutes. Again, with your hands, knead the dough for about 4 to 5 minutes
4. With a damp cloth, cover the dough and set aside in a warm place for about 30 minutes. Place the dough onto a lightly floured surface.
5. Divide the dough into 12 equal pieces and form each into a ball. Set the temperature of air fryer to 360°F. Grease an air fryer basket.
6. Arrange rolls into the prepared air fryer basket in 2 batches in a single layer. Air fry for about 15 minutes. Remove from the air fryer and serve warm.

Garlic Broccoli

(Prep + Cook Time: 35 minutes | Servings: 3)

Ingredients:
- 1 large head broccoli; cut into bite-sized pieces
- 3 garlic cloves, sliced
- 1 tbsp. fresh lemon juice
- 1 tbsp. butter
- 1/2 tsp. red pepper flakes; crushed
- 2 tsp. vegetable bouillon granules
- 1/2 tsp. fresh lemon zest, finely grated

Directions:
1. Set the temperature of air fryer to 355°F. In an air fryer pan, add the butter, bouillon granules and lemon juice and air fry for about 1 to 1 ½ minutes.
2. Stir in the garlic and air fry for about 30 seconds.
3. Stir in the broccoli and air fry for about 13 minutes.
4. Stir in the lemon zest and red pepper flakes and air fry for about 5 minutes.
5. Remove from air fryer and transfer the broccoli onto serving plates. Serve hot.

Veggies Stuffed Eggplants

(Prep + Cook Time: 34 minutes | Servings: 5)

Ingredients:
- 10 small eggplants, halved lengthwise
- 1 onion; chopped
- 1 tomato; chopped
- 1/4 cup cottage cheese; chopped
- 1/2 green bell pepper, seeded and chopped
- 2 tbsp. tomato paste
- 2 tbsp. fresh cilantro; chopped
- 1 tbsp. fresh lime juice
- 1 tbsp. vegetable oil
- 1/2 tsp. garlic; chopped
- Salt and ground black pepper; as your liking

Directions:
1. Carefully; cut a slice from one side of each eggplant lengthwise. Now; with a small spoon, scoop out the flesh from each eggplant leaving a thick shell.
2. Transfer the eggplant flesh into a bowl. Drizzle the eggplants evenly with lime juice.

3. Set the temperature of air fryer to 320°F. Grease an air fryer basket.
4. Arrange hollowed eggplants into the prepared air fryer basket in a single layer. Air fry for about 3 to 4 minutes.
5. Meanwhile; heat the oil in a skillet over medium heat and sauté the onion and garlic for about 2 minutes.
6. Add the eggplant flesh, tomato, salt and black pepper and sauté for about 2 minutes.
7. Stir in the cheese, bell pepper, tomato paste and cilantro and cook for about 1 minute. Remove the pan of veggie mixture from heat.
8. Stuff the hollowed eggplant shells with veggie mixture and close each with its cut part. Set the temperature of air fryer to 356°F. Grease the air fryer basket.
9. Arrange eggplant shells into the prepared air fryer basket in a single layer. Air fry for about 4 to 5 minutes.
10. Remove from air fryer and transfer the eggplants onto serving plates. Serve hot.

Cheese Stuffed Tomatoes

(Prep + Cook Time: 30 minutes | Servings: 2)

Ingredients:
- 1/2 cup cheddar cheese, shredded
- 2 large tomatoes
- 1/2 cup broccoli, finely chopped
- 1 tbsp. unsalted butter; melted
- 1/2 tsp. dried thyme; crushed

Directions:
1. Slice the top of each tomato and scoop out pulp and seeds. In a bowl; mix together the chopped broccoli and cheese.
2. Stuff each tomato evenly with broccoli mixture.
3. Set the temperature of air fryer to 355°F. Grease an air fryer basket.
4. Arrange tomatoes into the prepared air fryer basket. Drizzle evenly with butter. Air fry for about 12 to 15 minutes.
5. Remove from air fryer and transfer the tomatoes onto a serving platter.
6. Set aside to cool slightly. Garnish with thyme and serve.

Cheesy Brussel Sprouts

(Prep + Cook Time: 25 minutes | Servings: 3)

Ingredients:
- 1 lb. Brussels sprouts, trimmed and halved
- 1/4 cup whole wheat breadcrumbs
- 1/4 cup Parmesan cheese, shredded
- 1 tbsp. extra-virgin olive oil
- 1 tbsp. balsamic vinegar
- Salt and ground black pepper; as your liking

Directions:
1. Set the temperature of air fryer to 400°F. Grease an air fryer basket.
2. In a bowl; mix well Brussel sprouts, vinegar, oil, salt and black pepper.
3. Arrange Brussel sprouts into the prepared air fryer basket in a single layer. Air fry for about 5 minutes.
4. Remove from air fryer and flip the Brussel sprouts. Sprinkle the Brussel sprouts evenly with breadcrumbs, followed by the cheese.
5. Air fryer for about 5 more minutes. Remove from air fryer and transfer the Brussels sprouts onto serving plates. Serve hot.

Broccoli with Olives

(Prep + Cook Time: 34 minutes | Servings: 4)

Ingredients:

- 2 lbs. broccoli, stemmed and cut into 1 inch florets
- 1/4 cup Parmesan cheese; grated
- 1/3 cup Kalamata olives, halved and pitted
- 2 tbsp. olive oil
- 2 tsp. fresh lemon zest; grated
- Salt and ground black pepper; as your liking

Directions:

1. In a pan of boiling water, add the broccoli and cook for about 3 to 4 minutes. Drain the broccoli well.
2. Set the temperature of air fryer to 400°F. Grease an air fryer basket.
3. In a bowl; mix together broccoli, oil, salt and black pepper.
4. Arrange broccoli into the prepared air fryer basket.
5. Air fry for about 15 minutes, tossing once halfway through.
6. Remove from air fryer and immediately stir in the olives, lemon zest and cheese. Serve immediately.

Oatmeal Stuffed Bell Peppers

(Prep + Cook Time: 31 minutes | Servings: 2)

Ingredients:

- 2 large red bell peppers, halved lengthwise and seeded
- 2 cups cooked oatmeal
- 4 tbsp. canned red kidney beans, rinsed and drained
- 4 tbsp. coconut yogurt
- 1/4 tsp. smoked paprika
- 1/4 tsp. ground cumin
- Salt and ground black pepper; as your liking

Directions:

1. Set the temperature of air fryer to 355°F. Grease an air fryer basket.
2. Arrange bell peppers into the prepared air fryer basket, cut-side down.
3. Air fry for about 8 minutes. Remove from the air fryer and set aside to cool. Meanwhile; in a bowl; mix well oatmeal, beans, coconut yogurt and spices.
4. Stuff each bell pepper half with the oatmeal mixture. Now; set the air fryer to 355°F.
5. Arrange bell peppers into the air fryer basket and air fry for about 8 minutes.
6. Remove from air fryer and transfer the bell peppers onto a serving platter. Set aside to cool slightly. Serve warm.

Parmesan Asparagus

(Prep + Cook Time: 25 minutes | Servings: 3)

Ingredients:

- 1 lb. fresh asparagus, trimmed
- 1 tbsp. butter; melted
- 1 tbsp. Parmesan cheese; grated
- 1 tsp. garlic powder
- Salt and ground black pepper; as your liking

Directions:

1. In a bowl; mix together the asparagus, cheese, butter, garlic powder, salt and black pepper.
2. Set the temperature of air fryer to 400°F. Grease an air fryer basket.
3. Arrange asparagus into the prepared air fryer basket. Air fry for about 10 minutes.
4. Remove from air fryer and transfer the asparagus onto serving plates. Serve hot.

Basil Tomatoes

(Prep + Cook Time: 20 minutes | Servings: 2)

Ingredients:

- 2 tomatoes, halved
- 1 tbsp. fresh basil; chopped
- Olive oil cooking spray
- Salt and ground black pepper; as your liking

Directions:

1. Set the temperature of air fryer to 320°F. Grease an air fryer basket.
2. Spray the tomato halves evenly with cooking spray and sprinkle with salt, black pepper and basil.
3. Arrange tomato halves into the prepared air fryer basket, cut sides up. Air fry for about 10 minutes or until desired doneness.
4. Remove from air fryer and transfer the tomatoes onto serving plates. Serve warm.

Buttered Broccoli

(Prep + Cook Time: 17 minutes | Servings: 4)

Ingredients:

- 4 cups fresh broccoli florets
- 1/4 cup water
- 2 tbsp. butter; melted
- Salt and ground black pepper; as your liking

Directions:

1. Set the temperature of air fryer to 400°F.
2. Grease an air fryer basket. In a bowl; mix well broccoli, butter, salt and black pepper.
3. In the bottom of air fryer pan, place the water. Arrange broccoli florets into the prepared air fryer basket in a single layer.
4. Air fry for about 7 minutes. Remove from air fryer and transfer the broccoli onto serving plates. Serve hot.

Brussel Sprout Salad

(Prep + Cook Time: 35 minutes | Servings: 4)

Ingredients:

For Salad:

- 1 lb. fresh medium Brussels sprouts, trimmed and halved vertically
- 2 apples, cored and chopped
- 4 cups lettuce, torn
- 1 red onion, sliced
- 3 tsp. olive oil
- Salt and ground black pepper; as your liking

For Dressing:

- 1 tbsp. apple cider vinegar
- 2 tbsp. fresh lemon juice
- 1 tbsp. honey
- 2 tbsp. extra-virgin olive oil
- 1 tsp. Dijon mustard
- Salt and ground black pepper; as your liking

Directions:

1. Set the temperature of air fryer to 360°F. For Brussels sprout: in a bowl; add the Brussels sprout, oil, salt and black pepper and toss to coat well.
2. Spread the Brussels sprouts onto a large baking sheet.
3. Arrange the baking sheet into air fryer basket and air fryer for about 15 minutes, flipping once halfway through.
4. Remove from air fryer and transfer the Brussel sprouts onto a plate. Set aside to cool slightly.
5. In a serving bowl; mix together the Brussel sprouts, apples, onion and lettuce.
6. **For the dressing:** in a bowl; add all the Ingredients and beat until well combined.
7. Add the dressing and gently, stir to combine. Serve immediately.

Mixed Veggie Salad

(Prep + Cook Time: 2 hour 10 minutes | Servings: 8)

Ingredients:

- 1 cup cherry tomatoes, quartered
- 2 red bell peppers, seeded and chopped
- 3 medium zucchinis, sliced into ½-inch thick rounds
- 3 small eggplants, sliced into ½-inch thick rounds
- 4 medium tomatoes, cut in eighths
- 4 fresh basil leaves; chopped
- 1/2 cup Parmesan cheese; grated
- 1/2 cup Italian dressing
- 2 tbsp. olive oil, divided
- Salt; as your liking

Directions:

1. Set the temperature of air fryer to 355°F. Grease an air fryer basket. In a bowl; mix together the zucchini and one tbsp. of oil.
2. Place zucchini slices into the prepared air fryer basket. Air fry for about 25 minutes.
3. Remove from air fryer and place the zucchini slices into a bowl.
4. Set aside. In another bowl; mix well eggplant and one tbsp. of oil.
5. Place eggplant slices into the greased air fryer basket. Air fry for about 30 to 40 minutes.
6. Remove from air fryer and place the eggplant slices into a bowl with zucchini. Set aside. Now; set the temperature of air fryer to 320°F.
7. Place tomatoes into the greased air fryer basket.
8. Air fry for about 30 minutes. Remove from air fryer and place the tomatoes into a bowl with veggies.
9. In the bowl of cooked vegetables, add the bell pepper, basil, salt, dressing and salt and gently, stir to combine.
10. Cover the bowl of salad and refrigerate for 2 hours before serving.
11. Garnish with Parmesan cheese and serve.

Cheese Stuffed Mushrooms

(Prep + Cook Time: 23 minutes | Servings: 4)

Ingredients:

- 4 fresh large mushrooms, stemmed and gills removed
- 2 garlic cloves; chopped
- 1/4 cup Parmesan cheese, shredded
- 4-oz cream cheese; softened
- 2 tbsp. sharp cheddar cheese, shredded
- 2 tbsp. white cheddar cheese, shredded
- 1 tsp. Worcestershire sauce
- Salt and ground black pepper; as your liking

Directions:

1. In a bowl; mix well cream cheese, Parmesan, cheddar cheeses, Worcestershire sauce, garlic, salt and black pepper.
2. Set the temperature of air fryer to 370°F. Grease an air fryer basket.
3. Stuff each mushroom with the cheese mixture.
4. Arrange stuffed mushrooms into the prepared air fryer basket. Air fry for about 8 minutes.
5. Remove from air fryer and transfer the mushrooms onto a serving platter.
6. Set aside to cool slightly. Serve warm.

Veggie Stuffed Bell Peppers

(Prep + Cook Time: 45 minutes | Servings: 6)

Ingredients:

- 6 large bell peppers
- 1/2 cup fresh peas, shelled
- 2 garlic cloves, minced
- 1 onion, finely chopped
- 1 potato; peeled and finely chopped
- 1/3 cup cheddar cheese; grated
- 1 bread roll, finely chopped
- 1 carrot; peeled and finely chopped
- 2 tsp. fresh parsley; chopped
- Salt and ground black pepper; as your liking

Directions:

1. Remove the tops of each bell pepper and discard the seeds. Finely chop the bell pepper tops.
2. In a bowl; mix well chopped bell pepper tops, loaf, vegetables, garlic, parsley, salt and black pepper.
3. Stuff each bell pepper with the vegetable mixture. Set the temperature of air fryer to 350°F. Grease an air fryer basket.
4. Arrange peppers into the prepared air fryer basket. Air fry for about 20 minutes.
5. Remove the air fryer basket and top each bell pepper with cheese.
6. Air fry for 5 more minutes. Remove from air fryer and transfer the bell peppers onto a serving platter. Set aside to cool slightly. Serve warm.

Cheesy Dinner Rolls

(Prep + Cook Time: 15 minutes | Servings: 2)

Ingredients:

- 1/2 cup Parmesan cheese; grated
- 2 dinner rolls
- 2 tbsp. unsalted butter, melted
- 1/2 tsp. garlic bread seasoning mix

Directions:

1. Cut the dinner rolls into cross style, but not the all way through. Stuff the slits evenly with cheese.
2. Coat the tops of each roll with butter and then, sprinkle with the seasoning mix.
3. Set the temperature of air fryer to 355°F. Grease an air fryer basket.
4. Arrange dinner rolls into the prepared air fryer basket.
5. Air fry for about 5 minutes or until cheese melts completely. Remove from the air fryer and serve hot.

Spiced Soy Curls

(Prep + Cook Time: 20 minutes | Servings: 2)

Ingredients:

- 4-oz soy curls
- 1/4 cup nutritional yeast
- 3 cups boiling water
- 1/4 cup fine ground cornmeal
- 1 tsp. poultry seasoning
- 2 tsp. Cajun seasoning
- Salt and ground white pepper; as your liking

Directions:

1. In a heatproof bowl; add the boiling water and soak the soy curls for about 10 minutes. Through a strainer, drain the soy curls and then with a large spoon, press to release the extra water
2. In a bowl; mix well nutritional yeast, cornmeal, seasonings, salt and white pepper
3. Add the soy curls and generously coat with the mixture.
4. Set the temperature of air fryer to 380°F. Grease an air fryer basket. Arrange soy curls into the prepared air fryer basket in a single layer.
5. Air fry for about 10 minutes, shaking once halfway through
6. Remove from air fryer and transfer the soy curls onto serving plates. Serve warm.

Honey Glazed Carrots

(Prep + Cook Time: 27 minutes | Servings: 4)

Ingredients:

- 3 cups carrots; peeled and cut into large chunks
- 1 tbsp. fresh thyme, finely chopped
- 1 tbsp. honey
- 1 tbsp. olive oil
- Salt and ground black pepper; as your liking

Directions:

1. Set the temperature of air fryer to 390°F. Grease an air fryer basket. In a bowl; mix well carrot, oil, honey, thyme, salt and black pepper.
2. Arrange carrot chunks into the prepared air fryer basket in a single layer.
3. Air fry for about 12 minutes. Remove from air fryer and transfer the carrot chunks onto serving plates. Serve hot.

Zucchini Salad

(Prep + Cook Time: 45 minutes | Servings: 4)

Ingredients:

- 1 lb. zucchini; cut into rounds
- 5 cups fresh spinach; chopped
- 1/4 cup feta cheese, crumbled
- 2 tbsp. olive oil
- 2 tbsp. fresh lemon juice
- 1 tsp. garlic powder
- Salt and ground black pepper; as your liking

Directions:

1. Set the temperature of air fryer to 400°F. Grease an air fryer basket. In a bowl; mix together the zucchini, oil, garlic powder, salt and black pepper.
2. Arrange zucchini slices into the prepared air fryer basket in a single layer.
3. Air fry for about 30 minutes, tossing 3 times.
4. Remove from air fryer and transfer the zucchini slices onto a plate. Set aside to cool.
5. In another bowl; add the cooked zucchini slices, spinach, feta cheese, lemon juice, a little bit of salt and black pepper and toss to coat well. Serve immediately.

Sweet and Sour Brussel Sprouts

(Prep + Cook Time: 20 minutes | Servings: 2)

Ingredients:

- 2 cups Brussels sprouts, trimmed and halved lengthwise
- 1 tbsp. maple syrup
- 1 tbsp. balsamic vinegar
- Salt; as your liking

Directions:

1. Set the temperature of air fryer to 400°F. Grease an air fryer basket. In a bowl; add all the Ingredients and toss to coat well.
2. Arrange Brussels sprouts into the prepared air fryer basket in a single layer.
3. Air fry for about 8 to 10 minutes, shaking once halfway through.
4. Remove from air fryer and transfer the Brussels sprouts onto serving plates. Serve hot.

Sweet and Spicy Parsnips

(Prep + Cook Time: 59 minutes | Servings: 6)

Ingredients:

- 2 lbs. parsnip; peeled and cut into 1-inch chunks
- 2 tbsp. honey
- 1 tbsp. dried parsley flakes; crushed
- 1 tbsp. butter; melted
- 1/4 tsp. red pepper flakes; crushed
- Salt and ground black pepper; as your liking

Directions:
1. Set the temperature of air fryer to 355°F. Grease an air fryer basket. In a large bowl; mix together the parsnips and butter.
2. Arrange parsnip chunks into the prepared air fryer basket in a single layer. Air fry for about 40 minutes.
3. Meanwhile; in another large bowl; mix well remaining ingredients. After 40 minutes, transfer parsnips into the bowl of honey mixture and toss to coat well.
4. Again, arrange the parsnip chunks into air fryer basket in a single layer. Air fry for 3 to 4 more minutes.
5. Remove from air fryer and transfer the parsnip chunks onto serving plates. Serve hot.

Cheesy Spinach

(Prep + Cook Time: 30 minutes | Servings: 3)

Ingredients:
- 1 (10-oz) package frozen spinach, thawed
- 4-oz cream cheese; chopped
- 1/4 cup Parmesan cheese, shredded
- 1/2 cup onion; chopped
- 1/2 tsp. ground nutmeg
- 2 tsp. garlic, minced
- Salt and ground black pepper; as your liking

Directions:
1. In a bowl; mix well spinach, onion, garlic, cream cheese, nutmeg, salt and black pepper.
2. Set the temperature of air fryer to 350°F. Grease an air fryer pan. Place spinach mixture into the prepared air fryer pan.
3. Air fry for about 10 minutes. Remove from air fryer and stir the mixture well. Sprinkle the spinach mixture evenly with Parmesan cheese.
4. set the temperature of air fryer to 400°F and air fry for 5 more minutes.
5. Remove from air fryer and transfer the spinach mixture onto serving plates. Serve hot.

Pesto Tomatoes

(Prep + Cook Time: 21 minutes | Servings: 4)

Ingredients:
For Pesto:
- 1/2 cup plus 1 tbsp. olive oil, divided
- 1/2 cup Parmesan cheese; grated
- 1/2 cup fresh basil; chopped
- 1/2 cup fresh parsley; chopped
- 1 garlic clove; chopped
- 3 tbsp. pine nuts
- Salt, to taste

For Tomatoes:
- 8-oz feta cheese; cut into 1/2-inch-thick slices.
- 2 heirloom tomatoes; cut into 1/2-inch-thick slices
- 1/2 cup red onions, thinly sliced
- 1 tbsp. olive oil
- Salt, to taste

Directions:
1. Set the temperature of air fryer to 390°F. Grease an air fryer basket. In a bowl; mix together one tbsp. of oil, pine nuts and pinch of salt.
2. Arrange pine nuts into the prepared air fryer basket. Air fry for about 1 to 2 minutes.
3. Remove from air fryer and transfer the pine nuts onto a paper towel-lined plate.
4. In a food processor, add the toasted pine nuts, fresh herbs, garlic, Parmesan and salt and pulse until just combined.
5. While motor is running, slowly add the remaining oil and pulse until smooth.
6. Transfer into a bowl; covered and refrigerate until serving. Spread about one tbsp. of pesto onto each tomato slice.
7. Top each tomato slice with one feta and onion slice and drizzle with oil.
8. Arrange tomato slices into the prepared air fryer basket in a single layer. Air fry for about 12 to 14 minutes.

9. Remove from air fryer and transfer the tomato slices onto serving plates.
10. Sprinkle with a little salt and serve with the remaining pesto.

Herbed Carrots

(Prep + Cook Time: 29 minutes | Servings: 8)

Ingredients:
- 6 large carrots; peeled and sliced lengthwise
- 1/2 tbsp. fresh oregano; chopped
- 1/2 tbsp. fresh parsley; chopped
- 2 tbsp. olive oil
- Salt and ground black pepper; as your liking

Directions:
1. Set the temperature of air fryer to 360°F. Grease an air fryer basket. In a bowl; mix together the carrot slices and oil.
2. Arrange carrot slices into the prepared air fryer basket in a single layer. Air fry for about 12 minutes.
3. Remove from air fryer and sprinkle the carrots evenly with herbs, salt and black pepper.
4. Air fry for 2 more minutes. Remove from air fryer and transfer the carrot slices onto serving plates. Serve hot.

Spicy Potatoes

(Prep + Cook Time: 30 minutes | Servings: 6)

Ingredients:
- 1¾ lbs. waxy potatoes; peeled and cubed
- 1 tbsp. olive oil
- 1/2 tsp. ground cumin
- 1/2 tsp. ground coriander
- 1/2 tsp. paprika
- Salt and freshly ground black pepper; as your liking

Directions:
1. In a large bowl of water, add the potatoes and set aside for about 30 minutes.
2. Drain the potatoes completely and dry with paper towels. In a bowl; add the potatoes, oil and spices and toss to coat well.
3. Set the temperature of air fryer to 355°F. Grease an air fryer basket.
4. Arrange potato pieces into the prepared air fryer basket in a single layer.
5. Air fry for about 20 minutes. Remove from air fryer and transfer the potato pieces onto serving plates. Serve hot.

Tofu with Peanut Butter Sauce

(Prep + Cook Time: 35 minutes | Servings: 3)

Ingredients:
For Tofu:
- 1 (14-oz) block tofu, pressed and cut into strips
- 2 garlic cloves; peeled
- 2 tbsp. soy sauce
- 1 tbsp. maple syrup
- 2 tbsp. fresh lime juice
- 2 tsp. fresh ginger; peeled
- 1 tsp. Sriracha sauce

For Sauce:
- 1 (2-inches) piece fresh ginger; peeled
- 1/2 cup creamy peanut butter
- 2 garlic cloves; peeled
- 1 tbsp. soy sauce
- 1 tbsp. fresh lime juice
- 6 tbsp. of water
- 1 to 2 tsp. Sriracha sauce

Directions:
1. **For tofu:** in a food processor, put all the Ingredients except tofu and pulse until smooth. In a bowl; mix together the marinade and tofu
2. Set aside to marinate for about 20 to 30 minutes. Meanwhile; soak 6 bamboo skewers into water for about 30 minutes. With a cutter, cut each skewer in half.
3. Thread one tofu strip onto each little bamboo stick. Set the temperature of air fryer to 370°F. Grease an air fryer basket
4. Arrange tofu skewers into the prepared air fryer basket in a single layer. Air fry for about 15 minutes.
5. Remove from air fryer and transfer the tofu onto serving plates. Top with the sauce and serve
6. **For the sauce:** add all the Ingredients in a food processor and pulse until smooth.

Beans and Veggie Burgers

(Prep + Cook Time: 42 minutes | Servings: 4)

Ingredients:
- Olive oil cooking spray
- 1 cup fresh spinach; chopped
- 1 cup fresh mushrooms; chopped
- 6 cups fresh baby greens
- 1 cup cooked black beans
- 2 cups boiled potatoes; peeled and mashed
- 2 tsp. Chile lime seasoning

Directions:
1. In a large bowl; add the beans, potatoes, spinach, mushrooms and seasoning and with your hands, mix until well combined
2. Make 4 equal-sized patties from the mixture. Set the temperature of air fryer to 370°F. Grease an air fryer basket
3. Arrange patties into the prepared air fryer basket in a single layer and spray with the cooking spray. Air fry for about 12 minutes, shaking once halfway through.
4. Flip the patties and air fry for another 6 to 7 minutes
5. Now; set the temperature of air fryer to 90°F and air fry for 3 more minutes
6. Remove from air fryer and transfer the burgers onto serving plates. Serve warm alongside the baby greens.

Herbed Eggplant

(Prep + Cook Time: 30 minutes | Servings: 2)

Ingredients:
- 1 large eggplant, cubed
- 1/2 tsp. dried thyme; crushed
- 1/2 tsp. garlic powder
- 1/2 tsp. dried marjoram; crushed
- 1/2 tsp. dried oregano; crushed
- Olive oil cooking spray
- Salt and ground black pepper; as your liking

Directions:
1. Set the temperature of air fryer to 390°F. Grease an air fryer basket. In a small bowl; mix well herbs, garlic powder, salt and black pepper.
2. Spray the eggplant cubes evenly with cooking spray and then, rub with the herbs mixture.
3. Arrange eggplant cubes into the prepared air fryer basket in a single layer. Air fry for about 6 minutes.
4. Flip and spray the eggplant cubes with cooking spray. Air fry for another 6 minutes. Flip and again, spray the eggplant cubes with cooking spray.
5. Air fry for 2 to 3 more minutes. Remove from air fryer and transfer the eggplant cubes onto serving plates. Serve hot.

Stuffed Potatoes

(Prep + Cook Time: 46 minutes | Servings: 4)

Ingredients:

- 4 potatoes; peeled
- 1/2 cup Parmesan cheese; grated
- 1/2 of brown onion; chopped
- 2 tbsp. chives; chopped
- 2 to 3 tbsp. canola oil
- 1 tbsp. butter

Directions:

1. Set the temperature of air fryer to 390°F. Coat the potatoes with oil.
2. Arrange potatoes into the air fryer basket. Air fry for about 20 minutes, coating twice with the remaining oil.
3. Meanwhile; in a frying pan, melt the butter over medium heat and sauté the onion for about 4 to 5 minutes.
4. Remove from heat and transfer the onion into a bowl.
5. Remove the potatoes from air fryer and transfer onto a platter. Carefully; cut each potato in half. With a small scooper, scoop out the flesh from each half.
6. In the bowl of onion, add the potato flesh, chives and half of cheese and stir to combine. Stuff the potato halves evenly with potato mixture.
7. Sprinkle with the remaining cheese. Arrange potato halves into the air fryer basket. Air fry for another 6 minutes.
8. Remove from air fryer and transfer the potatoes onto a platter. Serve immediately.

Veggie Rice

(Prep + Cook Time: 38 minutes | Servings: 2)

Ingredients:

- 1 large egg, lightly beaten
- 2 cups cooked white rice
- 1/2 cup frozen peas, thawed
- 1/2 cup frozen carrots, thawed
- 1 tbsp. water
- 1 tbsp. vegetable oil
- 1 tsp. soy sauce
- 1 tsp. Sriracha sauce
- 2 tsp. sesame oil; toasted and divided
- 1/2 tsp. sesame seeds; toasted
- Salt and ground white pepper; as your liking

Directions:

1. In a large bowl; mix well rice, vegetable oil, one tsp. of sesame oil, water, salt and white pepper. Set the temperature of air fryer to 380°F. Lightly, grease an air fryer pan
2. Transfer rice mixture into the prepared air fryer pan. Air fryer for about 12 minutes, stirring once halfway through. Remove the pan from air fryer and place the beaten egg over rice
3. Air fry for another 4 minutes. Again, remove the pan from air fryer and stir in the peas and carrots. Air fry for 2 more minutes.
4. Meanwhile; in a bowl; mix together soy sauce, Sriracha sauce, sesame seeds and the remaining sesame oil. Remove from air fryer and transfer the rice mixture into a serving bowl.
5. Drizzle with the sauce and serve

Croissant Rolls

(Prep + Cook Time: 16 minutes | Servings: 8)

Ingredients:

- 4 tbsp. butter; melted
- 1 (8-oz) can croissant rolls

Directions:

1. Set the temperature of air fryer to 320°F. Grease an air fryer basket.
2. Arrange croissant rolls into the prepared air fryer basket. Air fry for about 4 minutes.
3. Flip the side and air fry for 1 to 2 more minutes.
4. Remove from the air fryer and transfer onto a platter.
5. Drizzle with the melted butter and serve hot.

170

Rice and Beans Stuffed Bell Peppers

(Prep + Cook Time: 30 minutes | Servings: 5)

Ingredients:

- 5 large bell peppers, tops removed and seeded
- 1/2 cup mozzarella cheese, shredded
- 1/2 small bell pepper, seeded and chopped
- 1 (15-oz) can red kidney beans, rinsed and drained
- 1 (15-oz) can diced tomatoes with juice
- 1 cup cooked rice
- 1 tbsp. Parmesan cheese; grated
- 1 ½ tsp. Italian seasoning

Directions:

1. In a bowl; mix well chopped bell pepper, tomatoes with juice, beans, rice and Italian seasoning. Stuff each bell pepper evenly with the rice mixture.
2. Set the temperature of air fryer to 360°F. Grease an air fryer basket.
3. Arrange bell peppers into the air fryer basket in a single layer.
4. Air fry for about 12 minutes. Meanwhile; in a bowl; mix together the mozzarella and Parmesan cheese.
5. Remove the air fryer basket and top each bell pepper with cheese mixture. Air fry for 3 more minutes.
6. Remove from air fryer and transfer the bell peppers onto a serving platter. Set aside to cool slightly. Serve warm.

Ratatouille

(Prep + Cook Time: 30 minutes | Servings: 4)

Ingredients:

- 1 zucchini; chopped
- 1 yellow bell pepper, seeded and chopped
- 1 eggplant; chopped
- 3 tomatoes; chopped
- 2 small onions; chopped
- 2 garlic cloves, minced
- 1 green bell pepper, seeded and chopped
- 1 tbsp. balsamic vinegar
- 2 tbsp. Herbs de Provence
- 1 tbsp. olive oil
- Salt and ground black pepper; as your liking

Directions:

1. Set the temperature of air fryer to 355°F. Grease a baking dish.
2. In a large bowl; add the vegetables, garlic, Herbs de Provence, oil, vinegar, salt and black pepper and toss to coat well.
3. Transfer vegetable mixture into the prepared baking dish. Arrange the baking dish into air fryer and air fry for about 15 minutes.
4. Remove from air fryer and transfer the vegetable mixture into a serving bowl. Serve immediately.

Breadcrumbs Stuffed Mushrooms

(Prep + Cook Time: 25 minutes | Servings: 4)

Ingredients:

- 16 small button mushrooms, stemmed and gills removed
- 1 garlic clove; crushed
- 1 ½ spelt bread slices
- 1 tbsp. flat-leaf parsley, finely chopped
- 1 ½ tbsp. olive oil
- Salt and ground black pepper; as your liking

Directions:

1. In a food processor, add the bread slices and pulse until fine crumbs form. Transfer the crumbs into a bowl. Add the garlic, parsley, salt and black pepper and stir to combine.
2. Stir in the olive oil. Set the temperature of air fryer to 390°F. Grease an air fryer basket.
3. Stuff each mushroom cap with the breadcrumbs mixture.
4. Arrange mushroom caps into the prepared air fryer basket. Air fry for about 9 to 10 minutes.
5. Remove from air fryer and transfer the mushrooms onto a serving platter.

Glazed Veggies

(Prep + Cook Time: 40 minutes | Servings: 4)

Ingredients:

- 2-oz cherry tomatoes
- 1 large zucchini; chopped
- 1 large carrot; peeled and chopped
- 1 green bell pepper, seeded and chopped
- 1 large parsnip; peeled and chopped
- 6 tbsp. olive oil, divided
- 3 tbsp. honey
- 1 tsp. garlic paste
- 1 tsp. Dijon mustard
- 1 tsp. mixed dried herbs
- Salt and ground black pepper; as your liking

Directions:

1. Set the temperature of air fryer to 350°F. Grease an air fryer pan.
2. Arrange vegetables into the prepared air fryer pan and drizzle with 3 tbsp. of oil. Air fry for about 15 minutes.
3. Meanwhile; in a baking dish, mix well remaining oil, honey, mustard, herbs, garlic, salt and black pepper.
4. Remove the vegetables from air fryer. Transfer the vegetables into baking dish with honey mixture and mix until well combined.
5. set the temperature of air fryer to 392°F. Arrange the baking dish into air fryer and air fry for about 5 minutes. Remove from air fryer and transfer the vegetable mixture into a serving bowl. Serve immediately.

Jacket Potatoes

(Prep + Cook Time: 30 minutes | Servings: 2)

Ingredients:

- 2 potatoes
- 3 tbsp. sour cream
- 1 tbsp. butter; softened
- 1 tbsp. mozzarella cheese, shredded
- 1 tsp. chives, minced
- Salt and ground black pepper; as your liking

Directions:

1. Set the temperature of air fryer to 355°F. Grease an air fryer basket.
2. With a fork, prick the potatoes. Arrange potatoes into the prepared air fryer basket.
3. Air fry for about 15 minutes. In a bowl; add the remaining Ingredients and mix until well combined.
4. Remove from air fryer and transfer the potatoes onto a platter.
5. Open potatoes from the center and stuff them with cheese mixture. Serve immediately

Salsa Stuffed Eggplants

(Prep + Cook Time: 40 minutes | Servings: 2)

Ingredients:

- 1 large eggplant
- 8 cherry tomatoes, quartered
- 2 tbsp. tomato salsa
- 1/2 tbsp. fresh parsley
- 2 tsp. fresh lemon juice, divided
- 2 tsp. olive oil, divided
- Salt and ground black pepper; as your liking

Directions:

1. Set the temperature of air fryer to 390°F.
2. Grease an air fryer basket. Place eggplant into the prepared air fryer basket.
3. Air fry for about 15 minutes. Remove from air fryer and cut the eggplant in half lengthwise.
4. Drizzle the eggplant halves evenly with one tsp. of oil. Now; set the temperature of air fryer to 355°F. Grease the air fryer basket.
5. Arrange eggplant into the prepared air fryer basket, cut-side up. Air fry for another 10 minutes.
6. Remove eggplant from the air fryer and set aside for about 5 minutes.

7. Carefully; scoop out the flesh, leaving about ¼-inch away from edges.
8. Drizzle the eggplant halves with one tsp. of lemon juice. Transfer the eggplant flesh into a bowl.
9. Add the tomatoes, salsa, parsley, salt, black pepper, remaining oil and lemon juice and mix well.
10. Stuff the eggplant haves with salsa mixture and serve.

Herbed Potatoes

(Prep + Cook Time: 26 minutes | Servings: 4)

Ingredients:
- 6 small potatoes; chopped
- 2 tbsp. fresh parsley; chopped
- 3 tbsp. olive oil
- 2 tsp. mixed dried herbs
- Salt and ground black pepper; as your liking

Directions:
1. Set the temperature of air fryer to 356°F. Grease an air fryer basket. In a large bowl; add the potatoes, oil, herbs, salt and black pepper and toss to coat well.
2. Arrange the chopped potatoes into the prepared air fryer basket in a single layer.
3. Air fry for about 16 minutes, tossing once halfway through.
4. Remove from air fryer and transfer the potatoes onto serving plates. Garnish with parsley and serve.

Sautéed Green Beans

(Prep + Cook Time: 20 minutes | Servings: 2)

Ingredients:
- 8-oz fresh green beans, trimmed and cut in half
- 1 tsp. sesame oil
- 1 tbsp. soy sauce

Directions:
1. In a bowl; mix well green beans, soy sauce and sesame oil.
2. Set the temperature of air fryer to 390°F. Lightly, grease an air fryer basket.
3. Arrange green beans into the prepared air fryer basket. Air fry for about 10 minutes, tossing once halfway through.
4. Remove from air fryer and transfer the green beans onto serving plates. Serve hot.

Sesame Seeds Bok Choy

(Prep + Cook Time: 16 minutes | Servings: 4)

Ingredients:
- 4 bunches baby bok choy, bottoms removed and leaves separated
- 1 tsp. garlic powder
- Olive oil cooking spray
- 1 tsp. sesame seeds

Directions:
1. Set the temperature of air fryer to 325°F. Arrange bok choy leaves into the air fryer basket in a single layer.
2. Spray with the cooking spray and sprinkle with garlic powder.
3. Air fry for about 5 to 6 minutes, shaking after every 2 minutes.
4. Remove from air fryer and transfer the bok choy onto serving plates. Garnish with sesame seeds and serve hot.

Stuffed Okra

(Prep + Cook Time: 27 minutes | Servings: 2)

Ingredients:

- 8-oz large okra
- 1/4 of onion; chopped
- 1/4 cup chickpea flour
- 2 tbsp. coconut; grated freshly
- 1 tsp. garam masala powder
- 1/2 tsp. ground turmeric
- 1/2 tsp. red chili powder
- 1/2 tsp. ground cumin
- Salt, to taste

Directions:

1. With a knife, make a slit in each okra vertically without cutting in 2 halves. In a bowl; mix together the flour, onion; grated coconut and spices.
2. Stuff each okra with the mixture. Set the temperature of air fryer to 390°F. Grease an air fryer basket.
3. Arrange stuffed okra into the prepared air fryer basket. Air fry for about 12 minutes.
4. Remove from air fryer and transfer the okra onto serving plates. Serve hot.

Almond Asparagus

(Prep + Cook Time: 21 minutes | Servings: 3)

Ingredients:

- 1 lb. asparagus
- 1/3 cup almonds, sliced
- 2 tbsp. balsamic vinegar
- 2 tbsp. olive oil
- Salt and ground black pepper; as your liking

Directions:

1. In a bowl; mix together the asparagus, oil, vinegar, salt and black pepper. Set the temperature of air fryer to 400°F. Grease an air fryer basket.
2. Arrange asparagus into the prepared air fryer basket in a single layer and top with the almond slices.
3. Air fry for about 5 to 6 minutes.
4. Remove from air fryer and transfer the asparagus onto serving plates. Serve hot.

Stuffed Tomatoes

(Prep + Cook Time: 37 minutes | Servings: 4)

Ingredients:

- 4 tomatoes
- 1 carrot; peeled and finely chopped
- 1 onion; chopped
- 1 cup frozen peas, thawed
- 1 garlic clove, minced
- 2 cups cold cooked rice
- 1 tbsp. soy sauce
- 1 tsp. olive oil

Directions:

1. Cut the top of each tomato and scoop out pulp and seeds. In a skillet, heat oil over low heat and sauté the carrot, onion, garlic and peas for about 2 minutes.
2. Stir in the soy sauce and rice and remove from heat. Set the temperature of air fryer to 355°F. Grease an air fryer basket.
3. Stuff each tomato with the rice mixture.
4. Arrange tomatoes into the prepared air fryer basket. Air fry for about 20 minutes.
5. Remove from air fryer and transfer the tomatoes onto a serving platter. Set aside to cool slightly. Serve warm.

Spicy Tofu

(Prep + Cook Time: 20 minutes | Servings: 2)

Ingredients:

- 1 (14-oz) block extra-firm tofu, pressed and cut into ¾-inch cubes
- 1 ½ tbsp. avocado oil
- 1 tsp. onion powder
- 1 tsp. garlic powder
- 3 tsp. cornstarch
- 1 ½ tsp. paprika
- Salt and ground black pepper; as your liking

Directions:

1. In a bowl; mix well tofu, oil, cornstarch and spices. Set the temperature of air fryer to 390°F.
2. Grease an air fryer basket.
3. Arrange tofu pieces into the prepared air fryer basket in a single layer. Air fry for about 13 minutes, shaking twice halfway through.
4. Remove from air fryer and transfer the tofu onto serving plates. Serve hot.

Sweet and Spicy Cauliflower

(Prep + Cook Time: 45 minutes | Servings: 4)

Ingredients:

- 1 head cauliflower; cut into florets
- 3/4 cup onion, thinly sliced
- 2 scallions; chopped
- 5 garlic cloves, finely sliced
- 1 tbsp. hot sauce
- 1 tbsp. rice vinegar
- 1 ½ tbsp. soy sauce
- 1 tsp. coconut sugar
- Pinch of red pepper flakes
- Ground black pepper; as your liking

Directions:

1. Set the temperature of air fryer to 350°F. Grease an air fryer pan. Arrange cauliflower florets into the prepared air fryer pan in a single layer.
2. Air fry for about 10 minutes. Remove from air fryer and stir in the onions.
3. Air fry for another 10 minutes. Remove from air fryer and stir in the garlic.
4. Air fry for 5 more minutes. Meanwhile; in a bowl; mix well soy sauce, hot sauce, vinegar, coconut sugar, red pepper flakes and black pepper.
5. Remove from the air fryer and stir in the sauce mixture. Air fry for about 5 minutes.
6. Remove from air fryer and transfer the cauliflower mixture onto serving plates. Garnish with scallions and serve.

Tofu with Capers Sauce

(Prep + Cook Time: 40 minutes | Servings: 4)

Ingredients:
For Marinade:

- 1/4 cup fresh lemon juice
- 1 garlic clove; peeled
- 2 tbsp. fresh parsley
- Salt and ground black pepper; as your liking

For Tofu:

- 1 (14-oz) block extra-firm tofu, pressed and cut into 8 rectangular cutlets
- 1/2 cup mayonnaise
- 1 cup panko breadcrumbs

For Sauce:

- 1 garlic clove; peeled
- 1 cup vegetable broth
- 1/4 cup lemon juice
- 2 tbsp. fresh parsley
- 2 tbsp. capers
- 2 tsp. cornstarch
- Salt and ground black pepper; as your liking

Directions:
1. **For marinade:** in a food processor, add all the Ingredients and pulse until smooth. In a bowl; mix together the marinade and tofu.
2. Set aside for about 15 to 30 minutes. In two shallow bowls, place the mayonnaise and panko breadcrumbs respectively.
3. Coat the tofu pieces with mayonnaise and then, roll into the panko. Set the temperature of air fryer to 375°F. Grease an air fryer basket.
4. Arrange tofu pieces into the prepared air fryer basket in a single layer.
5. Air fry for about 20 minutes, shaking once halfway through.
6. Meanwhile; for the sauce: add broth, lemon juice, garlic, parsley, cornstarch, salt and black pepper in a food processor and pulse until smooth.
7. Transfer the sauce into a small pan and stir in the capers. Place the sauce over medium heat and bring to a boil.
8. Reduce the heat to low and simmer for about 5 to 7 minutes, stirring continuously.
9. Remove the tofu from air fryer and transfer onto serving plates. Top with the sauce and serve.

Spiced Butternut Squash

(Prep + Cook Time: 35 minutes | Servings: 4)

Ingredients:
- 1 medium butternut squash, peeled, seeded and cut into chunk
- 2 tbsp. pine nuts
- 2 tbsp. fresh cilantro; chopped
- 1 tbsp. olive oil
- 1/8 tsp. chili flakes; crushed
- 1/8 tsp. garlic powder
- 2 tsp. cumin seeds
- Salt and ground black pepper; as your liking

Directions:
1. Set the temperature of air fryer to 375°F. Grease an air fryer basket. In a bowl; mix together the squash, spices and oil.
2. Arrange butternut squash chunks into the prepared fryer basket. Air fry for about 20 minutes, flipping occasionally.
3. Remove from air fryer and transfer the squash chunks onto serving plates.
4. Garnish with pine nuts and cilantro. Serve.

Herbed Veggies Combo

(Prep + Cook Time: 50 minutes | Servings: 4)

Ingredients:
- 1 lb. yellow squash, sliced
- 1/2 lb. carrots; peeled and sliced
- 1 lb. zucchini, sliced
- 1/2 tbsp. tarragon leaves; chopped
- 1/2 tbsp. fresh basil; chopped
- 6 tsp. olive oil, divided
- Salt and ground white pepper; as your liking

Directions:
1. Set the temperature of air fryer to 400°F. In a bowl; mix together 2 tsp. of oil and carrot slices.
2. Place carrot slices into the air fryer basket Air fry for about 5 minutes.
3. Meanwhile; in a large bowl; add the remaining oil, yellow squash, zucchini, salt and white pepper and toss to coat well. Transfer the zucchini mixture into air fryer basket with carrots.
4. Air fry for about 30 minutes, tossing 2 to 3 times. Remove from air fryer and transfer the vegetable mixture into a serving bowl.
5. Add the herbs and mix until well combined. Serve.

Broccoli with Cauliflower

(Prep + Cook Time: 35 minutes | Servings: 4)

Ingredients:
- 1 ½ cups cauliflower; cut into 1-inch pieces
- 1 ½ cups broccoli; cut into 1-inch pieces
- 1 tbsp. olive oil
- Salt; as your liking

Directions:
1. In a bowl; add the vegetables, oil and salt and toss to coat well.
2. Set the temperature of air fryer to 375°F. Grease an air fryer basket.
3. Arrange veggie mixture into the prepared air fryer basket. Air fry for about 15 to 20 minutes, tossing once halfway through.
4. Remove from air fryer and transfer the veggie mixture onto serving plates. Serve hot.

Sautéed Spinach

(Prep + Cook Time: 24 minutes | Servings: 2)

Ingredients:
- 1 garlic clove, minced
- 6-oz fresh spinach
- 1 small onion; chopped
- 2 tbsp. olive oil
- Salt and ground black pepper; as your liking

Directions:
1. Set the temperature of air fryer to 340°F. In an air fryer pan, heat the oil for about 2 minutes.
2. Add the onion and garlic and air fry for about 3 minutes.
3. Add the spinach, salt and black pepper and air fry for about 4 more minutes.
4. Remove from air fryer and transfer the spinach mixture onto serving plates. Serve hot.

Crispy Marinated Tofu

(Prep + Cook Time: 35 minutes | Servings: 3)

Ingredients:
- 1 (14-oz) block firm tofu, pressed and cut into 1-inch cubes
- 1 tbsp. cornstarch
- 2 tbsp. low sodium soy sauce
- 1 tsp. seasoned rice vinegar
- 2 tsp. sesame oil; toasted

Directions:
1. In a bowl; mix well tofu, soy sauce, sesame oil and vinegar. Set aside to marinate for about 25 to 30 minutes. Coat the tofu cubes evenly with cornstarch.
2. Set the temperature of air fryer to 370°F. Grease an air fryer basket. Arrange tofu pieces into the prepared air fryer basket in a single layer.
3. Air fry for about 20 minutes, shaking once halfway through.
4. Remove from air fryer and transfer the tofu onto serving plates. Serve warm.

Spices Stuffed Eggplants

(Prep + Cook Time: 27 minutes | Servings: 4)

Ingredients:
- 8 baby eggplants
- 3/4 tbsp. ground coriander
- 3/4 tbsp. dry mango powder
- 1/2 tsp. ground cumin
- 1/2 tsp. ground turmeric
- 1/2 tsp. garlic powder
- 4 tsp. olive oil, divided
- Salt, to taste

Directions:
1. In a small bowl; mix together one tsp. of oil and spices. From the bottom of each eggplant, make 2 slits, leaving the stems intact.

2. With a small spoon, fill each slit of eggplants with spice mixture. Now; brush the outer side of each eggplant with remaining oil.
3. Set the temperature of air fryer to 369°F. Grease an air fryer basket.
4. Arrange eggplants into the prepared air fryer basket in a single layer.
5. Air fry for about 8 to 12 minutes. Remove from air fryer and transfer the eggplants onto serving plates. Serve hot.

Tofu in Sweet and Spicy Sauce

(Prep + Cook Time: 43 minutes | Servings: 3)

Ingredients:
For Tofu:
- 1/2 cup arrowroot flour
- 1 (14-oz) block firm tofu, pressed and cubed
- 1/2 tsp. sesame oil

For Sauce:
- 2 large garlic cloves, minced
- 2 scallions (green part); chopped
- 1 ½ tbsp. chili sauce
- 1 tbsp. agave nectar
- 4 tbsp. low-sodium soy sauce
- 1 ½ tbsp. rice vinegar
- 1 tsp. fresh ginger; peeled and grated

Directions:
1. In a bowl; mix together the tofu, arrowroot flour and sesame oil. Set the temperature of air fryer to 360°F. Generously, grease an air fryer basket
2. Arrange tofu pieces into the prepared air fryer basket in a single layer
3. Air fry for about 20 minutes, shaking once halfway through.
4. Meanwhile; for the sauce: in a bowl; add all the Ingredients except scallions and beat until well combined.
5. Remove from air fryer and transfer the tofu into a skillet with sauce over medium heat and cook for about 3 minutes, stirring occasionally. Garnish with scallions and serve hot

Rice Flour Crusted Tofu

(Prep + Cook Time: 43 minutes | Servings: 3)

Ingredients:
- 1 (14-oz) block firm tofu, pressed and cubed into ½-inch size
- 1/4 cup rice flour
- 2 tbsp. olive oil
- 2 tbsp. cornstarch
- Salt and ground black pepper; as your liking

Directions:
1. In a bowl; mix together cornstarch, rice flour, salt and black pepper.
2. Coat the tofu evenly with flour mixture. Drizzle the tofu with oil.
3. Set the temperature of air fryer to 360°F. Grease an air fryer basket.
4. Arrange tofu cubes into the prepared air fryer basket in a single layer.
5. Air fry for about 14 minutes per side. Remove from air fryer and transfer the tofu onto serving plates. Serve warm.

Mushrooms with Peas

(Prep + Cook Time: 30 minutes | Servings: 4)

Ingredients:

- 16-oz cremini mushrooms, halved
- 4 garlic cloves, finely chopped
- 1/2 cup soy sauce
- 1/2 cup frozen peas
- 4 tbsp. maple syrup
- 4 tbsp. rice vinegar
- 1/2 tsp. ground ginger
- 2 tsp. Chinese five spice powder

Directions:

1. In a bowl; mix well soy sauce, maple syrup, vinegar, garlic, five spice powder and ground ginger. Set the temperature of air fryer to 350°F. Grease an air fryer pan.
2. Arrange mushroom into the prepared air fryer pan in a single layer. Air fry for about 10 minutes.
3. Remove from air fryer and stir the mushrooms.
4. Add the peas and vinegar mixture and stir to combine. Air fry for about 5 more minutes.
5. Remove from air fryer and transfer the mushroom mixture onto serving plates. Serve hot.

Desserts

Fruity Oreo Muffins

(Prep + Cook Time: 25 minutes | Servings: 6)

Ingredients:

- 1 banana; peeled and chopped
- 1 pack Oreo biscuits; crushed
- 1 apple, peeled, cored and chopped
- 1 cup milk
- 1 tsp. honey
- 1 tsp. fresh lemon juice
- 1 tsp. cocoa powder
- 1/4 tsp. baking soda
- 1/2 tsp. baking powder
- A pinch of ground cinnamon

Directions:

1. In a bowl; add the milk, biscuits, cocoa powder, baking soda and baking powder. Mix until a smooth mixture forms
2. Set the temperature of air fryer to 320°F. Grease 6 muffin cups. Place mixture evenly into the prepared muffin cups. Arrange the muffin cups into an air fryer basket. Air fry for 10 minutes or until a toothpick inserted in the center comes out clean
3. Remove from air fryer and place the muffin cups onto a wire rack to cool slightly.
4. Meanwhile; in another bowl; mix together the banana, apple, honey, lemon juice and cinnamon.
5. Carefully; scoop some portion of muffins from the center to make a cup. Fill each cup with fruit mixture. Refrigerate to chill before serving

Sweet Potato Pie

(Prep + Cook Time: 85 minutes | Servings: 6)

Ingredients:

- 1 (9-inches) prepared frozen pie dough, thawed
- 1/4 cup heavy cream
- 2 large eggs
- 6-oz sweet potato
- 1/2 tsp. ground cinnamon
- 1/8 tsp. ground nutmeg
- 3/4 tsp. vanilla extract
- 1 tsp. olive oil
- 1 tbsp. light brown sugar
- 2 tbsp. maple syrup
- 1 tbsp. butter; melted
- Salt, to taste

Directions:

1. Set the temperature of air fryer to 400°F. Coat the sweet potato evenly with oil. Arrange the sweet potato into an air fryer basket. Air fry for about 30 minutes. Remove from air fryer and set aside to cool completely
2. Peel the sweet potato and mash it completely. Place the pie dough onto a floured surface and cut into 8-inch pie shell.
3. Arrange the dough shell into a greased pie pan. In a large bowl; add the mashed sweet potato and remaining Ingredients and mix until well combined
4. Place sweet potato mixture evenly over the pie shell. Set the temperature of air fryer to 320°F.
5. Arrange the pie pan into an air fryer basket. Air fry for about 30 minutes. Remove from air fryer and place the pie pan onto a wire rack to cool for about 10 to 15 minutes before serving. Serve warm.

Brownies Muffins

(Prep + Cook Time: 20 minutes | Servings: 12)

Ingredients:

- 1/3 cup vegetable oil
- 1/4 cup walnuts; chopped
- 1 package Betty Crocker fudge brownie mix
- 1 egg
- 2 tsp. water

Directions:

1. In a bowl; mix well all the ingredients. Set the temperature of air fryer to 300°F.
2. Grease 12 muffin molds. Place mixture evenly into the prepared muffin molds
3. Arrange the molds into an Air Fryer basket. Air fry for 10 minutes or until a toothpick inserted in the center comes out clean
4. Remove the muffin molds from air fryer and place onto a wire rack to cool for about 10 minutes.
5. Finally, invert the muffins onto wire rack to completely cool before serving.

Yogurt Cake

(**Prep + Cook Time:** 35 minutes | **Servings:** 8)

Ingredients:

- 8 oz. canned pumpkin puree
- 1/2 tsp. vanilla extract
- 1/2 tsp. baking powder
- 3/4 cup sugar
- 1 banana; mashed
- 1 egg
- 1½ cups white flour
- 1 cup Greek yogurt
- 1 tsp. baking soda
- 2 tbsp. vegetable oil
- Cooking spray

Directions:

1. In a bowl, combine all ingredients (except the cooking spray) and stir well.
2. Pour the mixture into a cake pan greased with cooking spray and put it in your air fryer's basket
3. Cook at 330°F for 30 minutes. Cool down, slice and serve

Fruity Crumble

(Prep + Cook Time: 35 minutes | Servings: 4)

Ingredients:

- 1/2 lb. fresh apricots, pitted and cubed
- 7/8 cup flour
- 1/4 cup chilled butter, cubed
- 1/3 cup sugar, divided
- 1 cup fresh blackberries
- 1 tbsp. cold water
- 1 tbsp. fresh lemon juice
- Pinch of salt

Directions:

1. Set the temperature of air fryer to 390°F. Grease a baking pan. In a large bowl; mix well apricots, blackberries, 2 tbsp. of sugar and lemon juice. Spread apricot mixture into the prepared baking pan. In another bowl; add the flour, remaining sugar, salt, water and butter. Mix until a crumbly mixture forms.
2. Spread the flour mixture evenly over apricot mixture. Place the pan in an air fryer basket.
3. Air fry for about 20 minutes. Remove the baking pan from air fryer and place onto a wire rack to cool for about 10 minutes. Serve warm

Apple Cake

(Prep + Cook Time: 60 minutes | Servings: 6)

Ingredients:

- 1/3 cup brown sugar
- 1 cup all-purpose flour
- 2 cups apples, peeled, cored and chopped
- 1 egg
- 5 tbsp. plus 1 tsp. vegetable oil
- 1 tsp. ground cinnamon
- 1/2 tsp. baking soda
- 3/4 tsp. vanilla extract
- 1 tsp. ground nutmeg
- Salt, to taste

Directions:

1. In a bowl; mix well flour, sugar, spices, baking soda and salt. In another bowl; add the egg and oil and whisk until smooth. Add the vanilla extract and whisk well. Slowly, add the flour mixture, whisking continuously until well combined.
2. Fold in the chopped apples. Set the temperature of air fryer to 355°F. Lightly, grease a cake pan. Place mixture evenly into the prepared cake pan
3. With a piece of foil, cover the pan and poke some holes using a fork. Arrange the cake pan into an air fryer basket. Now; set the temperature of air fryer to 320°F. Air fry for about 40 minutes
4. Remove the foil and air fry for another 5 minutes or until a toothpick inserted in the center comes out clean. Remove the cake pan from air fryer and place onto a wire rack to cool for about 10 minutes.
5. invert the cake onto wire rack to completely cool before slicing. Cut the cake into desired size slices and serve.

Butter Cake

(Prep + Cook Time: 30 minutes | Servings: 6)

Ingredients:

- 3-oz butter; softened
- 1 ⅓ cups plain flour, sifted
- 1/2 cup milk
- 1/2 cup caster sugar
- 1 egg
- 1 tbsp. icing sugar
- A pinch of salt

Directions:

1. In a bowl; add the butter and sugar and whisk until light and creamy. Add in the egg and whisk until smooth and fluffy. add the flour and salt and mix well alternately with the milk. Set the temperature of air fryer to 350°F. Grease a small Bundt cake pan
2. Place mixture evenly into the prepared cake pan. Arrange the cake pan in an air fryer basket. Air fry for about 15 minutes or until a toothpick inserted into the center comes out clean
3. Remove the cake pan from air fryer and place onto a wire rack to cool for about 10 minutes. Now; invert the cake onto wire rack to completely cool before slicing. Dust the cake with icing sugar and cut into desired size slices. Serve.

Apple Crumble

(Prep + Cook Time: 35 minutes | Servings: 4)

Ingredients:

- 1 (14-oz) can apple pie filling
- 1/4 cup butter; softened
- 7 tbsp. caster sugar
- 9 tbsp. self-rising flour
- Pinch of salt

Directions:

1. Set the temperature of air fryer to 320°F. Lightly, grease a baking dish. Place apple pie filling evenly into the prepared baking dish. In a medium bowl; add the remaining Ingredients and mix until a crumbly mixture forms. Spread the mixture evenly over apple pie filling
2. Arrange the baking dish in an air fryer basket. Air fry for about 25 minutes

3. Remove the baking dish from air fryer and place onto a wire rack to cool for about 10 minutes. Serve warm.

Crispy Banana Split

(Prep + Cook Time: 19 minutes | Servings: 8)

Ingredients:

- 4 bananas; peeled and halved lengthwise
- 1 cup panko breadcrumbs
- 1/2 cup corn flour
- 3 tbsp. coconut oil
- 2 tbsp. walnuts; chopped
- 2 eggs
- 3 tbsp. sugar
- 1/4 tsp. ground cinnamon

Directions:

1. In a medium skillet, heat the oil over medium heat and cook breadcrumbs for about 3 to 4 minutes or until golden browned and crumbled, stirring continuously. Transfer the breadcrumbs into a shallow bowl and set aside to cool. In a second bowl; place the corn flour. In a third bowl; whisk the eggs
2. Coat the banana slices with flour and then, dip into eggs and finally, coat evenly with the breadcrumbs. In a small bowl; mix together the sugar and cinnamon
3. Set the temperature of air fryer to 280°F. Grease an air fryer basket. Arrange banana slices into the prepared air fryer basket in a single layer and sprinkle with cinnamon sugar
4. Air fry for about 10 minutes. Remove from air fryer and transfer the banana slices onto plates to cool slightlySprinkle with chopped walnuts and serve

---

Layered Cake

(Prep + Cook Time: 45 minutes | Servings: 8)

Ingredients:

For Cake:

- 3 ½-oz plain flour
- 3 ½-oz butter; softened
- 2 medium eggs
- 7 tbsp. sugar
- 1 tsp. ground cinnamon
- Pinch of salt

For Filling:

- 2/3 cup icing sugar
- 1¾-oz butter; softened
- 2 tbsp. strawberry jam
- 1 tbsp. whipped cream

Directions:

1. In a large bowl; mix well flour, cinnamon and salt. In another bowl; add the sugar and butter and whisk until creamy. Add in the eggs and whisk until well combined. Slowly, add the flour mixture whisking continuously until well combined Set the temperature of air fryer to 355°F. Grease a cake pan
2. Place mixture evenly into the prepared cake pan. Air fry for about 15 minutes and then, another 10 minutes at 335°F
3. Remove the cake pan from air fryer and place onto a wire rack to cool for about 10 minutes. Now; invert the cake onto wire rack to completely cool before filling. After cooling, cut the cake into 2 equal-sized portions.
4. **For filling:** in a bowl; add the butter and whisk until creamy. Add the cream and icing sugar and whisk until a thick creamy mixture forms. Place one cake portion onto a serving platter, cut side up.
5. Spread the jam evenly over cake and top with butter mixture. Arrange another cake over filling, cut side down. Cut the cake into desired size slices and serve

Walnut Brownies

(Prep + Cook Time: 37 minutes | Servings: 4)

Ingredients:
- 1/2 cup chocolate; roughly chopped
- 1 egg, beaten
- 1/4 cup walnuts; chopped
- 1/3 cup butter
- 5 tbsp. self-rising flour
- 5 tbsp. sugar
- 1 tsp. vanilla extract
- A pinch of salt

Directions:
1. In a microwave-safe bowl; add the chocolate and butter. Microwave on high heat for about 2 minutes, stirring after every 30 seconds. Remove from microwave and set aside to cool. Now; in a bowl; add the sugar, egg, vanilla extract and salt and whisk until creamy and light
2. Add the chocolate mixture and whisk until well combined. Add the flour and walnuts and mix until well combined. Set the temperature of air fryer to 355°F. Line a baking pan with a greased parchment paper.
3. Place mixture evenly into the prepared pan and with the back of spatula, smooth the top surface
4. Arrange the baking pan into an air fryer basket. Air fry for about 20 minutes
5. Remove the baking pan from air fryer and set aside to cool completely. Cut into 4 equal-sized squares and serve.

Lava Cake

(Prep + Cook Time: 27½ minutes | Servings: 4)

Ingredients:
- 2 large eggs
- 2 large egg yolks
- 1/3 cup all-purpose flour plus more for dusting
- 1 cup confectioners' sugar
- 1/3 cup fresh raspberries
- 2/3 cup chocolate chips
- 1/2 cup unsalted butter; softened
- 2 tbsp. powdered sugar
- 1 tsp. peppermint extract

Directions:
1. In a microwave-safe bowl; put the chocolate chips and butter. Microwave on high heat for about 30 seconds. Remove the bowl from microwave and stir the mixture well. Add the eggs, egg yolks and confectioners' sugar and whisk until well combined. Add the flour and gently, stir to combine
2. Set the temperature of air fryer to 375°F. Grease 4 ramekins and dust each with a little flour. Place mixture evenly into the prepared ramekins.
3. Arrange the ramekins into an air fryer basket. Air fry for about 10 to 12 minutes. Remove from air fryer and place the ramekins onto a wire rack for about 5 minutes
4. Carefully run a knife around sides of each ramekin several times to loosen the cake. Finally, invert each cake onto a dessert plate and dust with powdered sugar. Garnish with raspberries and serve immediately.

Orange Cake

(**Prep + Cook Time:** 30 minutes | **Servings:** 3)

Ingredients:
- 4 tbsp. flour
- 1 egg
- 2 tbsp. orange juice
- 4 tbsp. sugar
- 2 tbsp. vegetable oil
- 4 tbsp. milk
- 1 tbsp. cocoa powder
- 1/2 tsp. orange zest
- 1/2 tsp. baking powder

Directions:
1. Place all of the ingredients in a bowl and mix well.
2. Divide the mixture between 3 ramekins and place them in your air fryer
3. Cook at 320°F for 20 minutes. Serve the cakes warm and enjoy!

Passion Fruit Pudding Recipe

(Prep + Cook Time: 50 Minutes | **Servings:** 6)

Ingredients:
- 1 cup Paleo passion fruit curd
- 3 ½-ounce almond milk
- 1/2 cup almond flour
- 4 passion fruits; pulp and seeds
- 3 ½-ounce maple syrup
- 3 eggs
- 2-ounce ghee; melted
- 1/2 tsp. baking powder

Directions:
1. In a bowl; mix the half of the fruit curd with passion fruit seeds and pulp; stir and divide into 6 heat proof ramekins
2. In a bowl; whisked eggs with maple syrup, ghee, the rest of the curd, baking powder, milk and flour and stir well
3. Divide this into the ramekins as well, introduce in the fryer and cook at 200°F, for 40 minutes. Leave puddings to cool down and serve!

Pear Pastry Pouch

(Prep + Cook Time: 30 minutes | Servings: 4)

Ingredients:
- 2 small pears, peeled, cored and halved
- 2 cups vanilla custard
- 4 puff pastry sheets
- 1 egg, lightly beaten
- 2 tbsp. whipped cream
- 2 tbsp. sugar
- Pinch of ground cinnamon

Directions:
1. Carefully; make small cuts in each pear half. In the center of each pastry sheet, place a spoonful of vanilla custard and top with a pear half. In a bowl; mix together the sugar and cinnamon. Sprinkle the sugar mixture evenly over pear halves. Pinch the corners to shape into a pouch
2. coat each pear with egg. Set the temperature of air fryer to 330°F. Lightly, grease an air fryer basket. Arrange pear pouches into the prepared air fryer basket in a single layer. Air fry for about 15 minutes.
3. Remove from air fryer and transfer the pear pouches onto a platter. Top with whipped cream and serve with the remaining custard

Chocolate Yogurt Muffins

(Prep + Cook Time: 25 minutes | Servings: 9)

Ingredients:
- 1/4 cup mini chocolate chips
- 1 cup yogurt
- 1 egg
- 1/3 cup vegetable oil
- 1/4 cup pecans; chopped
- 1 ½ cups all-purpose flour
- 1/4 cup sugar
- 2 tsp. baking powder
- 1/2 tsp. salt
- 2 tsp. vanilla extract

Directions:
1. In a bowl; mix well flour, sugar, baking powder and salt. In another bowl; add the yogurt, oil, egg and vanilla extract and whisk until well combined. Add the flour mixture and mix until just combined. Fold in the chocolate chips and pecans. Set the temperature of air fryer to 355°F. Grease 9 muffin molds
2. Place mixture evenly into the prepared muffin molds. Arrange the muffin molds into an air fryer basket. Air fry for 10 minutes or until a toothpick inserted in the center comes out clean
3. Remove the muffin molds from air fryer and place onto a wire rack to cool for about 10 minutes. Finally, invert the muffins onto wire rack to completely cool before serving.

Cinnamon Apples

(**Prep + Cook Time:** 20 minutes | **Servings:** 4)

Ingredients:
- 4 apples; peeled, cored and cut into wedges
- 3 tbsp. cinnamon sugar
- 3 tbsp. butter; melted

Directions:
1. In a pan that fits your air fryer, mix the apples with the sugar and the butter; toss
2. Place the pan in the fryer and cook at 370°F for 15 minutes. Serve warm

Shortbread Fingers

(Prep + Cook Time: 27 minutes | Servings: 10)

Ingredients:
- 1 2/3 cups plain flour
- 3/4 cup butter
- 1/3 cup caster sugar

Directions:
1. In a large bowl; mix together the sugar and flour. Add the butter and mix until a smooth dough forms. Cut the dough into 10 equal-sized fingers. With a fork, lightly prick the fingers. Set the temperature of air fryer to 355°F. Lightly, grease a baking sheet.
2. Arrange fingers into the prepared baking sheet in a single layer. Arrange the baking sheet into an air fryer basket
3. Air fry for about 12 minutes. Remove the baking sheet from air fryer and place onto a wire rack to cool for about 5 to 10 minutes. invert the short bread fingers onto wire rack to completely cool before serving. Serve

Pecan Pie

(Prep + Cook Time: 50 minutes | Servings: 5)

Ingredients:
- 2 large eggs
- 3/4 cup brown sugar
- 1 cup pecan halves
- 1 frozen pie crust, thawed
- 1/4 cup caster sugar
- 1/3 cup butter; melted
- 1 tbsp. milk
- 1¾ tbsp. flour
- 1 tsp. vanilla extract

Directions:
1. In a large bowl; mix well sugars and butter. Add the eggs and whisk until foamy. Add the flour, milk and vanilla extract and whisk until well combined. Fold in the pecan halves. Set the temperature of air fryer to 300°F. Grease a pie pan. Arrange the crust in the bottom of prepared pie pan
2. Transfer pecan mixture evenly over the crust. Arrange the pan in an air fryer basket. Air fry for about 22 minutes and then, another 13 minutes at 285°F
3. Remove from air fryer and place the pie pan onto a wire rack to cool for about 10 to 15 minutes before serving. Serve warm.

Milky Doughnuts

(Prep + Cook Time: 39 minutes | Servings: 12)

Ingredients:
For Doughnuts:
- 1 cup all-purpose flour
- 1/2 cup milk
- 1 cup whole wheat flour
- 3/4 cup sugar
- 1 egg
- 1 tbsp. butter; softened
- 2 tsp. vanilla extract
- 2 tsp. baking powder
- Salt, to taste

For Glaze:
- 1 tbsp. cocoa powder
- 2 tbsp. icing sugar
- 2 tbsp. condensed milk

Directions:
1. In a large bowl; mix well flours, baking powder and salt. In another bowl; add the sugar and egg. Whisk until fluffy and light. Add the flour mixture and stir until well combined. Add the butter, milk and vanilla extract and mix until a soft dough forms
2. Refrigerate the dough for at least 1 hour. Now; put the dough onto a lightly floured surface and roll into ½-inch thickness.
3. With a small doughnut cutter, cut 24 small doughnuts from the rolled dough. Set the temperature of air fryer to 390°F. Grease an air fryer basket
4. Place doughnuts into the prepared air fryer basket in 3 batches. Air fry for about 6 to 8 minutes. Remove from air fryer and transfer the doughnuts onto a platter to cool completely. In a small bowl; mix together the condensed milk and cocoa powder. Spread the glaze over doughnuts and sprinkle with icing sugar. Serve

Vanilla Soufflé

(Prep + Cook Time: 54 minutes | Servings: 6)

Ingredients:
- 4 egg yolks
- 5 egg whites
- 1/4 cup all-purpose flour
- 1 cup milk
- 1/2 cup plus 2 tbsp. sugar, divided
- 1/4 cup butter; softened
- 2 tbsp. powdered sugar plus extra for dusting
- 3 tsp. vanilla extract, divided
- 1 tsp. cream of tartar

Directions:
1. In a bowl; add the butter and flour and mix until a smooth paste forms. In a medium pan, mix together 1/2 cup of sugar and milk over medium-low heat and cook for about 3 minutes or until the sugar is dissolved, stirring continuously
2. Add the flour mixture, whisking continuously and simmer for about 3 to 4 minutes or until mixture becomes thick. Remove from the heat and stir in 1 tsp. of vanilla extract.
3. Set aside for about 10 minutes to cool. In a bowl; mix together the egg yolks and 1 tsp. of vanilla extract. Add the egg yolk mixture into milk mixture and mix until well combined
4. In another bowl; add the egg whites, cream of tartar, remaining sugar and vanilla extract and whisk until stiff peaks form.
5. Fold the egg whites mixture into milk mixture. Set the temperature of air fryer to 330°F. Grease 6 ramekins and sprinkle each with a pinch of sugar
6. Place mixture evenly into the prepared ramekins and with the back of a spoon, smooth the top surface. Arrange the ramekins into an air fryer basket in 2 batches. Air fry for about 14-16 minutes. Remove from air fryer and set aside to cool slightly. Sprinkle with the powdered sugar and serve warm.

Red Velvet Cupcakes

(Prep + Cook Time: 32 minutes | Servings: 12)

Ingredients:
For Cupcakes:
- 3/4 cup peanut butter
- 2 cups refined flour
- 3/4 cup icing sugar
- 3 eggs
- 2 tsp. beet powder
- 1 tsp. cocoa powder

For Frosting:
- 4 ½ cups powdered sugar
- 1 (8-oz) package cream cheese; softened
- 1 cup butter
- 2 tsp. vanilla extract
- 1/4 tsp. salt

For Garnishing:
- 1/2 cup fresh raspberries

Directions:
1. **For cupcakes:** in a bowl; put all the Ingredients and with an electric whisker, whisk until well combined. Place the mixture into silicon cups. Set the temperature of air fryer to 340°F. Arrange the silicon cups into an air fryer basket
2. Air fry for about 10 to 12 minutes or until a toothpick inserted in the center comes out clean. Remove the silicon cups from air fryer and place onto a wire rack to cool for about 10 minutes
3. invert the cupcakes onto wire rack to completely cool before frosting
4. **For frosting:** in a large bowl; mix well butter, cream cheese, vanilla extract and salt. Add the powdered sugar, one cup at a time, whisking well after each addition. Spread frosting evenly over each cupcake. Garnish with raspberries and serve.

White Chocolate Cheesecake

(Prep + Cook Time: 54 minutes | Servings: 6)

Ingredients:
- 3 eggs, whites and yolks separated
- 1 cup white chocolate; chopped
- 1/2 cup cream cheese; softened
- 1/4 cup apricot jam
- 2 tbsp. powdered sugar
- 2 tbsp. cocoa powder

Directions:
1. In a bowl; add the egg whites and refrigerate to chill before using. In a microwave-safe bowl; add the chocolate and microwave on high heat for about 2 minutes, stirring after every 30 seconds.
2. In the bowl of chocolate, add the cream cheese and microwave for about 1 to 2 minutes or until cream cheese melts completely
3. Remove from microwave and stir in cocoa powder and egg yolks
4. Remove the egg whites from refrigerator and whisk until firm peaks form. Add 1/3 of the mixed egg whites into cheese mixture and gently, stir to combine.
5. Fold in the remaining egg whites. Set the temperature of air fryer to 285°F.
6. Place the mixture into a 6-inch cake pan. Arrange the cake pan into an air fryer basket
7. Air fry for about 30 minutes. Remove from the air fryer and set aside to cool completely. Refrigerate to chill before serving. Just before serving, dust with the powdered sugar. Finally, spread the jam evenly on top and serve.

Raspberry Cupcakes

(Prep + Cook Time: 30 minutes | Servings: 10)

Ingredients:
- 1/2-ounce cream cheese; softened
- 4¾-oz butter; softened
- 4¼-oz caster sugar
- 1/2 cup fresh raspberries
- 2 eggs
- 4 ½-oz self-rising flour
- 1/2 tsp. baking powder
- 2 tsp. fresh lemon juice
- A pinch of salt

Directions:
1. In a bowl; mix well flour, baking powder and salt. In another bowl; mix together the cream cheese and butter. Add the sugar and whisk until fluffy and light. Now; place the eggs, one at a time and whisk until just combined
2. Add the flour mixture and stir until well combined. Stir in the lemon juice. Place the mixture evenly into silicon cups and top each with 2 raspberries
3. Set the temperature of air fryer to 365°F. Arrange the silicon cups into an air fryer basket
4. Air fry for about 15 minutes or until a toothpick inserted in the center comes out clean. Remove the silicon cups from air fryer and place onto a wire rack to cool for about 10 minutes. invert the cupcakes onto wire rack to completely cool before serving.

Maple Apples

(**Prep + Cook Time:** 20 minutes | **Servings:** 4)

Ingredients:

- 5 apples; cored and cut into wedges
- 1/4 cup brown sugar
- 1/2 tsp. nutmeg powder
- 2 tsp. cinnamon powder
- 1 tbsp. maple syrup
- 4 tbsp. butter

Directions:

1. In a pan that fits your air fryer, mix the apples with the other ingredients and toss
2. Place the pan in the fryer and cook at 360°F for 10 minutes. Divide into cups and serve.

Apple Tart

(Prep + Cook Time: 35 minutes | Servings: 3)

Ingredients:

- 1 large granny smith apple, peeled, cored and cut into 12 wedges
- 1-ounce sugar
- 2 ½-oz butter; chopped and divided
- 3 ½-oz flour
- 1 egg yolk

Directions:

1. In a bowl; add half of the butter, flour and egg yolk and mix until a soft dough forms. Now; put the dough onto a floured surface and roll into a 6-inch round circle. Set the temperature of air fryer to 390°F. In a baking pan, add the remaining butter and sprinkle with sugar
2. Top with the apple wedges in a circular pattern. Place the rolled dough over apple wedges and gently press along the edges of the pan. Arrange the pan into an air fryer basket. Air fry for about 25 minutes. Remove from the air fryer and serve warm

Double Chocolate Muffins

(Prep + Cook Time: 50 minutes | Servings: 12)

Ingredients:

- 2 ½-oz milk chocolate, finely chopped
- 3 ½-oz butter
- 1 ⅓ cups self-rising flour
- 2 medium eggs
- 2/3 cup plus 3 tbsp. caster sugar
- 5 tbsp. milk
- 2 ½ tbsp. cocoa powder
- 1/2 tsp. vanilla extract
- Water, as required

Directions:

1. In a bowl; mix well flour, sugar and cocoa powder. With a pastry cutter, cut in the butter until a breadcrumb like mixture forms. In another bowl; mix together the milk and eggs. Add the egg mixture into flour mixture and mix until well combined
2. Add the vanilla extract and a little water and mix until well combined. Fold in the chopped chocolate.
3. Set the temperature of air fryer to 355°F. Grease 12 muffin molds. Transfer mixture evenly into the prepared muffin molds
4. Arrange the molds into an air fryer basket in 2 batches. Air fry for about 9 minutes.
5. Now; set the temperature of air fryer to 320°F. Air fry for another 6 minutes or until a toothpick inserted in the center comes out clean
6. Remove the muffin molds from air fryer and place onto a wire rack to cool for about 10 minutes. Now; invert the muffins onto wire rack to cool completely before serving.

Chocolate Cake

(Prep + Cook Time: 55 minutes | Servings: 4)

Ingredients:

For Cake:

- 1/3 cup plain flour
- 2 egg yolks
- 1/2 ounce caster sugar
- 3¾ tbsp. milk

- 1 ½ tbsp. unsweetened cocoa powder
- 2 tbsp. vegetable oil
- 1/4 tsp. baking powder
- 1 tsp. vanilla extract

For Meringue:

- 2 egg whites
- 1 ounce caster sugar

- 1/8 tsp. cream of tartar

Directions:

1. **For cake:** in a bowl; sift together the flour, baking powder and cocoa powder. In another bowl; add the remaining Ingredients and whisk until well combined. Add the flour mixture and whisk until well combined.
2. **For meringue:** in a clean glass bowl; add all the Ingredients and with an electric whisker, whisk on high speed until stiff peaks form
3. Place 1/3 of the meringue into flour mixture and with a hand whisker, whisk well. Fold in the remaining meringue. Set the temperature of air fryer to 355°F. Place the mixture into an ungreased chiffon pan.
4. With a piece of foil, cover the pan tightly and poke some holes using a fork. Arrange the cake pan into an air fryer basket.
5. set the temperature of air fryer to 320°F. Air fry for about 30 to 35 minutes. Remove the piece of foil and set the temperature to 285°F
6. Air fry for another 5 minutes or until a toothpick inserted in the center comes out clean. Remove the cake pan from air fryer and place onto a wire rack to cool for about 10 minutes.
7. invert the cake onto wire rack to completely cool before slicing. Cut the cake into desired size slices and serve.

Fried Apples

(**Prep + Cook Time:** 27 Minutes | **Servings:** 4)

Ingredients:

- 4 big apples; cored
- 1 tbsp. cinnamon; ground

- A handful raisins
- Raw honey to the taste

Directions:

1. Fill each apple with raisins, sprinkle cinnamon, drizzle honey, put them in your air fryer and cook at 367°F, for 17 minutes. Leave them to cool down and serve.

Strawberry Cheesecake

(Prep + Cook Time: 1 hour 57 minutes | Servings: 15)

Ingredients:

For Crust:

- 1 tbsp. honey
- 2 tbsp. natural peanut butter

- 7 tbsp. almond flour

For Filling:

- 2 scoops vanilla whey protein powder
- 10½-oz plain Greek yogurt
- 10½-oz cream cheese
- 1 cup fresh strawberries, hulled and sliced

- 2 eggs
- 2 tbsp. strawberry preserves
- 2 tbsp. Splenda
- 1/4 tsp. vanilla extract

For Topping:
- 2 tbsp. vanilla whey protein powder
- 2 tbsp. fat-free plain Greek yogurt
- 1 tbsp. Splenda

Directions:
1. Line a greased round baking pan with a parchment paper
2. **For crust:** in a bowl; add all the Ingredients and mix until a dough ball forms. Place the dough ball in the center of prepared baking pan. With your fingers, press downwards until the dough spreads evenly in the bottom of pan
3. Set the temperature of air fryer to 248°F. Arrange the baking pan into an air fryer basket. Air fry for about 7 minutes.
4. Remove the crust from air fryer and set aside to cool slightly. Meanwhile; for filling: in a large bowl; put all the Ingredients except strawberries and whisk until smooth
5. Fold in the strawberries. Place strawberry mixture evenly over the crust. With the back of spatula, smooth the top surface of strawberry mixture.
6. Again, set the temperature of air fryer to 248°F. Arrange baking pan into the air fryer basket. Air fry for about 30 minutes and then, another 1 hour at 195°F.
7. Remove from the air fryer and set aside for about 1 to 2 hours to cool
8. **For the topping:** in a bowl; put all the Ingredients and mix well. After cooling, top the cheesecake with topping mixture. Refrigerate for about 4 to 8 hours before serving.

Strawberry Cupcakes

(Prep + Cook Time: 28 minutes | Servings: 10)

Ingredients:

For Cupcakes:
- 2 eggs
- 7/8 cup self-rising flour
- 1/2 cup caster sugar
- 7 tbsp. butter
- 1/2 tsp. vanilla essence

For Frosting:
- 1 cup icing sugar
- 3 ½ tbsp. butter
- 1 tbsp. whipped cream
- 1/4 cup fresh strawberries, pureed
- 1/2 tsp. pink food color

Directions:
1. In a bowl; add butter and sugar and whisk until fluffy and light. Then, add the eggs, one at a time and whisk until well combined. Stir in the vanilla extract. Gradually, add the flour whisking continuously until well combined. Place the mixture into silicon cups
2. Set the temperature of air fryer to 340°F. Arrange the silicon cups into an air fryer basket. Air fry for about 8 minutes or until a toothpick inserted in the center comes out clean
3. Remove the silicon cups from air fryer and place onto a wire rack to cool for about 10 minutes. Now; invert the cupcakes onto wire rack to completely cool before frosting
4. For frosting: in another bowl; add the icing sugar and butter and whisk until fluffy and light.
5. Add the whipped cream, strawberry puree and color. Mix until well combined. Fill the pastry bag with icing and decorate the cupcakes.

Strawberry Cream

(**Prep + Cook Time:** 20 minutes | **Servings:** 6)

Ingredients:
- 8 oz. cream cheese
- 4 oz. strawberries
- 1/2 tbsp. lemon juice
- 1/2 cup heavy cream
- 2 tbsp. water
- 1 tsp. gelatin
- 1/4 tsp. sugar

Directions:
1. Place all ingredients in your blender and pulse
2. Divide the mixture into 6 ramekins and place them in your air fryer
3. Cook at 330°F for 15 minutes. Refrigerate (or place briefly in freezer) and serve the cream really cold.

Mini Apple Pies

(Prep + Cook Time: 50 minutes | Servings: 6)

Ingredients:
For Crust:
- 1/2 cup unsalted butter
- 1 ½ cups flour
- 1/4 cup chilled water
- 1 tsp. sugar
- Salt, to taste

For Filling:
- 4 Granny Smith apples; peeled and finely chopped
- 1/4 cup Nutella
- 2 tbsp. flour
- 2 tbsp. fresh lemon juice
- 2 tbsp. butter
- 2 ½ tbsp. sugar
- 1/4 tsp. ground nutmeg
- 1 tsp. ground cinnamon
- 1 tsp. fresh lemon zest, finely grated
- Salt, to taste

For Topping:
- 3 tbsp. sugar
- 1 egg, beaten
- 1 tsp. ground cinnamon

Directions:
1. In a bowl; mix well flour, sugar, butter and salt. With a pastry cutter, cut in the butter. Add the chilled water and mix until a dough forms. With a plastic wrapper, cover the bowl and refrigerate for about 30 minutes.
2. Meanwhile; for filling: in a large bowl; mix well all the ingredients. Set aside. Now; place the dough onto a lightly floured surface and roll into ½-inch thickness
3. With a ramekin, cut 12 circles from the dough. Place 6 circles in the bottom of 6 ramekins and press slightly.
4. Add the filling mixture evenly into the ramekins and top with the remaining circles. Pinch the edges to seal the pies. Carefully; cut 3 slits in each pie and coat evenly with the beaten egg
5. **For topping:** in a small bowl; mix together the cinnamon and sugar
6. Sprinkle each pie with the cinnamon sugar. Set the temperature of air fryer to 350°F. Arrange the ramekins into an air fryer basket. Air fry for about 30 minutes. Remove the ramekins from air fryer and place onto a wire rack to cool for about 10 to 15 minutes before serving. Serve warm.

Stuffed Apples

(Prep + Cook Time: 28 minutes | Servings: 4)

Ingredients:
For Stuffed Apples:
- 1/2 cup blanched almonds
- 1/2 cup golden raisins
- 4 small firm apples, cored
- 2 tbsp. sugar

For Vanilla Sauce:
- 2 tbsp. sugar
- 1/2 tsp. vanilla extract
- 1/2 cup whipped cream

Directions:
1. In a food processor, add raisins, almonds and sugar and pulse until chopped. Carefully; stuff each apple with raisin mixture. Set the temperature of air fryer to 355°F. Line a baking dish with a parchment paper. Now; place apples into the prepared baking dish

2. Arrange the baking dish into an air fryer basket. Air fry for about 10 minutes. Meanwhile; for vanilla sauce: in a pan, add the cream, sugar and vanilla extract over medium heat and cook for about 2 to 3 minutes or until sugar is dissolved, stirring continuously
3. Remove the baking dish from air fryer and transfer the apples onto plates to cool slightlyTop with the vanilla sauce and serve.

Simple Cheesecake

(Prep + Cook Time: 34 minutes | Servings: 14)

Ingredients:
- 1 lb. cream cheese; softened
- 1/2 cup sugar
- 2 large eggs
- 1 cup honey graham cracker crumbs
- 2 tbsp. unsalted butter; softened
- 1/2 tsp. vanilla extract

Directions:
Line a round baking dish with parchment paper
1. **For crust:** in a bowl; add the graham cracker crumbs and butter
2. Place the crust into baking dish and press to smooth. Set the temperature of air fryer to 350°F. Arrange the baking dish into an air fryer basket. Air fry for about 4 minutes.
3. Remove the crust from air fryer and set aside to cool slightly. Meanwhile; in a bowl; add the cream cheese and sugar and whisk until smooth
4. place the eggs, one at a time and whisk until mixture becomes creamy. Add the vanilla extract and mix well.
5. Place the cream cheese mixture evenly over the crust. Arrange baking dish into the air fryer basket. Air fry for about 15 minutes. Remove from the air fryer and set aside for about 1 to 2 hours to cool. Refrigerate to chill for about 3 hours before serving

Cream Doughnuts

(Prep + Cook Time: 31 minutes | Servings: 8)

Ingredients:
For Doughnuts:
- 2¼ cups plain flour
- 1/2 cup sour cream
- 1/2 cup sugar
- 2 egg yolks
- 2 tbsp. butter; softened
- 2 tbsp. butter; melted
- 1 ½ tsp. baking powder
- 1 tsp. salt

For Topping:
- 1 tsp. cinnamon
- 1/3 cup caster sugar

Directions:
1. In a large bowl; add the sugar and 2 tbsp. of softened butter and whisk until crumbly mixture forms. Add the egg yolks and whisk until well combined. In another bowl; sift together the flour, baking powder and salt. Divide the flour mixture in 3 portions
2. Add first portion of flour mixture and ½ of sour cream in the bowl of sugar mixture and mix well. Add the second portion of flour mixture and remaining sour cream and mix well.
3. add the remaining portion and mix until a dough forms. Refrigerate the dough before rolling. Now; put the dough onto a lightly floured surface and roll into 2-inch thickness
4. With a floured doughnut cutter, cut the dough. Set the temperature of air fryer to 355°F. Grease an air fryer basket.
5. Coat both sides of the doughnut with melted butter. Arrange doughnuts into the prepared air fryer basket in 2 batches
6. Air fry for about 8 minutes or until golden brown. Meanwhile; in a bowl; mix together the sugar and cinnamon. Remove from air fryer and transfer the doughnuts onto a platter to cool completely. Sprinkle the doughnuts with cinnamon sugar and serve

Chocolate Cream Cake

(Prep + Cook Time: 40 minutes | Servings: 6)

Ingredients:

- 2/3 cup sugar
- 1/2 cup sour cream
- 1/2 cup butter; softened
- 1 cup flour
- 1/3 cup cocoa powder
- 3 eggs
- 2 tsp. vanilla extract
- 1 tsp. baking powder
- 1/2 tsp. baking soda
- 1/8 tsp. salt

Directions:

1. In a large bowl; mix well flour, cocoa powder, baking powder, baking soda and salt. Add the remaining Ingredients and with an electric whisker, whisk on low speed until well combined
2. Set the temperature of air fryer to 320°F. Lightly, grease a cake pan
3. Place mixture evenly into the prepared cake pan. Arrange the cake pan into an air fryer basket. Air fry for about 25 minutes or until a toothpick inserted in the center comes out clean.
4. Remove the cake pan from air fryer and place onto a wire rack to cool for about 10 minutes
5. Now; invert the cake onto wire rack to completely cool before slicing. Cut the cake into desired size slices and serve.

Cinnamon Pears

(**Prep + Cook Time:** 20 minutes | **Servings:** 4)

Ingredients:

- 2 pears; halved
- 2 tbsp. sugar
- 1/2 tsp. cinnamon powder

Directions:

1. Put the pears in your air fryer and sprinkle the cinnamon and the sugar all over
2. Cook at 320°F for 15 minutes. Serve these pears warm and enjoy!

Chocolate Mug Cake

(Prep + Cook Time: 28 minutes | Servings: 1)

Ingredients:

- 1/4 cup self-rising flour
- 3 tbsp. coconut oil
- 3 tbsp. whole milk
- 1 tbsp. cocoa powder
- 5 tbsp. caster sugar

Directions:

1. In a shallow mug, add all the Ingredients and mix until well combined
2. Set the temperature of air fryer to 392°F
3. Arrange the mug into an air fryer basket. Air fry for about 13 minutes. Remove from the air fryer and serve warm

Fruity Tacos

(Prep + Cook Time: 15 minutes | Servings: 2)

Ingredients:

- 2 soft shell tortillas
- 1/4 cup raspberries
- 1/4 cup blueberries
- 2 tbsp. powdered sugar
- 4 tbsp. strawberry jelly

Directions:

1. Set the temperature of air fryer to 300°F. Lightly, grease an air fryer basket. Arrange the tortillas onto a smooth surface. Spread two tbsp. of strawberry jelly over each tortilla and top each with berries. Sprinkle each with the powdered sugar

2. Arrange tortillas into the prepared air fryer basket. Air fry for about 5 minutes or until crispy. Remove from the air fryer and transfer the tortillas onto a platter. Serve warm

Fudge Brownies

(Prep + Cook Time: 35 minutes | Servings: 8)

Ingredients:
- 1/2 cup flour
- 1/3 cup cocoa powder
- 1 cup sugar
- 1/2 cup butter; melted
- 2 eggs
- 1 tsp. vanilla extract
- 1 tsp. baking powder

Directions:
1. Set the temperature of Air fryer to 350°F. Grease a baking pan. In a large bowl; add the sugar and butter and whisk until light and fluffy. Add the remaining Ingredients and mix until well combined. Place mixture evenly into the prepared pan and with the back of spatula, smooth the top surface
2. Arrange the baking pan into an air fryer basket. Air fry pan for about 20 minutes
3. Remove the baking pan from air fryer and set aside to cool completely. Cut into 8 equal-sized squares and serve.

Chocolate Soufflé

(Prep + Cook Time: 31 minutes | Servings: 2)

Ingredients:
- 3-oz semi-sweet chocolate; chopped
- 2 eggs, egg yolks and whites separated
- 1/4 cup butter
- 2 tbsp. all-purpose flour
- 3 tbsp. sugar
- 1 tsp. powdered sugar plus extra for dusting
- 1/2 tsp. pure vanilla extract

Directions:
1. In a microwave-safe bowl; put the butter and chocolate. Microwave on high heat for about 2 minutes or until melted completely, stirring after every 30 seconds. Remove from microwave and stir the mixture until smooth. In another bowl; add the egg yolks and whisk well
2. Add the sugar and vanilla extract and whisk well. Add the chocolate mixture and mix until well combined. Add the flour and mix well. In a clean glass bowl; add the egg whites and whisk until soft peaks form.
3. Fold the whipped egg whites in 3 portions into the chocolate mixture. Set the temperature of air fryer to 330°F. Grease 2 ramekins and sprinkle each with a pinch of sugar
4. Place mixture evenly into the prepared ramekins and with the back of a spoon, smooth the top surface. Arrange the ramekins into an air fryer basket. Air fry for about 14 minutes. Remove from air fryer and set aside to cool slightly. Sprinkle with the powdered sugar and serve warm.

Apple Pie

(Prep + Cook Time: 45 minutes | Servings: 6)

Ingredients:
- 1 large apple, peeled, cored and chopped
- 1 frozen pie crust, thawed
- 1 egg, beaten
- 1 tbsp. butter; chopped
- 3 tbsp. sugar, divided
- 1 tbsp. ground cinnamon
- 1/2 tsp. vanilla extract
- 2 tsp. fresh lemon juice

Directions:
1. Grease a pie pan. With a smaller baking tin, cut 1 crust from thawed pie crust about 1/8-inch larger than pie pan. cut the second crust from the pie crust a little smaller than first one. Arrange the large crust in the bottom of prepared pie pan
2. In a bowl; mix together the apple, 2 tbsp. of sugar, cinnamon, lemon juice and vanilla extract. Place apple mixture evenly over the bottom crust.

3. Add the chopped butter over apple mixture. Arrange the second crust on top and pinch the edges to seal.
4. Carefully; cut 3 to 4 slits in the top crust. Spread the beaten egg evenly over top crust and sprinkle with the remaining sugar
5. Set the temperature of air fryer to 320°F. Arrange the pie pan into an air fryer basket. Air fry for about 30 minutes.
6. Remove from air fryer and place the pie pan onto a wire rack to cool for about 10 to 15 minutes before serving. Serve warm

Apple Pastry Pouch

(Prep + Cook Time: 40 minutes | Servings: 2)

Ingredients:
- 2 small apples; peeled and cored
- 2 puff pastry sheets
- 2 tbsp. butter; melted
- 1 tbsp. brown sugar
- 2 tbsp. raisins

Directions:
1. In a bowl; mix together the sugar and raisins. Fill the core of each apple with raisins mixture. Place one apple in the center of each pastry sheet and fold dough to cover the apple completely. Then, pinch the edges to seal.
2. Coat each apple evenly with butter. Set the temperature of air fryer to 355°F. Lightly, grease an air fryer basket
3. Arrange apple pouches into the prepared air fryer basket in a single layer
4. Air fry for about 25 minutes. Remove from air fryer and transfer the apple pouches onto a platter. Serve warm.

Banana Cake

(Prep + Cook Time: 55 minutes | Servings: 6)

Ingredients:
- 3 medium bananas; peeled and mashed
- 1/4 cup walnuts; chopped
- 1/4 cup raisins; chopped
- 2 eggs
- 1/2 cup sugar
- 1 ½ cups cake flour
- 1/2 cup vegetable oil
- 1/2 tsp. vanilla extract
- 1 tsp. baking soda
- 1/2 tsp. ground cinnamon
- Salt, to taste

Directions:
1. In a large bowl; mix well flour, baking soda, cinnamon and salt. In another bowl; beat well eggs and oil. Add the sugar, vanilla extract and bananas. Whisk until well combined. Add the flour mixture and stir until just combined. Set the temperature of air fryer to 320°F. Grease a cake pan.
2. Place mixture evenly into the prepared cake pan and top with walnuts and raisins. With a piece of foil, cover the pan.
3. Arrange the cake pan into an air fryer basket. Now; set the temperature of air fryer to 300°F. Air fry for about 30 minutes
4. Remove the piece of foil and set the temperature to 285°F. Air fry for another 5 to 10 minutes or until a toothpick inserted in the center comes out clean.
5. Remove the cake pan from air fryer and place onto a wire rack to cool for about 10 minutes
6. Now; invert the cake onto wire rack to completely cool before slicing. Cut the cake into desired size slices and serve.

Strawberry Cobbler Recipe

(Prep + Cook Time: 35 Minutes | Servings: 6)

Ingredients:

- 3/4 cup sugar
- 6 cups strawberries; halved
- 1/2 cup flour
- 1/8 tsp. baking powder
- 1/2 cup water
- 3 ½ tbsp. olive oil
- 1 tbsp. lemon juice
- A pinch of baking soda
- Cooking spray

Directions:

1. In a bowl; mix strawberries with half of sugar, sprinkle some flour, add lemon juice, whisk and pour into the baking dish that fits your air fryer and greased with cooking spray.
2. In another bowl, mix flour with the rest of the sugar, baking powder and soda and stir well
3. Add the olive oil and mix until the whole thing with your hands
4. Add 1/2 cup water and spread over strawberries
5. Introduce in the fryer at 355°F and bake for 25 minutes. Leave cobbler aside to cool down, slice and serve.

Lemon Cake

(Prep + Cook Time: 22 minutes | Servings: 6)

Ingredients:

- 3 oz. brown sugar
- 3 oz. flour
- 1 tsp. dark chocolate; grated
- 3½ oz. butter; melted
- 3 eggs
- 1/2 tsp. lemon juice

Directions:

1. Mix all of the ingredients in a bowl.
2. Pour the mixture into a greased cake pan and place in the fryer
3. Cook at 360°F for 17 minutes. Let cake cool before serving

Pear Delight

(Prep + Cook Time: 25 minutes | Servings: 4)

Ingredients:

- 4 pears; peeled and roughly cut into cubes
- 1/4 cup brown sugar
- 4 tbsp. butter; melted
- 1 tbsp. maple syrup
- 2 tsp. cinnamon powder

Directions:

1. In a pan that fits your air fryer, place all the ingredients and toss.
2. Place the pan in the air fryer and cook at 300°F for 20 minutes. Divide into cups, refrigerate and serve cold

Butter Donuts

(Prep + Cook Time: 25 minutes | Servings: 4)

Ingredients:

- 8 oz. flour
- 4 oz. whole milk
- 1 egg
- 2½ tbsp. butter
- 1 tbsp. brown sugar
- 1 tbsp. white sugar
- 1 tsp. baking powder

Directions:

1. Place all of the ingredients in a bowl and mix well.
2. Shape donuts from this mix and place them in your air fryer's basket
3. Cook at 360°F for 15 minutes. Arrange the donuts on a platter and serve them warm

Apple Bread Pudding

(Prep + Cook Time: 59 minutes | Servings: 8)

Ingredients:

For Bread Pudding:
- 10½-oz bread, cubed
- 1 ½ cups milk
- 1/2 cup raisins
- 1/4 cup walnuts; chopped
- 3/4 cup water

For Topping:
- 3/5 cup brown sugar
- 1 ⅓ cups plain flour
- 1/2 cup apple, peeled, cored and chopped
- 5 tbsp. honey
- 2 tsp. ground cinnamon
- 2 tsp. cornstarch
- 1 tsp. vanilla extract

- 7 tbsp. butter

Directions:

1. In a large bowl; mix well bread, apple, raisins and walnuts. In another bowl; add the remaining pudding Ingredients and mix until well combined. Add the milk mixture into bread mixture and mix until well combined. Refrigerate for about 15 minutes, tossing occasionally

2. **For topping:** in a bowl; mix together the flour and sugar. With a pastry cutter, cut in the butter until a crumbly mixture forms. Set the temperature of air fryer to 355°F

3. Place the mixture evenly into 2 baking pans and spread the topping mixture on top of each. Place 1 pan into an air fryer basket. Air fry for about 22 minutes. Repeat with the remaining pan. Remove from the air fryer and serve warm.

Creamy Blackberry

(**Prep + Cook Time:** 18 minutes | **Servings:** 4)

Ingredients:
- 1 cup blackberries
- 1/2 cup heavy cream
- 5 tbsp. sugar
- 2 tsp. vanilla extract
- 2 tsp. baking powder
- 1/2 cup butter; melted
- 2 eggs

Directions:

1. Place all of the ingredients in a bowl and whisk well.
2. Divide the mixture between 4 ramekins and place the ramekins in the fryer
3. Cook at 320°F for 12 minutes. Refrigerate and serve cold

Cranberry Jam

(**Prep + Cook Time:** 25 minutes | **Servings:** 8)

Ingredients:
- 2 lbs. cranberries
- 4 oz. black currant
- 3 tbsp. water
- 2 lbs. sugar
- Zest of 1 lime

Directions:

1. In a pan that fits your air fryer, add all the ingredients and stir.
2. Place the pan in the fryer and cook at 360°F for 20 minutes. Stir the jam well, divide into cups, refrigerate and serve cold

Yummy Rice Pudding

(Prep + Cook Time: 25 minutes | **Servings:** 6)

Ingredients:
- 7 oz. white rice
- 1 tbsp. butter; melted
- 1 tbsp. heavy cream
- 16 oz. milk
- 1/3 cup sugar
- 1 tsp. vanilla extract

Directions:
1. Place all ingredients in a pan that fits your air fryer and stir well
2. Put the pan in the fryer and cook at 360°F for 20 minutes. Stir the pudding, divide it into bowls, refrigerate and serve cold.

Chocolate Pudding

(Prep + Cook Time: 34 minutes | Servings: 4)

Ingredients:
- 1/4 cup fresh orange juice
- 2/3 cup dark chocolate; chopped
- 1/2 cup butter
- 1/4 cup caster sugar
- 2 medium eggs
- 2 tbsp. self-rising flour
- 2 tsp. fresh orange rind, finely grated

Directions:
1. In a microwave-safe bowl; add the butter and chocolate. Microwave on high heat for about 2 minutes or until melted completely, stirring after every 30 seconds. Remove from microwave and stir the mixture until smooth. Add the sugar and eggs and whisk until frothy
2. Add the orange rind and juice, followed by flour and mix until well combined. Set the temperature of air fryer to 355°F. Grease 4 ramekins.
3. Divide mixture into the prepared ramekins about ¾ full. Air fry for about 12 minutes
4. Remove from the air fryer and set aside to completely cool before serving. Serve warm

Apple Doughnuts

(Prep + Cook Time: 25 minutes | Servings: 6)

Ingredients:
For Doughnuts:
- 1/2 cup brown sugar
- 1 cup apple cider
- 1/2 pink lady apple, peeled, cored and grated
- 2 ½ cups plus 2 tbsp. all-purpose flour
- 1 egg
- 2 tbsp. unsalted butter; softened
- 1 tsp. baking powder
- 1/2 tsp. baking soda
- 1/2 tsp. ground cinnamon
- 1/2 tsp. salt

For Topping:
- 3 tbsp. butter; melted
- 1/2 cup sugar
- 1/2 tbsp. ground cinnamon

Directions:
1. In a medium pan, add the apple cider over medium-high heat and bring it to a boil. Lower the heat and simmer for about 15 minutes or until the cider reduces to 1/4 cup. Remove the pan from heat and transfer the apple cider into a bowl. Refrigerate to cool. In a large bowl; mix well flour, baking powder, baking soda, cinnamon and salt
2. In another bowl; add the brown sugar and butter and with an electric hand mixer, whisk until light and fluffy. Add the egg and whisk well.
3. Add the cooled apple cider and mix well. Put the flour mixture and mix until well combined. Add the grated apple and mix until a dough forms.

4. put the dough onto a lightly floured surface and with your hands, knead until a soft dough comes together. With a plastic wrap, wrap the dough and refrigerate for about 30 minutes
5. place the dough onto a lightly floured surface and roll into 1-inch thickness. With a 3-inches doughnut cutter, cut the doughnuts.
6. Set the temperature of air fryer to 360°F for about 2 minutes. Grease an air fryer basket. Now; turn off the air fryer.
7. Arrange doughnuts into the prepared air fryer basket and let the dough rest in the turned off air fryer for about 5 minutes. Again, set the temperature of air fryer to 360°F
8. Air fry for about 5 minutes, flipping once halfway through. Meanwhile; in a shallow bowl; mix together the sugar and cinnamon. Remove from air fryer and transfer the doughnuts onto a platter. Brush both sides of doughnuts with melted butter and then, coat with the cinnamon sugar. Serve

Coffee Cheesecakes Recipe

(**Prep + Cook Time:** 30 Minutes | **Servings:** 6)

Ingredients:
For the cheesecakes:
- 2 tbsp. butter
- 3 tbsp. coffee
- 3 eggs

- 8-ounce cream cheese
- 1/3 cup sugar
- 1 tbsp. caramel syrup

For the frosting:
- 3 tbsp. caramel syrup
- 2 tbsp. sugar

- 3 tbsp. butter
- 8-ounce mascarpone cheese; soft

Directions:
1. In your blender, mix cream cheese with eggs, 2 tablespoon butter, coffee, 1 tablespoon caramel syrup and ⅓ cup sugar and pulse very well, spoon into a cupcakes pan that fits your air fryer, introduce in the fryer and cook at 320°F and bake for 20 minutes.
2. Leave aside to cool down and then keep in the freezer for 3 hours. Meanwhile; in a bowl, mix 3 tablespoon butter with 3 tablespoon caramel syrup, 2 tablespoon sugar and mascarpone, blend well, spoon this over cheesecakes and serve them

Grape Stew

(**Prep + Cook Time:** 20 minutes | **Servings:** 4)

Ingredients:
- 1 lb. red grapes
- 26 oz. grape juice

- Juice and zest of 1 lemon

Directions:
1. In a pan that fits your air fryer, add all ingredients and toss
2. Place the pan in the fryer and cook at 320°F for 14 minutes. Divide into cups, refrigerate and serve cold

Chocolate Banana Pastries

(Prep + Cook Time: 27 minutes | Servings: 4)

Ingredients:
- 2 bananas; peeled and sliced
- 1 puff pastry sheet

- 1/2 cup Nutella

Directions:
1. Cut the pastry sheet into 4 equal-sized squares. Spread Nutella evenly on each square of pastry. Divide the banana slices over Nutella. Fold each square into a triangle and with wet fingers, slightly press the edges. Then with a fork, press the edges firmly
2. Set the temperature of air fryer to 375°F. Lightly, grease an air fryer basket. Arrange pastries into the prepared air fryer basket in a single layer. Air fry for about 10 to 12 minutes. Remove from air fryer and transfer the pastries onto a platter. Serve warm

Raisin Bread Pudding

(Prep + Cook Time: 27 minutes | Servings: 3)

Ingredients:

- 2 bread slices; cut into small cubes
- 1 cup milk
- 1 egg
- 1 tbsp. brown sugar
- 2 tbsp. raisins, soaked in hot water for about 15 minutes
- 1 tbsp. chocolate chips
- 1 tbsp. sugar
- 1/2 tsp. ground cinnamon
- 1/4 tsp. vanilla extract

Directions:

1. In a bowl; mix well milk, egg, brown sugar, cinnamon and vanilla extract. Stir in the raisins
2. In a baking dish, spread the bread cubes and top evenly with the milk mixture. Refrigerate for about 15 to 20 minutes. Set the temperature of air fryer to 375°F. Remove from refrigerator and sprinkle with chocolate chips and sugar on top
3. Arrange the baking dish into an air fryer basket. Air fry for about 12 minutes. Remove from the air fryer and serve warm.

Apple and Cinnamon Sauce

(**Prep + Cook Time:** 40 minutes | **Servings:** 6)

Ingredients:

- 6 apples; peeled, cored and cut into wedges
- 1 cup red wine
- 1 cup sugar
- 1 tbsp. cinnamon powder

Directions:

1. In a pan that fits your air fryer, place all of the ingredients and toss
2. Place the pan in the fryer and cook at 320°F for 30 minutes. Divide into cups and serve right away

Raspberry Wontons

(Prep + Cook Time: 36 minutes | Servings: 12)

Ingredients:

For Wonton Wrappers:

- 18-oz cream cheese; softened
- 1/2 cup powdered sugar

For Raspberry Syrup:

- 1 (12-oz) package frozen raspberries
- 1/4 cup water
- 1 package of wonton wrappers
- 1 tsp. vanilla extract

- 1/4 cup sugar
- 1 tsp. vanilla extract

Directions:

1. **For wrappers:** in a bowl; add the sugar, cream cheese and vanilla extract and whisk until smooth. Place a wonton wrapper onto a smooth surface. Place one tbsp. of cream cheese mixture in the center of each wrapper. With wet fingers, fold wrappers around the filling and then, pinch the edges to seal
2. Set the temperature of air fryer to 350°F. Lightly, grease an air fryer basket. Arrange wonton wrappers into the prepared air fryer basket in 2 batches
3. Air fry for about 8 minutes. Meanwhile; for the syrup: in a medium skillet, add water, sugar, raspberries and vanilla extract over medium heat and cook for about 5 minutes, stirring continuously
4. Remove from the heat and set aside to cool slightly. Transfer the mixture into food processor and blend until smooth. Remove the wontons from air fryer and transfer onto a platter. Serve the wontons with topping of raspberry syrup.

Doughnuts Pudding

(Prep + Cook Time: 75 minutes | Servings: 4)

Ingredients:

- 6 glazed doughnuts; cut into small pieces
- 4 egg yolks
- 1/2 cup semi-sweet chocolate baking chips
- 1/4 cup sugar
- 1 ½ cups whipping cream
- 3/4 cup frozen sweet cherries
- 1/2 cup raisins
- 1 tsp. ground cinnamon

Directions:

1. In a large bowl; mix together doughnut pieces, cherries, raisins, chocolate chips, sugar and cinnamon. In another bowl; add the egg yolks and whipping cream and whisk until well combined. Add the egg yolk mixture into doughnut mixture and mix well. Set the temperature of air fryer to 310°F. Line a baking dish with a piece of foil
2. Place doughnuts mixture evenly into the prepared baking dish. Arrange the baking dish into an air fryer basket. Air fry for about 60 minutes. Remove from the air fryer and serve warm

Cinnamon Rolls

(**Prep + Cook Time:** 12 minutes | **Servings:** 8)

Ingredients:

- 1 lb. bread dough
- 3/4 cup brown sugar
- 1/4 cup butter; melted
- 1½ tbsp. cinnamon; ground

Directions:

1. Roll the dough on a floured working surface, shape a rectangle and brush with the butter.
2. In a bowl, combine the cinnamon and sugar and then sprinkle this over the dough
3. Roll the dough into a log, seal, cut into 8 pieces and leave the rolls to rise for 2 hours
4. Place the rolls in your air fryer's basket and cook at 350°F for 5 minutes on each side. Serve warm and enjoy!

Brioche Pudding

(**Prep + Cook Time:** 35 minutes | **Servings:** 4)

Ingredients:

- 3 cups brioche; cubed
- 2 cups half and half
- 2 cups milk
- 1/2 tsp. vanilla extract
- 1/2 cup raisins
- 1 cup sugar
- 4 egg yolks; whisked
- 2 tbsp. butter; melted
- Zest of 1/2 lemon

Directions:

1. In a bowl, add all of the ingredients and whisk well
2. Pour the mixture into a pudding mould and place it in the air fryer
3. Cook at 330°F for 30 minutes. Cool down and serve.

Pineapple and Carrot Cake

(**Prep + Cook Time:** 55 minutes | **Servings:** 6)

Ingredients:

- 5 oz. flour
- 1/4 cup pineapple juice
- 1/3 cup carrots; grated
- 1/3 cup coconut flakes; shredded
- 1/2 cup sugar
- 3/4 tsp. baking powder
- 1/2 tsp. baking soda
- 1/2 tsp. cinnamon powder
- 1 egg; whisked
- 3 tbsp. yogurt
- 4 tbsp. vegetable oil
- Cooking spray

Directions:
1. Place all of the ingredients (except the cooking spray) in a bowl and mix well.
2. Pour the mixture into a spring form pan, greased with cooking spray, that fits your air fryer
3. Place the pan in your air fryer and cook at 320°F for 45 minutes. Allow the cake to cool before cutting and serving

Rum Cheesecake

(Prep + Cook Time: 30 minutes | **Servings:** 6)

Ingredients:
- 16 oz. cream cheese; softened
- 2 eggs
- 1/2 tsp. vanilla extract
- 1/2 cup sugar
- 1/2 cup graham cookies; crumbled
- 2 tsp. butter; melted
- 1 tsp. rum

Directions:
1. Grease a pan with the butter and spread the cookie crumbs on the bottom.
2. In a bowl, mix all the remaining ingredients and whisk well; then spread this mixture over the cookie crumbs
3. Place the pan in your air fryer and cook at 340°F for 20 minutes. Let the cheesecake cool down, refrigerate and serve cold

Amaretto Cream

(Prep + Cook Time: 18 minutes | **Servings:** 8)

Ingredients:
- 12 oz. chocolate chips
- 1 cup heavy cream
- 1 cup sugar
- 1/2 cup butter; melted
- 2 tbsp. amaretto liqueur

Directions:
1. Place all of the ingredients in a bowl and stir
2. Pour the mixture into small ramekins and place in the air fryer
3. Cook at 320°F for 12 minutes. Refrigerate / freeze for a while... best when served really cold.

Oreo Cheesecake

(Prep + Cook Time: 30 minutes | **Servings:** 8)

Ingredients:
- 1 lb. cream cheese; softened
- 1/2 tsp. vanilla extract
- 4 tbsp. sugar
- 1 cup Oreo cookies; crumbled
- 2 eggs; whisked
- 2 tbsp. butter; melted

Directions:
1. In a bowl, mix the cookies with the butter and then press this mixture onto the bottom of a cake pan lined with parchment paper.
2. Place the pan in your air fryer and cook at 350°F for 4 minutes
3. In a bowl, mix the sugar with the cream cheese, eggs and vanilla; whisk until combined and smooth and spread this over the crust
4. Cook the cheesecake in your air fryer at 310°F for 15 minutes. Place the cheesecake in the fridge for a couple of hours before serving.

Cream of Tartar Bread

(Prep + Cook Time: 50 minutes | **Servings:** 6)

Ingredients:

- 3/4 cup sugar
- 1½ cups flour
- 1/3 cup milk
- 1/3 cup butter
- 2 zucchinis; grated
- 1 tsp. vanilla extract
- 1 egg
- 1 tsp. baking powder
- 1/2 tsp. baking soda
- 1½ tsp. cream of tartar

Directions:

1. Place all ingredients in a bowl and mix well.
2. Pour the mixture into a lined loaf pan and place the pan in the air fryer
3. Cook at 320°F for 40 minutes Cool down, slice and serve.

Pumpkin Cake

(Prep + Cook Time: 35 minutes | **Servings:** 8)

Ingredients:

- 8 oz. canned pumpkin puree
- 1/2 cup Greek yogurt
- 1 egg; whisked
- 3/4 cup sugar
- 3/4 tsp. pumpkin pie spice
- 1 tsp. baking powder
- 1 cup white flour
- Cooking spray

Directions:

1. Place all ingredients (other than the cooking spray) in a bowl and mix well.
2. Grease a cake pan with cooking spray, pour the cake batter inside and spread
3. Place the pan in the air fryer and cook at 330°F for 25 minutes. Let the cake cool down, slice and serve.

Made in the USA
Coppell, TX
08 December 2019